THE SUN BOAT
A Voyage of Discovery

By the same Author

IN THE WAKE OF ODYSSEUS
IN THE WAKE OF A WISH

Daphne *at Garf Husein's rock temple, Nubia*

THE SUN BOAT

A Voyage of Discovery

Göran Schildt

Translated from the Swedish by
ALAN BLAIR

STAPLES PRESS LIMITED
LONDON

To my shipmates
MONA, EDRIES, ALVAR,
JUAN, MAIRE *and* ÅKE

Contents

Illustrations

THE SUN BOAT
A Voyage af Discovery

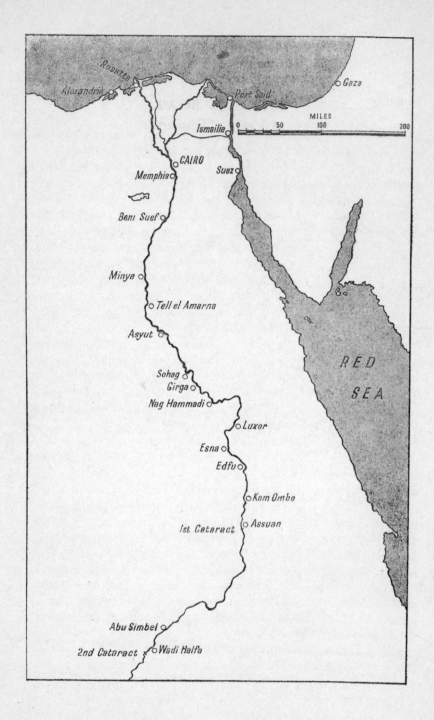

CHAPTER I

The Gateway to Egypt

Shoreless sea, overcast sky, a small motor-yacht labouring against wind and waves with two people on board.

Sitting at the tiller, with Mona at my side, I could not help wondering what we looked like to the passengers in the aeroplane that was thundering past above our heads. A picture with no meaning or context, a floating fragment impossible to understand. And yet this was the whole of the external truth about us: the sea, a few planks, the sails and two crouched figures in oilskins. Never before had I seen so plainly that we are something only in relation to where we have come from and where we are going, that the present comes to life only when linked with the past and the future.

The angry sea which we saw around us might have been any sea at all, but we knew what ports were waiting for us beyond the horizon; the wet deck, so uninviting to a stranger, was our *Daphne* and the person sitting beside me was Mona. Mona and *Daphne* – two powers which have determined my life and which have so long been part of it. If I am to explain why, on this November day, I found myself here, a hundred nautical miles south-east of Cyprus, it is with them I must begin.

There are many yachtsmen, but few who have a wife as much under the spell of sea and wind as they are themselves. For me, the fact that Mona loves the life of a sailing vagabond is fortunate but almost unaccountable. She does so in her own way; she takes no interest in nautical problems and is not an expert in handling the boat, she gets angry with me and scared the minute there is discomfort, trouble or danger, she is incapable of splicing a rope, telling a schooner from a cutter or fixing a compass bearing. But none is more eager than she to launch into the blue on a long and hazardous voyage and none is happier when we sail into a new port and make contact with the unknown that awaits us. She is not afraid of the lone night watches and her untiring care makes the boat a cosy, well-run home.

As for *Daphne*, all I will say of her is what a grateful husband might say of his wife after a long marriage. We met long ago, and the first fervent rapture, the time when everything is miraculous and one hardly dares to believe one's good fortune, has imperceptibly changed into mutual, matter-of-course possession. *Daphne* is no longer in the first flush of youth, the years and the hardships have left their mark and her lines are not those one sees in the fashion columns of the yachting magazines. Her bowsprit and low freeboard in particular proclaim that she came into being twenty years ago. But standing there in the shipyard in the spring, freshly painted and fitted out, she is still dazzlingly beautiful and when we return in the late autumn after the experiences of the summer I am vastly proud of her: hasn't she put up a better show than all the spoilt luxury boats in port? Experience – deep, fruitful, real – is a value that I set higher than all the qualities which are merely empty promises. Beauty, intelligence and skill are not to be despised as starting-points, but they do not acquire their full worth until they have gradually been changed into life's experiences and wisdom. *Daphne* is a well-tried boat and because of what we have gone through together we are bound to each other with indissoluble ties.

This may partly explain our situation on the boundless sea, but not the immediate circumstances. Why are we sailing from Beirut to Alexandria so full of expectations, anxiety, curiosity and recklessness? A long prelude has brought us here, a development along two lines which, in some strange way, are interwoven.

The first is an incorrigible love of adventure. I know that adventure is a flight from that which is our serious, real, everyday duty; it allows us to take everything lightly and irresponsibly because it keeps bringing us something new. Adventure is a multi-coloured thread which we eagerly grasp and which leads us to places which we should never have found on our own. For me, adventure has always been synonymous with sailing; I discovered its seduction as a boy when I headed out to the archipelago in my first sailing-boat, landed on unknown islands, went aground, got myself afloat, found birds' nests, talked to fishermen, spent the night in the boat, saw bathing girls on a rock and had to row home in a dead calm. The thread of adventure leads on the whole time by itself like a string of gaudy glass beads. *Vita Nuova* was the name of my first little boat, a name which the subsequent and larger ones would have had the same right to bear, for what does adventure give us if not the illusion of an ever-new life, of new possibilities and environments.

The years passed but the love of adventure remained the same. Each summer gave me a few weeks or months of the life it brings with it, often hard and exacting but in its essentials easy. My pretensions grew: first the Gulf of Finland, then the Baltic felt too cramped. In 1948 Mona and I were ready to take the plunge into waters more suited to our boat and to us: *Daphne* sailed to the Mediterranean. Since then we have followed adventure's twisting and enticing fairways down there. One summer they led us round Italy and Sicily, another to the big islands of the western Mediterranean and the east coast of Spain, a third to Greece, a fourth to Dalmatia . . . . Always new coasts, new harbours, new people, but the same open sea. Sometimes, after meeting one of those yachts that sail aimlessly about like the *Flying Dutchman* with a retired English couple on board who, year after year, find compensation for the hampering monotony of a long civil service career, I have seen Mona, *Daphne* and myself, gout-ridden and old, haunting the seas in the same situation. But on second thoughts I am convinced that we shall be spared this fate. For the very reason that we have always been able to satisfy our lust for adventure, we can hope that it will not obsess us. We are moderate adventurers: after three or four months' vagabondage we have always returned willingly to our duties and everyday life at home in the North. After our really long voyages we have even managed to stay at home over a summer, while *Daphne* has lain in the shipyard down in Italy.

One or two other extenuating circumstances may also be pleaded. If we have deserted everyday life through these journeys, we have, in different ways, tried to turn them to account after we got home. I have written books to retain the joy, to save the fleeting experiences from fading away like dreams. Only at my desk have our voyages taken on their full reality and meaning for me – to such an extent that it is the journey through France to Italy (described in *In the Wake of a Wish*) and the summer in Greece (*In the Wake of Odysseus*) which are still alive in my consciousness, while the Odysseys of the other summers have paled. When I now once more satisfy the need of reliving, interpreting and deepening the events of a voyage and, at my typewriter, transport myself in thought to sunny Egypt while the winter storms pile snowdrifts up outside my window, it is so that *Daphne*'s latest and most original voyage shall not slip through my fingers.

But if love of adventure has been the mainspring of our journeys, another factor has also been there from the beginning and determined their course. Our being *en route* to Egypt on this November day was no mere whim or chance but part of a set purpose. I presume that most people have a personal intellectual problem, some question they live with and try to intensify in some way. My problem has to do with the personality of Western man: what factors have created it, what traditions are worthwhile and alive for it, wherein are the difficulties and mistakes? This problem has accompanied me on all our journeys and has stimulated my interest not only in the living environments we have met with but also in art's testimonies of past generations' ideas and feelings. Europe has been a large book for me, a book in which I have learnt much that cannot be gleaned from ordinary books. In France I gained a new understanding of the Christian heritage and a lesson in the drawbacks of individualism, in Italy I came to know the most human and the happiest of all Europeans and in Greece I tasted of the Fount itself, from which our civilization springs.

It was this very visit to Greece which made me curious about that which is not Greece: because of my engrossment in the West I wanted to know what lay immediately outside and before the world created by the Greeks. It was in Crete that my interest for the not-so-distant Egypt awakened and we spoke for the first time of sailing on the Nile – the river from which the Greek Fount has so obviously borrowed some of its water, although it has filtered and transformed it.

Here, between Greece and Egypt, is the dividing line, and also a hidden but vital connection. Egypt, unlike China of old and the former civilizations of Central America, is a world that is not entirely strange to us: face to face with the kingdom of the Pharaohs we feel something awake and stir deep down in the semi-darkness of our creeds, myths and memories. We are like emigrant children, who in later years visit the land of their grandparents, dead long since; because of their parents and their

own lives they are strangers there, yet – doubtfully, wonderingly
– they recognize songs and fairy-tales they heard in their childhood. The Sphinx who asked riddles . . . Joseph and his brethren
. . . The God who died but rose again . . . On narrow, uncertain
paths we make our way back through our inner self to sunny,
ineffably peaceful days by the Nile.

For me this connection was essential, as I do not think we can
understand any culture other than our own. Or rather: if anything
is too strange, we can gain only knowledge about it, not experience, and that makes it worthless, at least to me. Experience is the
individual's reaction to what he meets, knowledge on the other
hand something which only refers to objects. Is there such a thing
as knowledge? Sometimes I am inclined to think that knowledge
is a special form of experience, the most dead, the most uninterest-
ing and the least effective experience.

But we are still far out to sea on board *Daphne* and the reader
does not know how we have got there.

In the early summer we had started from Venice, where *Daphne*
had lain waiting for us. Via Dalmatia and the Greek mainland we
had sailed as quickly as possible to Asia Minor and the islands of
the Aegean, where we had spent the whole summer on dazzling
voyages of discovery. The idea was that by October we should be
in the extreme east of the Mediterranean, from where we could
easily slip across to Egypt. An exchange of letters with the
president of the Cairo Yacht Club had made it clear to us that this
is the right moment to start a Nile trip: the summer heat is past,
the water level still high after the flooding, and the current not
too strong. Unfortunately, we did not carry out this well-advised
plan but dallied at anchor in the beguiling bays of Southern
Turkey, confident that November would be as fine as October.
Hardly had we got across to Cyprus when the weather changed:
rain and thunderstorms prevented us from leaving Famagusta's
harbour and the English meteorologists at the airfield confirmed
that the summer's stable high pressure belts had gone beyond
recall. This radical and very definite break in the weather between
summer and winter is typical of the Mediterranean and so dangerous to small boats that the ancient Greeks suspended all shipping
between November and February. We remembered how dearly
the apostle Paul had paid for his late start on his autumn journey

to Rome and we anxiously studied the chart, on which the distance to Alexandria, whichever way we turned the sheet, remained 350 nautical miles. For that stretch we needed at least four days of good weather. Four days and nights: it had suddenly become an impossibility after four months of steady summer. The calm, safe Nile seemed infinitely remote and our whole Egyptian voyage menaced. No wonder that our spirits became as gloomy and agitated as the sea thundering against the harbour pier, while the lightning flashed round the horizon. It was more to put an end to this stagnation than to get any nearer to our goal that we decided to sail across to Beirut. The distance from there to Alexandria is only a few miles shorter than from Famagusta, but from Beirut one can in an emergency follow the coast. Luck was with us and we crossed easily between two storms; the 110 nautical miles took us a good twenty-four hours and it felt much more hoepful to lie in a new port. For it is a fact that one takes root in ports: if one calls at them briefly to put a passenger ashore or to bunker, there is no difficulty in leaving them, but the longer one stays, the greater the effort needed to set sail again.

Unhappily, the weather made us take even firmer root in Beirut than in Famagusta. Each morning we were awakened by sunshine and looked hopefully out of the cabin, but above the high mountain ridges of Anti-Lebanon black clouds hung and above the horizon of the sea threatening thunderstorms piled up their gleaming formations. And each evening our meteorologist friends on the Cyprus radio repeated their formula of 'unsettled weather', their warning against 'thunderstorms and swells', their forecast of 45-knots wind.

Beirut has no yacht harbour and visiting small boats have an uncomfortable time, as they have to tie up right out in the middle of the main harbour basin; from there you have to row ashore in the dinghy to grimy wharves when you want to visit the town. We were fortunate in having kindly neighbours who could keep an eye on *Daphne* when we were away and who sympathetically shared our worries about the next part of the trip. To starboard lay a large, white schooner from Bermuda, owned by a wealthy Englishman who had left the boat here over the winter. It was called *Beegie* and was looked after by a crew of two, comprising a gout-ridden, crabby Spaniard and an ever-cheery, smiling Greek lad from Cyprus. They were both pessimists as regards our chances of sailing to Alexandria, a cruise which even in the summer could be tricky for a large boat like theirs. Our only hope, they said, was to follow the coast, with Haifa, Jaffa and Port Said as intermediate ports of call. But under prevailing war conditions, no ship which has been in Israel may call at an Arab port: if we put in at Jaffa we would be implacably refused admission to Egypt. The voyage was therefore unfeasible and we had better settle down to spend the winter in Beirut. The harbour wasn't so bad, the climate was sunny and the whisky cheap. Four months soon pass . . .

Our neighbour on the port side was a curious craft which at first sight seemed to be a cross between a veranda and a floating straw hat. Its name was written in elegant Arabic letters on the bows and we were given to understand it meant Puppy. We were also told that the owner was an Egyptian prince who was living in exile in Lebanon. The second we heard that *Puppy* was born on the Nile she took on an almost painful fascination for us: she now no longer resembled a straw hat but a sun boat. She was in the care of a small man by the name of Mustafa who went about dressed in turban and caftan and who spoke only Arabic. He interested us immoderately by his behaviour, equally dignified whether he was swabbing down *Puppy*'s deck, saying his prayers to Mecca or sitting under the awning with legs crossed, sewing at some mysterious handiwork. One thing was certain: Mustafa was not a real seaman, even if it was his calling. We wondered whether any Arab can be a good seaman. Does not his religion prevent him from being so? The complete subjection to God's will, the self-control and the indifference to material values characteristic of the Mohammedan make him a brave and patient warrior, a conqueror of desert wastes and often a harmonious everyday person as well, but the personal responsibility, the defiant spirit and the resolution of despair demanded of a genuine sailor are unknown to him. The maritime expeditions and privateering feats of the Arabs in past centuries, like those of the Turks, are no proof to the contrary, for their fleets were no doubt largely manned by Greeks.

Mustafa's story, told us by a Lebanese, fully confirmed what we thought. Formerly, when *Puppy* lay in Alexandria, Mustafa had no more put out to sea than he did here in Beirut, except in an absolutely dead calm with the help of the engine. But when the revolution came, the prince, from his refuge in Lebanon, sent a command to Mustafa in Alexandria: *Puppy* was to be sailed across the sea at once. Mustafa sighed, resigned himself into the hands of the Almighty and set out. When still only a few miles off Alexandria he ran into the most terrible storm and hid himself in the cabin to be spared the awful sight. For seven days *Puppy* drifted helplessly, Mustafa expecting every second to be swallowed by the waves, but at long last the storm abated as suddenly as it had arisen. Mustafa came up on deck to give thanks to Allah – and found that *Puppy* was lying only a few cable-lengths from the entrace to Beirut harbour.

For our part, we did not dare to trust in such pious miracles but sought help from science. Beirut has an airfield, which the Lebanese themselves claim is the finest in the western hemisphere and which we presumed must at least boast a few professional meteorologists. We went in search of a telephone and sure enough the weather prophet on duty was heard on the line. A forecast for the course to Alexandria? The reply was anything but encour-againg and in addition covered only the next twelve hours. What about the next four days – what weather could he offer for them? Regrettably, nothing at all, such long-period forecasts were quite outside the air station's province. I hung up dejectedly, but Mona was not to be put off so easily.

'Tomorrow morning we'll drive out to the airfield and talk sense to them', was her resolute comment, and so, having nothing better to do, out we went.

The airfield was indeed impressive. After we had been piloted up to a large office with glass walls, Mona began at once by telling the French-speaking meteorologists that her brother had the same job at Bromma airport in Stockholm and was a friend of Professor Bergeron's. The Frenchmen sprang to life. We were courteously invited to sit down and the entire staff set to work to compile the finest and most promising four-days' forecast possible: the weather had suddenly become ideal for a sailing trip to Alexandria. Who says it is not good to have connections! Happy and grateful, we hurried back to the harbour, arranged our clearance at express speed and only an hour later were heading out between Beirut's harbour piers on to a sea which, though still grey and sullen, we did not doubt would soon comply with the meteorologist's calculations.

The stretch of open sea that now lay ahead of us was the longest Mona and I had ever set off on alone. When *Daphne* sailed from Denmark to England we were three on board and the crossings Sicily-Greece, Sardinia-Mallorca, Ragusa-Brindisi, which we had previously made, were all shorter. But we had one advantage which we had lacked during previous voyages: a new and reliable engine. *Daphne* is built as a 'fifty-fifty boat', i.e. she is driven just as much by engine as by sail, but I stubbornly regard her as a sailing-boat with an auxiliary engine. This means that on principle I limit the stretches covered by engine to less than fifty per cent of a voyage's total distance. In previous years we often recorded still finer results, about twenty per cent engine operation, but that was due partly to our decrepit engine: either it didn't start at all or we held off as long as possible from trying to start it, afraid of the trouble and disappointment to which it so easily gave rise. This time the whole problem was changed and simplified through our having installed a Mercedes Benz thirty-four h.p. Diesel (a marine variation of the well-known private car 180 D's engine). It gives *Daphne*, despite her displacement of six and a half tons and anything but racer lines, a speed of seven and a half knots, which is also about the maximum when sailing; with half engine power we can do six knots, so that we nearly always go at this economic speed. When this story starts, the experiences of a long summer had already fulfilled all our expectations of the new engine, but its real testing-time awaited it down on the Nile.

We encountered only a light wind off Beirut but set our full 495 sq. ft. of sail as support in the heavy sea. This time we didn't hesitate to use the engine, all considerations of distance statistics went by the board. One thing only was important: to get down to Alexandria by every means available. After all the voyages and all the years Mona and I have sailed together we immediately fell into the right working routine. I set the course, 240°, put out the log and took bearings by the most convenient radio beacons; for the first time during the season we had invaluable help from our newly installed Aga direction-finding radio, which gave us frequent control bearings to Nicosia in Cyprus and the Beirut airfield astern. Mona lashed our motor scooter fast to its place in the saloon, put protective plastic covers over bookshelves, bunks and other parts of *Daphne*'s innards which were sensitive to water, and then despite the awkward motion of the boat got to work in the pantry to prepare a hot meal. The most important thing during a voyage like this is the condition of the crew and for this to be good one should have as regular meals as possible and get sufficient sleep. We always try, both by day and night, to sleep during the three hours when we take it in turns for the watch below, but this is after all the drawback of being only two on board. Unless the weather is ideal, there is very little sleep. This is all right for a day or two, but when you have not slept for four or five your power of resistance and fighting spirit are low. We have always been well aware that our long crossings have succeeded only because we had luck with the weather.

Even so, it was a relief to be on the move at last. No more doubt or uncertainty, it was up to us now to do our best. Imperceptibly we were filled with the sea's great peace, which is the same in storm and calm alike. Out here on the boundless wastes, where even the biggest breakers are merely a ripple on the surface and all the constant changes in cloud, wave and wind merely emphasize that the essentials are always the same, man too acquires a different and more steadfast outlook.

The first night at sea was rather trying. The wind, which was westerly and allowed us to stretch in the right direction, was still light but the waves grew bigger – evidently it was blowing hard somewhere south of Cyprus or near Crete. On the open Mediterranean the swell travels hundreds of miles from the local storm centres and you never know if it bodes bad weather or merely brings a greeting from it. It gets dark early in the late autumn – I had to put on the binnacle light about six o'clock – and the nights seem endless in a small boat which is tossed about from trough to trough in pitch-black darkness hour after hour. About nine o'clock we entered an area where the water was phosphorescent: every foaming crest gleamed white around us and sometimes we slid down a chute of luminosity which was so strong that the whole boat took on a ghostly glow.

Towards midnight rain squalls forced us to pay off a few points and to furl the mainsail. I will not deny that our spirits were low:

we knew quite well that we could not go on indefinitely tacking against a heavy sea with a small boat like *Daphne* and that we might have to turn right about and go back to Beirut. Without the engine we would presumably have lain pitching on the same spot, now we did at least make two knots against the waves, which broke more and more often over the deck. Sleep was out of the question and it seemed an eternity before the dawn came, grey and doubtful. It was about seven o'clock on this morning that the passenger plane from Tel Aviv to Cyprus thundered over our heads and I began to ponder about the invisible threads which bound us to more stable factors than the heaving sea around us.

The morning, when the rising sun has its say in the atmosphere's balance of power, is always the critical time for the weather and we waited on tenterhooks to know the verdict. This time it was Not Guilty. The clouds were raised like a curtain from the southern horizon, the wind died away and the sea was slowly smoothed out; we were plainly heading away from the storm area, which was left behind in the north. We had found our summery Mediterranean again. The sun shone, the engine hummed and as mile was added to mile I sat listening to the song of the bow-wave, far too conscious of our difficulties to be really care-free but feeling that every hour which passed like this was a gift. The Italian weather report in the afternoon was not promising: it spoke of '*mare agitato*' for the eastern Mediterranean, a grading which lies half way between '*mare mosso*' and the roughest sea '*mare molto agitato*'. The Cyprus radio in the evening predicted 'thunderstorms and local showers', but our own glass was rising. The second night at sea was just as calm as the first had been rough. With a slow, regular roll, as though she were breathing deeply, *Daphne* bore us south across the rippling sea.

The third day passed, calm and sunny. At sunset the sea took on the unmistakable opalescent shade that we recognized from Venice's lagoon and the Rhône estuary; this would have told us, if the radio direction finder had not done so, that we were approaching the Nile Delta, although the coast was so low-lying that we could not yet see it. But it sent us a greeting of another and far more evocative kind: as the short dusk of the south deepened, a land wind sprang up, enveloping us suddenly with smells so curious and unexpected that it was almost like a revelation. The chief ingredient was the pungent reek of swamps, but mixed with it was a smoky smell which we later learnt comes from the dried cakes of straw and manure which are the Egyptian fellah's main fuel. It was the supper-time smoke from the Delta villages which reached us, but on this evening at sea it seemed to us to be Egypt's own smell, a mixture of soil, temple incense, mummy-embalming spices and human sweat.

The night breeze from the land was strong after the hot day and gave us an excellent side-wind. We stopped the engine, which had been running without a break for three days and nights, and set course for the Rosetta lighthouse which had emerged in the dark. Our nautical manual had warned us of the extensive shoals in the estuary and we left a good wide margin – much too good, for we lost both the favourable course and the moderate sea inshore. The waves began to wash over us, the wind gradually veered until it was blowing head on and to our disgust we saw a large, lighted passenger ship pass several nautical miles nearer the lighthouse. Evidently we were not meant to reach our goal as easily as we had hoped: that night was one of the worst of the whole autumn. Twice we tacked towards the shore, but dared not go too near as we were uncertain of our exact position and there are perilous shoals far out to sea. In vain we peered for the lighthouse on Nelson Island – the little island from which the admiral led the devastating battle against Napoleon's fleet at Abu Quir. There was not the faintest sign of either Nelson Island's or Alexandria's lighthouse; all we could see was a host of fishing-boats, whose lanterns looked deceptively like flash-beacons as they bobbed up and down. There was nothing for it but to wait out at sea for the dawn: once again we drank the bitter draught, the Mediterranean's salt water. Wave after wave struck us in the face, forcing their way down our throats; soon a hard crust had formed on hands, face and oilskins.

This night off the Nile Delta gave us our first lesson about Egypt, a lesson which we should have missed had we arrived as ordinary tourists: we realized that the country is more isolated than an island, that no other country in the same way as ancient Egypt was a closed vessel into which outside influences could only seep by the drop. Modern Egypt has two gateways, both of

them of late date and opened by foreigners: the city founded by
Alexander the Great with the deliberate intention of breaking
down the barrier round antiquity's richest land, and Port Said,
built a century ago by Europeans. The old and natural approaches,
which were the only ones during Egypt's age of greatness, have
always been difficult to force: in the south the wild rapids of the
cataracts have hindered too close a contact with the interior of
Africa, in the east and west the deserts have formed frontiers more
insurmountable than snowclad Alps could do and in the north is
the low-lying, harbourless Delta coast with its dangerous sandbanks. That the Greeks during antiquity could force this approach
without the help of lighthouses or engines on the way to their
trading city of Naucratis in the Delta was a mystery and a wonder
to us on this gusty night at sea.

The dawn came at last and all the false beacons went out as
though by magic, only the real one was left like a wet, clear pearl
on the grey horizon. We were too tired to go down into the
pitching cabin to check the flashes in the list of lights. It must be
Nelson Island, we told ourselves, and headed towards the light.
We wanted to start the engine now, as we were making no headway in the choppy sea. I pressed the starter: no result. An inspection down in the engine-room showed that the battery, already
low, had been soaked during the night's wet passage and was too
weak to turn the starting motor. There was nothing for it but to
sail. The sun had risen and the flat coast appeared. At first we
thought we could make out sparse groups of trees, until all at
once the haze lifted and we found to our amazement that we were
in front of an endless city waterfront of tall modern buildings,
tasteless palace hybrids and, here and there, the minarets of a
mosque: Alexandria. During the night the current had borne us
westward; it was not Nelson Island but the big lighthouse at
Ras el Tin which we had sighted at dawn.

The wind developed into a kind of gale with sunshine which
reminded us very much of the mistral off Marseilles. We had a
stiff, wet tack before getting near enough to the city to distinguish
cars and people in the streets. While on the last tack up towards
Ras el Tin's point a V-formation of cranes suddenly flew in from
the sea, trumpeting loudly, and sank down to rest in the lee of the
shore. They were the same birds, the same cries we had heard on

so many clear autumn days at home in the far North, when they had started on their long flight to the South. These triumphant flocks, circling above us at the same moment we ourselves laboriously reached the coast of Africa, suddenly brought our distant homeland, lying now under the autumn frosts, strangely close.

The approach, or rather the approaches, to Alexandria are awkward, as in order to pass the dangerous shoals one must follow exactly one of the three leading lines marked out by means of tall seamarks on shore. A Yugoslavian tramp and a huge English liner were just on their way in and the pilot-boat which had met them came up to us and asked if we wanted help. After all the warnings and alarming descriptions we had heard of the rapacity of oriental authorities, shipbrokers and dragomans, we declined all assistance. With the help of charts and *The Mediterranean Pilot* we puzzled out by ourselves which buoys and marks were to be followed in order to come in through the relatively wide Boghaz channel. The blue waves gradually took on a more and more dirty-brown colour and by the time we had reached the entrance to the vast harbour, it was no longer the Mediterranean on which we sailed but the combined sewers of Alexandria with its million inhabitants.

Where were we to go among all the boats that were loading and unloading, all the shipyards, grimy wharves and endless warehouses? Quite at a loss, we scudded in with only the mainsail up, more vexed than ever that the engine would not start. The weather had suddenly turned hot, we took off our oilskins, gumboots and wet sheepskin jackets, and found that after our four days' sail we looked haggard, wild and windblown. A motorboat full of shouting men was bearing down on us. It boarded *Daphne* despite our vigorous protests and two orientals with portfolios stepped on to our deck – grasping shipbrokers, we thought. Three or four more boats turned up and for a moment we thought we were in for barefaced privateering, until we caught sight of uniforms and soldiers in red fezes. The Egyptian army now began to enter *Daphne* from all sides until every square inch of deck was occupied; at least forty strange men invaded our floating home. Had we by mistake sailed into a prohibited military area or had a new world war broken out unknown to us? Only when one of the soldiers saluted smartly and in broken English bade us welcome to Egypt, while flashlights went off right down a line of new motorboats, did I see that at any rate we had nothing to fear; a clump of journalists with pads and interview questions fully reassured us. While all this was going on, *Daphne* had continued scudding into the harbour by her mainsail, but as the press of people round me had blocked my view, we had got out of our course. Suddenly the main boom gybed. At one blow about thirty fezes were swept overboard – luckily nobody was hurt but the photographers probably got some amusing pictures.

By degrees it all became clear. We were welcomed in the kindest possible way by the Egyptian authorities and, to our utter astonishment, assumed the role of semi-official state guests that we learnt to play in less amateurish fashion during the months that followed. The background to our elevation was this:

Early in the year I had written to a Swedish business man in Cairo, Åke Norrby, and asked his advice about the trip we were planning. Norrby, in his capacity as representative in Egypt of Bofors, was on good terms with one of the 'new men' in the country, General Hassan Ragab, who happened to be very interested in sailing and had, among other things, founded the Egyptian Seascout League. The General at once looked upon our enterprise with a benign eye: it might well stimulate the seascouts to make similar river trips and show other countries how peaceful conditions in the new Egypt really were. He wrote us a letter, promising our expedition every possible support. We did not begin to suspect what this implied until here in Alexandria, where the authorities had already been on the *qui vive* for several weeks as the result of a telephone call from Cairo. Coastguards, lighthouse-keepers and pilots had been watching out for us day and night and as the General had not specified *Daphne*'s size or my degree of importance, they had been prepared for a luxury yacht with the tonnage of a small steamer and a potentate in a snow-white uniform. I must say that the reception committee put a good face on it and that the grey-haired, gold-braided harbour-master piloted us into the yacht harbour at Ras el Tin with great dignity.

Mona never really got over the shock of making her entrance on the Egyptian stage so unkempt, unpowdered and in all ways

27

so unprepared. To appear in the newspapers and in front of the authorities with her hair on end was bad enough, but having to step ashore at the yacht club in this condition was the last straw, and she could never forgive me for having arranged it all so stupidly. As regards luxury and fashionableness, Alexandria Yacht Club was far and away the grandest we had ever seen. The club had been the apple of King Farouk's eye and his enormous yacht *Mahrussa* was still moored to the quay. *Daphne* was shown to a place of honour at the jetty right below the restaurant and we knew greater comfort than in any club harbour we had previously visited. During the next few days we met many kind and friendly members of this club, mostly European families of a type that is common in Alexandria: they were Englishmen, Frenchmen, Italians and Greeks, many of them families who had come to Egypt three generations ago and founded businesses and industries here but who had assimilated the country's customs and interests to such a small degree that very often they could not even speak Arabic. They were now being shown, more and more clearly with every day that passed, that they were regarded as undesirable parasites in the new national state, that their residence permits might be withdrawn without warning, in short that the era of European enterprise in Egypt was at an end. As representatives of the new age, stiff groups of white-clad Egyptian officers sat at the lunch tables of the club restaurant, but on Sunday afternoons the club's well-tended garden terraces were still one big European garden party. I am not ashamed to admit the sympathy we showed these people who had had the misfortune to be born in the wrong country, so anguished under the care-free surface, but I do blush for the way in which we so naïvely accepted their descriptions of the good old days under Farouk.

It was the club, incidentally, which gave us our first insight – rather a comic one – into the social problems which are a legacy from the monarchy, or rather into the reluctance to see them. We had duly admired the restaurant's staff of perfect waiters, coal-black Nubians in ankle-length silk caftans and pleated turbans, who on swift and soundless feet bore the French chef's delicacies to the tables in the elegant dining-room. Judge of our amazement on the first evening when we came home from town after closing-time and passed the dining-room on our way to the quay: sleepy black heads were lifted from the tables, which had been converted into beds for the staff, who had nowhere to live but their place of work.

In so far as we had been expecting an oriental or ancient atmosphere in Alexandria, the city was a disappointment. It is a fairly typical Mediterranean port of nineteenth-century pattern, not unlike Piraeus, Barcelona or Marseilles. It is almost unbelievable that a two-thousand-year-old cultural metropolis could be so transformed into an upstart city lacking tradition, historic monuments or traces of the past. Yet Alexander the Great's embalmed body and unopened sarcophagus, together with most of the ancient Alexandria's ruins, lie hidden somewhere under the blocks of offices and the boulevards, if one can believe the testimony of historians and travellers of old. Alexander's tomb, down into which many a Roman emperor stepped during his royal progress in Egypt to pay homage to the world conqueror, was buried under temporary defence walls during the riots and sieges towards the end of the second century A.D. and was never found again. Tradition points out a spot just south of the present Fuad I Street underneath the Nebi Daniel mosque as the hiding-place of the tomb, but the Mohammedan priesthood has hitherto opposed every effort at research. Let us be thankful for this opposition: it is far more dignified for Alexander to rest in peace with a big city as a tombstone than to be exhibited in a museum.

What we saw most of in Alexandria was Egyptian government offices and civil servants. Despite the extreme benevolence of the authorities and their wish to facilitate our journey in every way, it was an unusual and intricate procedure to arrange a permit to import *Daphne* temporarily through the Egyptian customs, to get stamps and certificates from coastguards, ordinary police, secret police, harbour authorities, lock and bridge engineers, etc. In these delicate operations we had invaluable help from Sweden's excellent consul Emil Delin and mighty support from the head of the Egyptian Ports and Lights, Admiral Yusuf Hammad. At first these countless calls at civil service departments seemed an utter waste of time and we thought regretfully of all that we might have seen and learnt of Egypt instead. Had we known that this was only a beginning and that daily, for hours at a stretch, for the next four months we were to consume Coca Cola, tea or coffee during polite conversation with government officials, ranging from provincial governors and ministers to police officers and village chieftains, we might have turned tail in alarm. Only by degrees did we learn that this modern variation of old oriental courtesy, which makes it impossible to have a short and purely factual contact with a fellow human being, is something worthy of great respect. It means that one adheres to the human factor and the irrational essentials which we, in our efficient western communities, have done away with more and more. Hospitality offered and received, a drink consumed in common, conversation about the beauty of the country, are in themselves ceremonies of undeniable import, but more than anything else they are the means and the pretext for mutual investigation and indirect conclusions. These daily contacts, which, despite their transience, let us feel liking and understanding or dislike and criticism of so many varied members of the community whom we should not even have met in a western country, taught us more about Egypt than all the picturesque walks would have done. By degrees we developed it into a real sport to ask suitable questions, make indirect suppositions and, above all, to state as obvious facts everything that we wondered at. Presumably our interlocutors manoeuvred in the same way to sound our attitude: conversation is an art in the orient.

In this way we very soon found out that the Egyptian reality has two sides: the one you want people to believe in and which perhaps you hope you can soon bring about, and reality such as it is on account of unfortunate but understandable circumstances. This division occurs of course in most countries, but in a nation with so many unsolved internal and external problems, such newly-aroused national self-assertion and such impatient eagerness for reform as the Egyptian, it is particularly apparent. You visit a school and hear from the teachers that school is compulsory for all, that illiteracy is almost a thing of the past – but closer inspection shows that those who can read and write are few among the broad masses of the people. You visit a factory and are told that child labour is forbidden by law – which means that all the youngsters swarming among the machines have forged certificates (which no one believes in) saying they have turned sixteen. This duplicity is to be found more or less everywhere in the Egyptian society and lent no little psychological interest to our daily dealings with the authorities. Here in Alexandria we still believed all we were told; the next stage in our development was indignation at their barefaced mendacity, but at last we realized that it is not a question of deliberate lies but of a kind of word magic with ancient traditions: reality always shapes itself in time according to our way of describing it. In this current metamorphosis of their native land the Egyptian civil servant joins whole-heartedly.

But we were eager to leave Alexandria, to get all formalities and practical matters settled so that at last we could reach the real Egypt and start our Nile trip. After six days everything was ready, the exhausted batteries recharged, the engine overhauled by a Mercedes mechanic and the problem of finding an interpreter provisionally solved. We had been aware from the outset that it is not possible to travel about the Egyptian countryside without an interpreter; if you cannot speak the language of the country you need someone who can talk to the local inhabitants, help with purchases and other practical matters and also act as go-between with the authorities. It is not a question of xenophobia – of which we saw very little during our journey – but rather of a lack of that familiarity with foreigners which makes it possible to move about in European countries unmolested. A foreigner in an Egyptian village is seen only once in a blue moon and causes such a sensation that everyone has simply got to know who he is and what he does. If he can tell them himself or is already known, well and good; otherwise he must resign himself to the police turning out and to being detained and questioned. For us who were going to sail on the Nile, moreover, there was the added need of contact with other boats, with locksmen and with people at the places we called at. We were therefore very pleased when the eldest of the yacht club's boat watchmen, a sturdy little Arab by the name of Ibrahim who spoke tolerably good English, offered to come with us to Cairo for ten shillings a day plus his keep. He had recently done the same trip with a large motorboat and therefore said he could also act as pilot.

Originally we had intended following the Mahmoudie Canal, which links Alexandria with the Nile, but Admiral Hammad dissuaded us: not only was the canal barely deep enough for our five feet three inches, but it was so chock-full of barges and feluccas that we risked both untold delays and damage to the boat. The alternative was the sea route via the more westerly of the Nile's two mouths, the so-called Rosetta Mouth, a good forty nautical miles east of Alexandria. I will not deny that it went very much against the grain to embark on a new sea adventure – it had been such an enormous relief to us to leave the treacherous and perilous sea when we had sailed into Alexandria harbour, convinced that now, for a whole sunny winter, we would merely glide along on sheltered waters as smooth as glass. Rosetta Mouth was dangerous and in any case could only be passed in relatively calm weather. But when we were promised a reliable pilot, who would meet us out at sea, we gave in. The start was fixed for early in the morning of 14th November and Ibrahim set off by bus to Rosetta to make sure that the pilot really got under way.

The weather was overcast and a cutting wind was blowing when we left Alexandria at dawn and via the Frigate Channel came out on to the open sea. Without our engine there would have been no hope of getting to Rosetta by nightfall – now, with all sails set, we could stretch on the right course against the choppy sea. The coastline is so low that off the wide Abu Quir Bay we lost sight of it, but about three o'clock in the afternoon the Rosetta lighthouse appeared like a sharp pencil above the horizon. The sea also lessened by degrees – evidently the sandbanks extending for miles outside the river mouth gave a certain lee. When low-lying spits of sand emerged we began to take soundings – a wise precaution, as the first one showed a depth of two fathoms and soon only one. At the same moment we caught sight of a two-masted boat inshore of the lighthouse. We saw it sailing at incredible speed over the low banks – obviously it was on the river and was helped by the current. We anchored and soon it had got out to us. On the rounded deck sat two cross-legged Arabs in turbans and caftans, manoeuvring with great skill. They circled round *Daphne*'s stern so that one of them could hop on board and after he had greeted us in the name of Allah we weighed anchor. The flat-bottomed pilot boat went straight back to the lighthouse but *Daphne* was borne in a wide arc far out to sea, where a large fishing fleet lay tossing about. Then we followed a twisting course between a series of sandbanks marked by old petrol drums anchored as buoys. The drums have to be shifted every week or month as the channel changes – without a pilot it would have been impossible to get in here and even now the keel scraped bottom several times.

The shoals changed imperceptibly to low, sterile river banks; it began to get dark but we could still make out one or two cement buildings and a water tower which, to our archaeologically-tuned eyes, looked like a fantastic ancient Egyptian temple. For a good half-hour we had to lie out in the current with the engine running; a bunch of fishing-boats on their way home were thronging round a control station to get their papers stamped. Each boat had over twenty men on board – it takes time to get used to the density of population in this country, where five or six men always do the same work as one man with us. How the pilot could guide us into the town of Rosetta in the pitch darkness was a mystery, but after an hour and a half's journey upstream we tied up at the police jetty and were welcomed by Ibrahim and a jovial police sergeant in gold-green uniform. The latter shone his torch on three fierce, befezzed soldiers with rifles and heavy cartridge belts round their waists.

'Don't be afraid', he explained in broken English. 'We will keep guard all night, this is the government landing-stage and the police-station with other soldiers is just next door. You are in complete safety!'

A trifle bewildered, we withdrew into *Daphne*'s cosy cabin, where Mona got supper ready. After five months of adventure at sea it felt very nice to be resting on the calm waters of the great river, to have slunk in through the narrow gateway to Egypt's enclosed and sunny winter garden, away from the grey skies and cold of Europe, but we began to wonder if perhaps new forms of hardship did not lie ahead.

CHAPTER II

Delta Landscape

The Nile Delta is not a part of Egypt usually visited by tourists and one must admit that in two important respects it is overshadowed by the country's southern provinces. In the first place, there are very few ancient monuments here: temples and tombs have long since sunk down into the soft earth or been buried under the new layers of silt which the river is constantly bringing with it. In the second, the landscape itself is not remarkable; instead of the narrow river valley between cliffs and desert wastes which makes Upper Egypt an oasis 600 miles long and sometimes only a few yards wide, there is only a flat and fertile plain, crisscrossed by canals, railway lines and roads. There is nothing unusual about the climate either: the nearness of the sea makes clouds, mist and rain almost as common as in other Mediterranean countries.

Yet I like to think back on the five days that our journey to Cairo took: they initiated us into the timelessly formal atmosphere, so curiously composed of happiness and sorrow, that is Egypt. Nowhere have I known air so pure and easy to breathe or seen a landscape so vibrant with a garden of paradise's enchantment as in Egypt – nor have I been dogged so inescapably or nauseatingly by decay, excrement, feverish human suffering. Underlying all dazzling experiences is always the awareness that this world is ruthless, exacting and too strong for man. Yet it is man who has created it and set his stamp on it, perhaps as no other landscape has been created and influenced by its inhabitants. But it is not for themselves men have created Egypt – it is for someone else. The question that is unavoidable during a Nile trip is this: for whom has Egypt been created? for whom have these millions and millions of lives, cut off before their time, been sacrificed? who is the great lord who can live in the garden of paradise, breathing the pure desert air without being worried by the destitution? Partly, I suppose, it has been the Pharaohs, the sultans and viceroys, the big landowners, the village tyrants and, latterly, the wealthy foreign tourists, but they have all been really deputies for the actual lords of Egypt, those for whom this strange land was once created and who could enjoy it without inhibitions: the gods. Everything in Egypt speaks of them; they are necessary, in fact, for otherwise the superhuman beauty and the superhuman suffering would be meaningless. It is no wonder that the gods were the only living, real beings in ancient Egypt and that man could live only by putting himself in relationship to them. And one can see that they were succeeded by foreign conquerors and profiteers who set their own egotism in place of that of the gods. If it is really possible to bring about the social revolution in Egypt of which there has been so much talk lately and which is meant for the welfare of the majority, a radical change will have been made in the Nile country for the first time in history.

We were awakened early by the teeming life of Rosetta on this first morning on the Nile. The sun had just risen in a cloudless sky and was shining down from the other side of the river over clumps of Nile boats at their moorings, with sky-high masts, over the swarming crowds of people on the banks and over the hideous, utterly dreary brick buildings along the street by the river. Our guards were dozing under some large trees by the landing-stage, an overfull ferry put out from the shore and drifted obliquely with the current towards the palm-fringed east bank, while a motor barge chugged past on its way up towards the distant haze that hung over the river. We too would have preferred to start off at once on the adventure that was beckoning to us, but we were forced to be patient: *Daphne*'s masts were to be taken down for the trip to Cairo. Although all the bridges *en route* can be opened, they are so many and their opening times are so erratic that we were advised to be independent of them. After Cairo we could begin to sail again, as in Upper Egypt the bridges are often hundreds of miles apart.

The problem was how to dismantle the masts without a mast crane. But we had a brainwave. Ibrahim and Ahmed Sobh, a very amiable and obliging seascout whom we had met in Alexandria and who had come along to help us in Rosetta, had a word with the captain of a large two-masted Nile sailing-boat which lay nearby. *Daphne* was towed under its high bowsprit, to which a jack was fastened, and soon our masts lay happily on deck. They did stick out fore and aft, but our experience on the French canals had taught us that in spite of this we could manoeuvre quite well. During the work, *Daphne* was inundated by people who wanted to lend a hand and Ibrahim was anxious in case some of our equipment should vanish in the confusion, but when the job was done after two hours, sails and ropes stowed away, shroud-pulleys counted and the masts safely chocked up, nothing was missing. It was time to dole out to the forest of grasping, dirty hands the baksheesh that had been clamoured for ever since the work started.

Baksheesh – this word which the tourist in Egypt is soon sick of the sound of and which had met us in loud-voiced chorus on our very first walk in Alexandria – covers both the alms that the foreigner is expected to dispense at every step and the wage earned for small services, from willingness to stand as a model in front of the camera to payment for real work, such as this derigging. When you see the destitution in Egypt and realize that these few coppers mean a definite, though temporary, improvement in the family's living conditions, you put up more easily with the begging, which is really rife only along the well-beaten tourist tracks: in the villages at the foot of the Pyramids, at Luxor and Assuan. In ordinary villages we very seldom heard the demanding cry.

The police force in Egypt is a purely military organization composed of men armed with rifles and spruce officers who have badges of rank on their shoulders. We had been given a hint as to the expediency of paying a courtesy call on Rosetta's major in the adjacent police barracks, hereby beginning the intercourse with the high guardians of law and order which was to be our lot in so many Egyptian towns and villages. One bright spot was that all these officers turned out to speak English, so no interpreter was needed. They were also polite and helpful throughout. Rosetta's *mamour*, i.e. chief of police, wanted to do something special for us and after a voluble consultation on the telephone in Arabic he declared:

'You are to be shown our rice factory, which exports rice even to your homeland.'

The mamour himself and two other officers, plus five or six soldiers, came with us – it was our first walk under police escort but by no means our last. Everything was still new and unfamiliar to us; the stench, the flies, the misery, which we literally waded in as we picked our way along Rosetta's muddy streets, our own part as carefree, protected central figures in the sensational procession and perhaps most of all the behaviour of the police. Both in front of and behind us marched grim-faced soldiers armed with rifles and leather whips. We gazed open-mouthed at this last object, the so-called *courbasch*, which, as I found out later, has played such a leading part in Egypt's social history. It is very little exaggeration to say that for thousands of years it has formed the chief contact between the powers that be and the common people in this land. Probably with its help the Pyramids were built and right up to the nineteenth century it was in constant use every time a road or canal was built, in the collection of taxes and the administration of justice. The fact that one still sees it so often does not mean to say that it plays a much greater role than the sabres of the Swedish police: more and more it has come to be an attribute, the sign of authority. But the crack of its thongs in the air still creates a respectful vacuum in crowd-filled streets, as we saw for the first time here in Rosetta. We detested these walks under escort and avoided them as often as possible, but we soon learnt that an Egyptian police officer cannot imagine any other form of excursion. His kind offer to show us this or that sight within his district always resulted in such parades, which – at whip's length – hundreds of inquisitive people joined, so that often the entire village seemed on the point of rioting.

The rice factory was also a depressing experience. It lay some distance from the river, but a constant stream of men dressed in rags carried the heavy sacks from barges along sagging planks up to the flat roof of the factory, where the rice was dried in the sun: the building of the Pyramids must have presented much the same sight. The inside of the factory was a huge jumble of shafts, wheels and slapping belts. One felt surrounded by a hundred monsters with ravenous jaws. The owner, a small, befezzed man with a paunch, did admit that 'a few accidents do happen now and then'. But there was nothing wrong with the rice itself; it was well up to the standard of the world's leading brands.

On the way back we looked into a large, dilapidated mosque. Its wooden roof was supported by hundreds of columns, which had evidently been taken from various ancient buildings; several of them had double capitals, one below the rafters and one upside down on the floor. Otherwise Rosetta has no ancient monuments. The famous Rosetta Stone, which became the key with which Champollion solved the riddle of the hieroglyphics, was found all by itself a mile or two outside the town. It is hard to believe that even at the beginning of the nineteenth century Rosetta was still a larger and more important place than Alexandria. The impression of poverty and unhealthy dampness which now pervades the town seemed to us particularly strong in this abandoned mosque. There was not a soul to be seen inside, but out in the courtyard a lone man was lying like a discarded rag. As we walked past he raised himself painfully on his elbow; out of the waxy face, ravaged by disease, two large eyes stared at us, stared without seeing: a dying man alone with his god. But above him the sky arched its silk-blue bowl, the palms lifted their tall free trunks behind the wall of the mosque and outside – wide, generous and eternal – the river glided past.

It was half-past one before Mona, Ibrahim and I got away from our mooring by the police barracks. We were full of the solemnity of the moment: our Nile voyage was beginning. Rosetta disappeared behind a bend and we headed upstream between green, well-tilled banks. Here and there the desert sand had encroached from the west, seized a palm grove or a solitary marabout grave in its deadly embrace and was now cast in yellow dunes right down to the water. Then the fields began again. But there was almost more life on the water than on the banks. We met many craft of different types, small steamers, barges, rowing-boats, but mostly large sailing-boats with sky-high masts and bellying sails, fantastic, almost supernatural visions. The Nile boats, built to catch the light breezes above the high, steep banks and only to scud on ever-sheltered waters, are some of the most extraordinary craft in existence. At short intervals we passed villages which, with their low houses of sun-dried bricks and their free planning, had a much more pleasing appearance than the town of Rosetta. Round cakes of manure and dry maize straw were neatly stacked on the flat roofs for fuel, women dressed in black and men in light-coloured caftans, so-called *galabias*, were visible in the scant shade of the palms, and women with earthenware pitchers balanced on their heads kept making their way down the steep bank to fetch water. The whole scene had an air of dignity and peace which might well be called biblical; perhaps the idyllic impression was partly due to the fact that our field-glasses helped us to take part, without too intimate contact, in the women's conversation as they filled their pitchers, in the children's games in the village streets and in the men's work in the fields.

Towards evening we passed the big lock at Atfech, which had recently been completed. It was built to shut off the entire river channel between each flood period, so that none of the precious river water is lost and no sea water is forced up the irrigation channels during northerly storms. The lock was negotiated as easily as any on the Seine or Saône and we tied up in the middle of the little village just above the lock.

Sublime peace as the sun went down and the peasants, who had finished their day's work, came down to the river to wash, according to ritual, feet, arms, face and genitals. Then they drank Nile's water and, each by himself, said their prayers towards Mecca – the whole thing so dignified, so brimful of tradition, meaning and human beauty that only afterwards did we react to the hair-raising sanitary problems. The river is an appalling carrier of infection and bacilli, as it functions as a giant sewer for the greater part of Egypt's twenty-two million inhabitants, who are also in the habit of throwing all their dead oxen, camels, donkeys and other animals into the water, where you meet them as stinking rafts surrounded by vultures. You watch aghast as one fellah cups his hand to drink while another, only a few yards upstream, empties his bowels. In all my life I have never seen so many hairy human backsides as on this first day on the Nile: the river bank is one big public lavatory. With a certain wonderment I later read in Flaubert's and Maxime du Camp's accounts of their travels how the two friends, upon arrival in Egypt, hastened down to the Nile to drink its sacred waters: their salvation must have been the fact that Pasteur did not discover bacilli until some years later and that in those days there were only seven million Egyptians to contribute to the water's savoury taste.

It was still dark when we were aroused about six o'clock the next morning by the people on the neighbouring boats. They all washed themselves just as ritualistically as in the evening, after which prayers were said. To my astonishment I saw that open fires had been lighted down in the empty holds of the boats, where the crew crouched in a ring to warm themselves while breakfast, a kind of bean porridge called *foule*, was prepared. About half-past six the sun rose and we set off. The morning was very cold and a raw mist lay over the river, but this mist, out of which the patterns of the palm groves, the villages with the smoke curling up and the boats on the glassy water appeared like Chinese drawings, was incredibly beautiful – pearly-grey and dense for the first hour, but lighter and lighter as the sun rose, until all that was left was a faint shimmer above the river. The banks became as clear-cut as the reliefs of a burial chamber.

Almost inevitably, one compares the Nile shore's endless bands of rural scenes in silhouette against the background of desert or field with the reliefs of the old Egyptian tombs on a connecting base-line. When, in addition, one sees again the same occupations, the same tools and the same people one recognizes from re-productions in the art-history books, a voyage on the Nile becomes at the same time a voyage back into ancient Egypt. The naked fishermen wading about in the mud by the shore with nets stretched between long sticks had a particularly ancient air. Their powerful, straight shoulders, narrow hips and round heads were unmistakable: it is one of Egypt's greatest miracles that the race, the types of people, have so obviously been preserved unchanged for five thousand years, due no doubt to the country's isolated position. While the peoples in other parts of the world have flowed backwards and forwards like sea currents and mixed with each other, only small quantities of foreign blood have come into Egypt and they have been largely assimilated.

The same people, but a new land, one might say. For while man lives on, there is not one square foot of the old Egypt left. This is due partly to the river, which every year fetches new soil from the interior of Africa. The whole country is rising, the river-bed as much as its surroundings: the land of the Pharaohs lies about fifteen feet below the Egypt of today. But man himself has caused the greatest changes by cultivating, damming and irrigating the soft soil. In that way, in the dim dawn of time, Egypt once rose out of the endless marshes and as a result of man's continuous work the ancient conditions have in their turn been altered. The papyrus reeds, the lotus flowers, the crocodiles and the hippopotami, which for a long time lived on as memories of the old wilderness, have now gone for good and all. In our day, cotton and maize could serve as the country's heraldic plants, just as two animals, the camel and the water-buffalo, which were unknown to the old Egyptians, represent the most typical fauna.

The irrigation system itself, which for thousands of years was the unchanging basis of the country's agriculture, as it hardly ever rains in Egypt, has radically changed during the last hundred years. The old method of letting the Nile flood the fields each year, of sowing in its fat slime and in this way getting a good harvest, is nowadays used only in Upper Egypt and, like the papyrus, crocodiles and marshes, will probably soon be something which lives on only in the distant Sudan. The many dams that have been built in the Nile, chiefly the big Delta dam near Cairo, have made possible the building of a wide network of canals, which are kept filled with water all the year round without the fields being flooded. From these canals suitable quantities of water are drawn off regularly for the crops and the earth gives unbroken harvests – three or four – depending on what is grown. It is this rationalized agriculture which has allowed Egypt's population to leap up to twenty-two millions, – ten times as many as lived here during Napolean's campaigns and three times the highest population figure of antiquity. The Delta is that part of the country which has been most profoundly changed by the new irrigation system; the actual character of the landscape has become so uncertain that now you think you are passing through Holland with sailing-boats high above the fields, now through France with rustling avenues of poplars, now through England with shady parks and ugly factories – to be transported once more to Africa.

On this particular morning we got some idea of how Egypt's unchanging population in an unchanged way meets this changed world: in front of a modern brick-works a motor barge was loading. A flock of women and children, of whom the youngest was perhaps five, moving at the double carried bricks on their heads down springing planks, while a grim-looking sheik type with a stick in his hand stood on deck supervising the work.

Ibrahim looked after the tiller all day, which gave me a welcome chance of writing up the log-book, reading and attending to

Daphne. Otherwise our interpreter was of little pleasure to us. Before he moved on board Mona had made up his bed with sheets in the after-saloon and been worried about the kind of food he would like. As it turned out, he not only preferred to sleep on top of the quilt and to eat his own food that he had brought with him, but he had very little time at all for the Nordic democracy's forms of expression. In fact, we had a strong suspicion that he disliked Europeans, thought us unclean from a religious point of view and was determined to do no more than the work he had undertaken, – to pilot *Daphne* safely to Cairo. He was neither friendly nor unfriendly, gay nor sad, merely matter-of-fact. The encounter with the oriental self-control in Ibrahim's person was a lesson to us with our mania for making friends: we saw that we would never know what he thought and that it was probably best for us.

About eleven o'clock in the morning we passed a comparatively big town. The banks were chock-a-block with people and hundreds of boats lay in dense clusters on the river. What did this mean? A big fair and religious festival which took place here in Desouk every year, Ibrahim informed us. He must have regretted his talkativeness when we instantly decided to stop and have a look at the town, but his warnings and protests could not deter us.

'Well, don't blame me,' he said as we tied up beside a big barge, but he did promise to guard the boat while we went ashore.

With the camera – regarded with such suspicion in Mohammedan countries – hidden in Mona's handbag, we balanced our way across the many boat-decks and climbed the high, muddy bank, a target for staring eyes from countless crouching figures on the boats. At the top of the bank was a labyrinth of temporary dwellings made of canvas and sacking, where a compact mass of fellah families lived, men in light-coloured galabias, women in black gowns, but unveiled as the custom is in the country, and a swarm of children of all ages. Farther away we came across large tents where acrobats, sword-swallowers and jugglers appeared, and lions, strong men and legless women were on show; there were merry-go-rounds, rifle-ranges, try-your-strength machines, all of the most primitive and simple kind, such as were to be seen

at country fairs in Europe before electricity was invented and
naive surprise disappeared. For those familiar with the problems
of Italian over-population and unemployment it was touching to
find at this wretched fellah fair a tent with the inscription
TROUPE ACROBATICA ITALY and MUR DE LA MORT
– some Italian cyclist acrobats were trying their luck here as the
only Europeans among nothing but orientals. The most Egyptian
of all the performers were perhaps the stick-fighters from Upper
Egypt who, surrounded by dense rings of spectators, showed
their strange, stylized battles. Local colour of another kind was
provided by the large, magnificently equipped stalls, where
bottles of eye medicine were sold as if they had been the elixir of
life; Egypt is the classic land of eye diseases and we were struck by
the large number of people at the fair with blind or blighted eyes.

The temptation to capture some of all this on film was strong.
Cautiously drawing out the camera, I first photographed – on
the basis of what the history of art teaches about the motifs in
Islamic reproductions – only inanimate objects, a few water
pitchers, an inscription. So far so good, nobody reacted hostilely.
Then I went on to animals: a performing monkey, some camels
with splendid trappings which were making their way through
the sea of people. But when I pointed the lens at a group of women
they raised loud cries and hid their faces in their hoods. A
ferocious giant, perhaps the husband of the women, rushed up
to us and a crowd collected. Fortunately there were some policemen in red fezzes nearby. They saved us from the mob, but led
us away instead. Were we under arrest? On the way we were
stopped by a young man, under whose plain clothes two long
pistol barrels stuck out. He asked curtly in English if we had any
papers. Luckily, we had equipped ourselves with three documents
in Alexandria: one from Admiral Hammad to the police, another
to the bridge, harbour and lock authorities and a third from the
Swedish Embassy, all in Arabic and obviously eloquent. The
plain-clothes policeman introduced himself politely as chief of
the secret police and told us that he had been ordered here during
the fair from his permanent post in Port Said. As he seemed a
pleasant sort of person and could give us interesting information,
we resigned ourselves with a good grace to being escorted by
him from then on.

The fair at Desouk is really an annual pilgrims' gathering at the tomb of a holy man, the Sheik Ibrahim. Our escort, who evidently had some education, told us that, like the even larger fair at Tantah, it is a direct continuation of the ancient Egyptian festivals at Busiris and Bubastis, familiar from the vivid descriptions of Herodotus. At present there were about 25,000 fellahs collected in the town, but tomorrow, the big festival day, there would be considerably more. We elbowed our way to the mosque, a cupola-crowned and comparatively modern building which we were allowed to enter, thanks to our detective. That is to say, Mona was no more allowed to enter the mosque itself than any other woman, but was conducted by two police by an outer way to the burial chapel. As we stood in a queue at the door, an enormous American car stopped in the street, a bowing servant opened the car door and the doorkeeper of the mosque hurried up to kiss the hand of the man getting out. He was a portly Egyptian in European dress who graciously allowed himself to be divested of his shoes before entering the mosque in his socks.

'A holy man, a sheik,' I heard to my astonishment, thereby learning two new things: that holiness and material prosperity do not exclude each other in Mohammedan countries, and that the word sheik, which means chieftain or elder, is also used to denote those who have come farthest in religion.

Inside the mosque a host of cripples, beggars and sick people had encamped. The dectective and I were borne along by the stream of pilgrims to the burial chapel, right up to the grating which protected the actual coffin. Along the other side of the coffin, behind a trellis screen, the women with their children filed past. They stroked the iron grating passionately, and then passed their hands across their sexual organs to become fertile. Here I heard for the first time the weird trill of exaltation called *zagarit*, which so obviously reaches us through thousands of years that my blood ran cold with a sacred terror. After that we heard it often during our voyage – even in such profane contexts as when a ferry started after a long wait or a chieftain condescended to show himself in a village, but like its opposite, the women's ancient wail of lament at a death or a funeral, it never left us unmoved.

DELTA LANDSCAPE

Our detective friend now insisted that we go with him to the police station, a sight not to be missed, so he said. He really wanted to show us to the chief of police, a fat and sweaty major who sat behind a rickety table in the town's bus garage which had been turned into a temporary police station. The major was greatly put out by our presence; our entire stock of credentials plus passports were copied out word by word, and while we sipped a courteously proffered Coca Cola we had ample time to study the pickpockets, short-weight vendors and bloodstained fighters who were set down in an unceasing stream at the door and collected inside awaiting examination, while their wives, children and friends, praying or resigned, jostled outside. No shadow of tragedy hung over the police station, rather an atmosphere of the market hubbub of former times in our own homeland, the brawling of boisterous village lads and the barefaced tricks of the out-and-out rogues.

After at least an hour we were allowed to proceed, still under detective escort. We now admired the magnificent rest tents which village chieftains and other potentates, vying nobly with each other, had erected and into which anyone at all could go and sit down on the gilded chairs and be offered refreshment. This hospitality is not a form of charity to the poor but a form of intercourse between men from all classes of society in the spirit of Mohammedan brotherliness. The beggar in rags is just as well-mannered here as the sheik and all join in the conversation. The westerner cannot help pausing to search his heart; is this not an example of practical equality and very real education of the masses which we have nothing to equal?

To round off our visit to the fair we squashed in among naive peasant girls and excited children in a tent made of sacking to watch a shimmy-dancer. The music alone, executed on half a dozen instruments by two men with the help of mouths, hands and feet, was worth the few coppers we paid for admission and we capitulated utterly when a ripe beauty who must have weighed at least fifteen stone began to jerk her bared stomach about with a vigour which was almost military – first standing up, then on her knees and at last lying down with only her trunk moving and a stereotyped expression of bliss on her heavily painted face. The whole thing was so candid and so unashamedly obscene that

45

it became innocent, and the children, who without a doubt had learnt everything about love's gestures in their overcrowded living conditions, applauded as enthusiastically as the grown-ups.

Then we picked our way home through the camp area, carefully avoiding sleeping people, dishes of food spread out on the ground for sale and the human excrement that was dotted about everywhere. This time we happened to pass through a cluster of tents where smiling young women drew aside the sacking and beckoned us. For two northerners, unused to so much compact humanity as the last few hours had thrust upon us, it felt like a privilege to step once more on board our welcoming *Daphne* and steer out on to the open waters of the river. We all three felt an urgent need of sorting ourselves out and regaining our mental balance. Ibrahim, who was quite anxious by this time, was almost cordial to us; I went and stood in the bows to be alone and to breathe the pure desert air and Mona, unable to clean up Egypt, set to work to clean the already neat and tidy *Daphne*.

Yet we were glad we had stopped at Desouk. From that day we felt attached to the fellah with the strong bands of solidarity and compassion. Perhaps it is possible to feel this solidarity with everyone provided you can get close enough to them – so close that you recognize in them your own will to live, create and develop yourself, this power within, which is common to us all and which is expressed in so many different ways according to our various external potentialities. But the small differences in these expressions are often a greater hindrance to our understanding than the large ones. It is not because the fellah's life resembles ours that we identify ourselves so deeply with him but because his elementary need of security, love, holiness and success has taken on such different forms: we cannot stop at this meagre exterior but go straight to the core. Compassion needs no explanation: the boundless joy we had witnessed at the paltry delights of Desouk was a plain enough pointer to the sorrows in these lives. Statistics about the enormous prevalence of the various endemic diseases, about the scarcity of food, the tyrannic power of superstition and about the average length of life as being twenty-eight years, cannot add anything essential to what we saw here with our own eyes.

After that day in Desouk we could not see the burning problems of Egypt from any other angle but the social, and our attitude
to the new regime was based entirely on what we thought it could
do for the fellahs. Are they themselves at last to have the benefit of
their work, does the government really feel responsible for them,
or are they expected to go on suffering in order that a handful of
officers with a lust for power can build up a modern but unnecessary army and lead Egypt towards the sterile sacrifices of war?

It was four o'clock before we got away from Desouk, and
Ibrahim, who was evidently prone to nervous fears, soon had a
new problem to worry about: where were we to shelter for the
night? To us, used only to thinking of a harbour's safety as regards
wind and sea, this anxiety was very odd. Couldn't we drop anchor
anywhere at all and hang out a riding-light as a warning? Ibrahim
snorted: if we *must* spend the night out on the river, then it was
best not to have a light which would give us away. But nobody
does anchor on the Nile – you tie up at the bank, preferably in a
large village where there are police. Why? Ibrahim refused to go
into any details, he merely mumbled something about there being
so many 'bad people'. Darkness began to fall, but there was no sign
of a town or village. Soon we were steering through dense
darkness which was alive with sailing-boats floating soundlessly
along without any navigation lights. Evidently Ibrahim too was
uncertain of the way, he began to call out to other boats and when
an uncommonly friendly voice answered from a large two-master
he conjured me to take a pilot. With his galabia tucked up to his
thighs, a gaunt man leapt over on to *Daphne* and took over the
helm. After an uneventful two hours we reached the town of
Kafr ez Zaiyat and tied up on the outside of a moored river
steamer.

As usual we were roused at dawn by chattering and shouting.
The river steamer was filling up with passengers long before the
hour of departure. In the dawn light Kafr ez Zaiyat looked, if
possible, even drearier than Rosetta and we had no wish to
accompany Ibrahim when he went ashore to buy eggs and fruit.
Instead, we studied the passengers on the river boat with the
same naive curiosity as they studied us. The steamer had no
cabins, only two flat, veranda-like decks one above the other and
the better-class passengers emphasized their splendid isolation by

47

spreading out white mats on which they sat with crossed legs. Not one person in European dress, not one prosaic suitcase, only galabias and turbans, saddle-bags and chests. Stately patriarchs walked gravely across the gangway, followed by two or three humble wives dragging the baggage.

We started about half-past seven together with the river steamer, but it soon lagged behind on its zig-zag trip between the various villages. Up to now we had light-heartedly steered along in midstream and always had deep water under our keel, but on this day we experienced for the first time something which we were blissfully unaware was to be a daily occurrence during the months that followed. *Daphne* skipped gently over something at once firm and elastic, lurched – and continued after a further jog or two if the shoal was small or stuck fast if it increased. In the latter case we were usually swung round ninety degrees by the current, the boat heeled over on her keel and we listed heavily. I now know that one should not sail on the Nile at all with a keel-boat – least of all if it has a draught like ours. It is not mere chance that *Daphne* is the only yacht to have ascended the Nile to Assuan and Wadi Halfa – at least neither I nor our friends at the Cairo Yacht Club have heard of any predecessor.

On this first day we took our groundings calmly and put them down to our inexperience. If, later on, we occasionally saw the foolhardiness of our enterprise we never for one moment thought of giving in: difficulties made the sport better, the trip more varied and the satisfaction of winning through greater. A redeeming feature of navigation on the Nile is also the fact that you never run aground on rocks or stones, only on soft sandbanks – with the possible exception of sunken craft. A less redeeming feature is the uncertainty in which you live regarding glass, china, saucepans, books and cameras which are not properly stowed: more than one temptingly served meal has slid meanly to the deck instead of down our throats.

South of Kafr ez Zaiyat the Nile is unexpectedly desolate, most of the villages are on the irrigation canals some little distance from the river and you steer along between high, grass-covered banks as though in a gigantic ditch. About one o'clock we decided to put in by the bank to let the engine rest for a while and to have a look at the landscape above the ditch. While Ibrahim stayed on

48

board as guard, Mona and I climbed the bank to a road, on the other side of which the ground again sloped steeply downwards. We were standing on an embankment which had been built along the river as a dike against the floods; fertile fields stretched away at our feet to another embankment which screened off the landscape. On top of it evidently ran a large irrigation canal, as tall sails could be glimpsed between the trees. We followed the road towards a little village and as we strolled through the still landscape we were seized more and more by a mood which we could not explain. It was rather as when you get a familiar taste in the mouth but cannot at once place it. Trees which had newly burst into leaf, tender crops sprouting out of the black soil, exultant birdsong and peasants harrowing the fields . . . However bewildering it was after the long summer to think of spring in the middle of November, it was yet inescapable: nature's great miracle of renewal was in progress, quite out of keeping with conditions in the normal countries of the northern hemisphere.

The scouts of the village, the children at play, caught sight of us long before we reached the first houses and soon we had a numerous and merry retinue. It was the irrigation canal and its boats which interested us, but to reach them we had to pass through the outskirts of the village. Rather doubtfully we greeted the fellahs with a *salamaleikum*, which to our ears sounded like a joke but was received very well and was answered by long tirades. One fellah took us eagerly by the hand and managed at length to make us understand what he wanted: we were to drink a cup of tea with him. Curious to see the interior of a house, we accepted, but two chairs were brought out and we had to sit in the village street, stared at by a dense crowd of spectators as though we were Martians, while the fellah's invisible wife made tea inside. The fellahs make tea by letting the tea leaves stand and simmer for hours in order to brew the black and bitter drink they call tea. Fortunately we had a packet of cigarettes with which we could repay the kindness before going on to the canal. This turned out to be one of the main arteries which conducts the water from the big dam at Cairo. From this, water can easily be drawn off all the year round down on to the fields according to the intricate distribution system so vital to the fellahs which ensures water to each plot of land at least every eighteen days. There are no locks

D

leading down from here to the Nile, otherwise it would have been
ideal for us to make our way to Cairo through an idyllic and leafy
inner Egypt.

Hundreds of inquisitive villagers accompanied us back to
Daphne and witnessed our start. The afternoon brought several
more groundings, but we were beginning to learn how to avoid
them. The most important thing, of course, is to take soundings;
we did so with our maritime plumb-line, which Ibrahim at first
despised. The Nile boats have, since the time of the Pharaohs,
sounded with a long, narrow stick, which is worked by a man
in the bows. But our plummet was much easier to handle; we
had the satisfaction of converting not only Ibrahim but also, later
on, real Nile skippers. But of what help is the plummet when it is
shallow everywhere and you must nevertheless make headway?
On such thresholds the current is strong, often five or six knots.
There are two rules. The first is to keep away from flat, shallow
banks or low sandbanks and instead follow the steep, deeply
hollowed-out sides. The second is that the strongest current also
marks the greatest depth, for it is the force of the water which
shapes the loose sand. But the exceptions are many and it is
especially difficult to find the way when you come to parts of the
river with islands or sharp bends.

At sunset Ibrahim began to worry again about where to spend
the night. He had not the vaguest idea where we were and as we
had only the Guide Bleu's sketchy general map we did not know
if there was any town within reach. At all events it was plain to
us all that we could not keep moving on the shoal-filled river after
nightfall. A large rowing-boat of the primitive kind used as a
ferry across the Nile lay moored between two projecting stone
jetties built to check the onslaught of the current at the floods.
We made straight for it to get advice and information from the
ferryman. He was sitting half asleep in his craft, a grey-haired
giant with muscular arms and a fierce expression who instantly
made us think of his fellow craftsman Charon. He must have
inspired Ibrahim with confidence all the same, for the upshot of
their talk was that we took shelter for the night under his wing.

There was still time for an evening stroll and Mona and I were
not slow to seize the opportunity. Here too a road followed the
Nile on top of the high embankment. Far away in a bend of the

river we caught a glimpse of a white domed tomb surrounded by palms, one of these many lonely shrines called *marabouts* containing the earthly remains of a holy sheik. Why not visit it? . . . We followed the road, which seemed built as a bridge across a pleasure-garden: at our feet lay on one side the majestic Nile and on the other fertile fields, where the peasants said their prayers after their day's work and the cattle wandered homewards, while a sunset sky full of dramatic clouds arched above our heads. Everything breathed such peace, the air was so light and balmy, life so transfigured that we could have walked for mile after mile.

The marabout shrine was crumbling away but as a ruin perhaps gave more eloquent witness of its god than it had done when the cupola was new. I thought how very different ruins appear in western and eastern surroundings. With us, the ancient monuments are resigned relics of a golden age beyond recall or background atmosphere to the sermon of life's rebirth through primitivism, as shown by the ruin landscapes of European art with shepherds, robbers or Italian *lazzaroni*. For the adherents of Islam, whose countries are so full of building fragments from Egyptian, Greek, Roman and Byzantine antiquity, they speak another tongue: the oriental ruin is most often to be found in the desert, where whitened bones stick up out of the sand, encircled by screeching vultures and proving indisputably that all earthly striving is vanity. When a European building decays or a grave is forgotten, it is a defeat for the human initiative we believe in; the equivalent decay in Mohammedan countries is a natural victory for the power that is indifferent to man's ambitions and to which everything is subordinate.

Night was falling as we strolled home and soon the daylight lingered only as a gleaming reflection in the dark water of the rice-fields. Small fires of maize stalks were flickering in front of the huts by the wayside, the fellahs were cooking their supper and our greeting was answered with an invitation to share their repast. We thought of Spain, where the same courtesy is common, no doubt a legacy from the Arabic conquerors. On reaching the little bend where *Daphne* and the ferry-boat lay snugly side by side, we could see from up on the embankment that our neighbour Charon had also lighted a fire in the bottom of his craft. One or two men from the village, together with Ibrahim, were sitting as guests in a circle round the fire, deep in animated conversation. We ate our supper and turned in, to read for a while before falling asleep, but even in our sleep we were half conscious that the men sat on: the fire crackled faintly and they talked, talked interminably as one can only talk in the orient.

It was only six o'clock when Ibrahim roused us and insisted that we make a start at once even though it was hardly light. Shivering and sleepy, I started the engine, Charon twisted his face into a farewell smile and we headed out on to the grey Nile. Hardly had the sun risen when a dense mist settled down over the river and there was nothing for it but to anchor. I could control my bad morning humour no longer:

'Couldn't we have had another hour's sleep after the night's coughing and talking! Why on earth did you sit up all night instead of telling the others to be quiet?'

Ibrahim gave me a look that was both hurt and ironic:

'Do you know what we were talking about for so long and why I wanted to start? They wanted to plunder your boat and everything in it, but I persuaded them not to. I told them what protectors you have and that you have come here as guests. I made friends with them and got them to give up the idea. But they said we must be off before any more men came from the village.'

At last the scales fell from our eyes. In our guilelessness we had not understood the risks implied in mooring a boat laden with tempting riches by the banks of black need. We had misjudged Ibrahim and his anxiety and perhaps he had even saved our lives by playing the part of Scheherazade and all through the night telling tales which had put off a decision. From now on we listened to his warnings with greater respect, both in the matter of shelter for the night and navigation.

The mist lifted by degrees, revealing a village where a small ferry, perhaps forty feet long, was just putting out across the river. It was a miracle ferry, for it was packed to overflowing when we first saw it, but an unending stream of people, donkeys, camels and oxen kept making their way down the steep bank, and we had the impression that they were spirited away the second they got on board. At last, however, a donkey did get left with its hind legs hanging over the side and the ferry began to move.

We too started off and headed upstream the whole day with varied success. We had one rather troublesome grounding, but also two hours' care-free progress in the wake of a motor barge which showed us the way. About three o'clock we began to wonder how much farther it was to the big dam at the fork of the Delta, which we hoped to reach before nightfall. We decided to ask the men on some barges which were unloading stones by the bank. Four hours, they said. It was only two hours until sunset and according to them no villages on the river before the dam. Problems about where to spend the night piled up in our minds in all their bleakness: we had not forgotten Charon's ferry. After a few moment's consultation we agreed to stop by the barges, which belonged to a large company: their crew would hardly dare to harm us.

This time our evening walk led us to a grove of huge trees a mile or two from our mooring place. They surrounded a deserted factory which had been invaded by a little village. Inquisitive heads peeped out of windows and doors which had been hacked out of the brick wall at random, and it was not long before the obligatory police appeared, this time only an old, gout-ridden country constable, a so-called *gaffir*, with a flint-lock blunderbus on his back and a turban on his head. He made vigorous signs to us to go with him: we must needs meet someone whom he called *omda*. We thus made the acquaintance of a person to be found in every Egyptian village and who in his little world is more important than both the head of state and the prime minister in theirs. The village chieftain, formerly called *sheik el beled* and nowadays *omda*, is no longer the tyrant with power over life and death that he was in practice up to fifty years ago, but in most villages he is still the authorities' only representative, the chief of the *gaffirs*, elected for life and usually the son of the previous *omda*, as only the biggest landowners can put up for this unsalaried, but indirectly lucrative, post.

Our first omda, who was sitting in the shade of a gnarled tree, clad in a dressing-gown, was far and away the poorest we met, just as his village was the smallest we visited, but there was nothing wrong with his authority. With a dignified gesture he invited us to sit down on the mud-brick bench beside him and the old gaffir, who sprang to attention every time he was addressed, was sent at the double to the omda's home with orders for tea to be made. He himself carried out from the dark depths of his office his two greatest treasures: a gramophone and a telephone. The former, one of the old kind with a horn, was instantly set going and rasped out an Arabic song. We quite saw that this technical wonder established the omda's position in the eyes of the villagers as a pioneer of the new era. But the aged telephone, which had no wires and had evidently been out of order for many decades, what was its function? We should never have found out had not two youths of about fourteen, with a smattering of English and dressed in striped pyjamas (quite a usual garment in which to pay a call), appeared. They went to school in Cairo and were on a short visit to relatives in the village. With their help we could exchange a few phrases with the omda, among other things concerning the telephone. What was it used for?

'It is my connection with the government and the governor. I report everything that happens here in the village and what the people do ...'

I could never make out whether the omda himself was a victim of his illusion or whether the dodge with the telephone was merely intended to raise his prestige, but I saw at once that we had lighted upon the material for a short story in the spirit of Gogol or one of the other Russian satirists of society – profoundly grave in its robust humour. It is easy to imagine the scenes when the omda threatens a stubborn miscreant or rewards virtue by speaking of the matter into the telephone in the presence of respectfully listening witnesses, or when a man unjustly accused in desperation snatches the mute mouthpiece from the tyrant's hand and speaks the truth into it. The belief that someone hears us, is interested in us and judges us by our deeds can never be merely ridiculous.

We had great difficulty in getting away from our omda, who conducted us to his home, showed us his white-faced wife, worn out by child-bearing and work, and his windowless bedroom stinking of filth: here we were to sleep tonight, he and his wife would give up their own bed to us, he would not hear of our spending the night on a small boat on the river. At the risk of his reporting our stiff-necked ingratitude on the miraculous telephone, we took our leave, however, and were escorted back to *Daphne* by the gaffir.

Ibrahim was right: the bargees did not set upon us during the night, but as we could not be quite sure of this before dawn, none of us got much sleep. We were late off the mark – a mist again came down as the sun went up – but nevertheless without mishap reached the big dam at the Delta fork about noon. Here the Nile divides into the two arms which, via Rosetta and Damietta, reach the sea. A mass of boats were waiting for lockage, but, urged on by Ibrahim, we calmly steered past them to the lock-chamber, which was instantly opened to the accompaniment of courteous greetings: privileges are still a matter of course in Egypt. The architecture of the dam was in a curious feudal Gothic style with crenellations, turrets and drawbridges, which I took to be the fruits of an ill-advised artistic game until I discovered in an old guide-book that they had been very seriously meant by the viceroy Said Pascha who was desperately interested in fortifications and who completed the dam in the 1850s. Huge trees, green lawns, riverside cafes and small sailing-boats nowadays make the Delta fork a shady park, a favourite objective for a day's outing from Cairo.

The deep and almost current-free water above the dam made the last lap to Cairo easy and pleasant to cover. The banks, however, became more and more depressing and suburban, littered with dreary factories and stinking dumping-grounds, but instead the silhouette of a high hill emerged, the Muqattam Hill, with Mohammed Ali's cupola mosque. Here, some little way above the Nile fork, the Delta ends and the Nile Valley begins, this canyon which the river has carved out of the desert plateau right from the great marshes deep in the Sudan, this narrow strip of fertile soil, which sometimes almost disappears when the cliffs come up to the river and sometimes spreads out into small plains when they withdraw. Just as it was natural for the old Egypt's first big national capital city, Memphis, to grow up here in the border zone between the Delta and the river valley, so it is strategically, politically and economically understandable that Egypt's Arabic capital Cairo has come to be situated here.

We scanned the horizon in vain for the Pyramids on the right bank, but they lie somewhat to the south of the city and away from the river and we did not see them until the following day, when we climbed up to the Mohammed Ali mosque and gazed out across the sea of houses to the edge of the desert: there they were, perhaps no longer so overwhelmingly huge beside the factories and skyscrapers which have sprung up in Cairo, but large and majestic by reason of their form, the most stable any building can have.

By now we had imperceptibly entered Cairo itself. The bridges we passed vibrated under heavy traffic and on the banks there was a seething mixture of light galabias and European dress, American cars and shaggy camels. At the large Gezira Island we chose the west arm of the river, which borders the Doqqi quarter of the city. We steered along between two unbroken lines of houseboats moored to the bank, most of them inhabited and many with a neat little garden on the sloping shore. We, as Nile travellers, could not have arranged a more suitable meeting: here they all lay as though in an open-air museum, all the old *dahabias* and paddle-steamers which are the leading figures in the homely nineteenth-century Egyptian travel books. Their curved masts bear sails no longer and the paddles are eaten away with rust, but the carved verandas and the poetic names *Lotus, Sesostris, Cleopatra,* are still there. The blocks of flats lining the river, on the other hand, were completely modern and might have been in any western capital at all.

Beyond Gezira Island the river widened so that it looked almost like a lake. On the east bank we glimpsed the Egyptian Museum, the broad, teeming streets leading in to the business centre and down by the water the Hotel Semiramis. Where should we tie up?

'That's the yacht club over there,' Ibrahim said, pointing to a barge anchored by the west bank, almost on the border of the Doqqi and Giza quarters of the town.

Sure enough, we made out a small armada of sailing-dinghies reflecting their white hulls in the river in the flow of the afternoon sun, and on the veranda deck of the club barge men and women sat at small tables drinking tea, while others set off on a little sailing trip. The moment could not have been more opportune if we had wanted the greatest possible notice to be taken of our arrival at the Cairo Yacht Club: it was Friday, a Mohammedan holiday, when most of the offices are shut and an unusually large number of members had collected. In all the yacht clubs we have visited in the Mediterranean, *Daphne* has been a small and insignificant craft, an ugly duckling among the swans. Here, among these yachtsmen who kept between two bridges and had only dinghies at their disposal, she was The Great Ship from the Far Distant Seas.

We moored at the little pontoon bridge and tried to appear as unassuming as possible.

CHAPTER III

Cairo's Four Worlds

Rome is usually regarded as a somewhat inaccessible city: only to those who live there for many years and imbibe its infinitely complex atmosphere, its 2,500-year-old history and wealth of contrasting monuments, does the eternal city reveal its uniqueness as the heart of European culture. What, by comparison, is one to say of Cairo? Here one meets a history that is twice as long and cultural strata that are four times as complicated; for instead of Rome's spiritual continuity, in Cairo four civilizations without any organic connection have been laid one on top of the other. Ancient Egypt, the Hellenistic-Coptic age, the Arabic era and now a violently expanding western awakening have all set their stamp on this strange city without even superficially blending.

For us, who in ten hectic days tried to get a general view of Cairo's resources, our stay here was a continuous exercise in dizzy mental leaps: the dividing-line is absolute when you step from the city square with its bus traffic, blocks of offices and the newly-built Home Office into the Egyptian Museum with its stone effigies and mummies, and it is just as strongly marked between the formless quarters in old Cairo, teeming with oriental life, and the stylized, apocalyptic world inside the Coptic Museum's door. None of these worlds has evolved out of the others, they are all isolated in an odd way. It is therefore natural for me to divide my description of Cairo into four different sections, beginning with the stratum which lies on the surface – the modern city.

We could not have had more delightful headquarters than our peaceful moorings by the pontoon bridge in front of the Cairo Yacht Club. Gently – and but rarely – rocked by the wash from some passing barge, we awakened each morning with the same joy, the same fresh appetite for new experiences. The winter nights in Egypt are starry and chilly: we had a small spirit stove which warmed the cabin. The mornings are often damp with dripping dew and light veils of mist, but the sun, as it blazed down on to the river bank, gave us courage to sprint to the cold shower in the barge, and over our morning coffee on *Daphne*'s deck we revelled in the champagne-like air of an Egyptian winter. Until the afternoon we had the club entirely to ourselves, including telephone, restaurant and all conceivable help from the five dark-skinned Nubian servants, who were kindness itself. They were hard at it painting and rigging the club's small boats, as it is now, at the end of November when the river sinks back into its normal channel after the flooding and the current lessens, that the sailing season in Cairo begins. They lent a hand in re-erecting *Daphne*'s masts so that she would look more beautiful in port and be ready to continue the voyage, and they carried ashore our motor scooter, which was an enormous asset to us during our stay in Cairo. Pyramids, mosques, museums, authorities and newly-acquired friends were all easy of access thanks to the Lambretta, despite the big distances – added to which was the stimulating pleasure of riding about on our own wheels to explore this city of surprises.

But the yacht club was our headquarters in more ways than one; in addition to being a haven it was also the focal point of most of our contacts in town. Among friends and acquaintances, we must give pride of place to the General, who was the club's president and our mighty patron even before we had met him. General Hassan Ragab does not belong to the revolutionary council which governs the country after the fall of the monarchy, but he is in close touch with 'the new men', who seem to value his technical knowledge, idealistic character and winning personality. The General is tirelessly active in the big industrial and social transformation which is going on in Egypt, but as by nature he is the prototype of a scout leader he has not been slow to become one in practice besides his other duties: he has started and leads the Egyptian Seascout Corps with which we were to be so pleasantly associated. I do not know if one can judge the other men in charge of the country by General Ragab. In him, at all events, we saw two traits which one is glad to meet in oriental countries: he had very definite western leanings and he was democratic to his finger-tips, simple in his way of life and in constant touch with every stratum of the community. During his holidays he is in the habit of sailing about the country's waterways, dressed as a seaman, with some of his seascouts in order to get to know conditions in the country districts as they really are. This is especially salutary in a land like Egypt, where contact between town and country, between the privileged and the exploited, between the government and the people, is so perilously meagre. After all the kindness and help we received from General Ragab during our journey it would have been difficult for me to give such an outspokenly realistic description of what we saw in Egypt if I did not know his own attitude and was not aware that, to the limit of his powers, he is fighting the very conditions that distressed us.

It is obviously General Ragab's influence which has made Cairo Yacht Club a very unusual club in the city: here, Europeans and Egyptians, wealthy people and ordinary office clerks or students, can not only meet but really associate. The members are few enough for all to know each other and they often – but always in all simplicity – arrange parties and dances. We were very kindly received into this circle and also invited home by several families, beginning with the General himself, who showed us films he had taken of a scout camp on the wonderfully beautiful coast of the Red Sea. Many of the members lived near the club in the Doqqi quarter, and here too we had our nearest contacts among fellow-countrymen: the Swedish Legation with its kind and helpful Minister, Mr Weidel, from whose flat we had a view of the Pyramids; Finland's Consul-General, Eric Ahlquist, whose charming wife sewed half a dozen new pages into my passport for the many new permits and stamps, and Åke Norrby, whose encouraging letter and good advice had drawn us to Egypt.

Of everything the General helped us with, three things in particular are outstanding, as our continued journey would have been impossible without them. First, he procured maps for us, which was no small matter. There was not one to be had in the bookshops and none of our friends at the club had a detailed map of Egypt. On the sheets from the War Ministry which the General rather anxiously entrusted to us in exchange for a formally signed receipt, was the eloquent stamp – SECRET. They were twenty quite ordinary maps of the Nile Valley with all villages and roads marked, but with no details of channels or depth of water, which unfortunately change far too swiftly to be charted. A second and greater problem was shelter for the night during the rest of the trip. After a talk with the Home Secretary, the General not only obtained the necessary permission for us to make the Nile trip at all, but also a promise of police protection for *Daphne* at every place we touched at. Finally, the most difficult and vital problem, that of our interpreter, was solved most happily.

'I have already picked out your travelling companion,' the General informed us the first evening we met. 'Edries will go with you, he is one of my best lads and I think you will like him.'

Edries! Looking back, I think of you with an affection and an anxiety which are almost paternal. During the four months you lived with us, sharing all our experiences, you grew so close to us that we really got to know both your many good sides and your few failings. We saw you change through your contact with us, we went through together the crises of friendship that our dissimilarities made unavoidable and we were moved by the pure, white soul behind your dark face, which sometimes reminded us of the young Pharaoh Iknaton, sometimes of the wild children of nature in the land of your black father, the Sudan. It would be unfair to call you the born scout, though you did take your scoutship more seriously than any European youth of your age. At heart it was not excellence as a scout you sought, but an idealistic western plan of life, you wanted companions who did not look down on your dark skin and who, like yourself, wanted to build up a new Egypt. That life is not a scout movement, the goals not so easily defined and the leaders not always such paragons, you will find out in due course. Our anxiety for you is because of your incorruptibility, your moral courage, your burning zeal to spread your ideas: with such an attitude one risks the disfavour of all authorities and especially those who themselves wish to monopolize popular enlightenment, progress and truth.

Edries was twenty-one years old and the son of one of those countless Nubians who had come to Cairo to go into service with wealthy families, but as his grandfather was a village chieftain in Nubia and his father was employed by a prince, he had grown up with the feeling of being an aristocrat in his own circle. The shadow over his life was that his mother had died when he was ten and he found it impossible to live with his stepmother. He was now therefore living in a small cabin on the seascouts' barge *Haris*, where he was a kind of salaried clubmaster at the same

61

time as he was a free student. *Haris* was the Cairo Yacht Club barge's next-door neighbour, and the day after our arrival Edries came over to *Daphne*, dressed in full scout uniform and with eyes shining with expectation of the adventures shimmering ahead. He told us that all his pals were envious of him: none of the seascouts had ever had a chance of making such a cruise up the Nile.

Cairo of today is a western metropolis of the unpruned, half-barbaric type to be seen in South America: straggling rows of tall buildings with towers and breaches of style, streets in bad repair, seething traffic, speculators' housing projects which spring up from the ground like mushrooms and grim slums in the suburbs. The worst sides of the new age have asserted themselves here, thanks to cheap labour and sudden expansion; industrialism's many problems of adjustment, which Europe has struggled with for more than a century, have still to be solved. For the majority of the population – former fellahs who have lost the security of the village community, the remains of the artisan and small-tradesman classes who are being squeezed harder and harder by industrialization, the workers who as yet have no class consciousness, the civil servants who exist on starvation wages and the many indefinable individuals swarming in the streets who have only one big problem, how to get enough to eat – for all these Caironians their city is no doubt a dreary stone waste which they need all the fatalism of Islam to endure.

For a small circle of wealthy people – both Egyptian and foreign business men and diplomats – Cairo is, on the other hand, acknowledged to be a pleasant city with many resources. By force of circumstances it was mostly in this world that we chanced to move; we were invited to cocktail parties in tents which had been erected on the desert plateau by the Pyramids, we heard of the excellent duck-shooting in various game preserves which were visited at week ends, we discussed in luxury flats by the Nile the government's disturbing policy and the worsening business prospects for foreign enterprisers, we trod the soft carpets of the Hotel Semiramis, saw shimmy-dancers at night clubs and 'the last dancing Dervish' at a private party in a mysterious Arabic mansion.

Cairo's fashionable centre is the Gezira Sporting Club on the leafy island in the heart of the city, formerly a purely European and very exclusive club, nowadays somewhat democratized and open also to Egyptians, who will no doubt soon predominate. Granted, it is very nice to have lunch at Gezira beside the green-gleaming swimming-pool, wave to friends who have come from a game of tennis, gossip about the latest party at so-and-so's. Granted, it is convenient for the young wives of diplomats to deposit their children at the Gezira playground while they go off on a round of shopping. But we had not come to Egypt to get to know this *milieu* and we felt both indignant and anti-western when we heard arguments such as these at the lunch-tables:

'Egypt's big problem is over-population. It's madness to raise the standard of living and improve the national health: why, even the present twenty millions are more than the country can feed.'

'Oh yes, the people are in a bad way all right, but let's face it, they don't deserve any better. You should have seen them that ghastly time they burnt Europeans outside Shepherd's. They're primitive and incapable of learning anything except what they've been doing for thousands of years: tilling the soil, digging canals and hewing stone.'

'Their knavery and begging is beyond belief. The minute you go out duck-shooting, the blighters slink out of every bush and show you bleeding sores which they make out are gunshot but which they have inflicted themselves.'

No, problems are not lacking in modern Egypt.

*   *   *   *   *

But below the surface of the western metropolis lives another Cairo, the old Mohammedan city.

The first we saw of Cairo as we came up the river was the Mohammed Ali mosque, whose cupolas and minarets emerged out of the mist high up on the Muqattam Hill like a supernatural vision. Its power of suggestion was so strong that all the factory chimneys and radio masts were transformed into a forest of minarets, and if previously I had been more inclined to think that we were approaching the old Memphis and the capital of modern Egypt, I saw now in a flash that we were really drawing near to the city where the Thousand and One Nights was written. True, this book – or rather this world built of words – contains Persian tales refashioned in Bagdad and legends which have found their way along the caravan routes from India, but it obtained its final shape, and several of its main stories, in Egypt, whose hidden treasures, dark soil and hot blood have coloured the whole of this work, as endless and drawn-out as the Nile itself.

At first we were misled by Cairo's seemingly modern appearance, its blocks of flats, business streets, cars and cinemas. We sought the Thousand and One Nights only in the scattered relics from the past: in beautifully ornamented wells, in the gleaming goldsmiths' shops in the bazaars and in broken tombs of caliphs, where green turbans droop over narrow coffins. So little is needed to stir the imagination: a young veiled woman on a camel, a closed garden gate in a crumbling wall, old oil lamps in a bazaar stall or a merchant's wise and dignified face – instantly one thinks of princesses as slender as the letter alif, of enchanted gardens, of genii imprisoned in bottles and of caliphs in disguise. Yet it is not in these external things that Cairo's oriental atmosphere lies: the world of the Arabian Nights lives on chiefly in the hearts of the people.

Twice during our stay in Cairo we went up to the Citadel and from the terrace by the Mohammed Ali mosque looked out over the city, the Nile Valley and the desert plateau on the other side of the river, where the triangles of the Pyramids rest. The first time we thought that Cairo looked like a modern city with the mosques interspersed as the remains of a sunken world: in the background the venerable Ibn Tulun mosque from the ninth century and in the foreground the mighty cubes of the Sultan Hassan and Rifayeh mosques, graver and prouder than the cupola mosques of Istambul. The second time we climbed up here – it was shortly before our departure – we seemed instead to be looking out over a city which, in its essentials, was still oriental. Was it the dusk deepening over the sea of roofs, the desert's majesty stealing in from the empty wastes in the west or our experiences of the past days which influenced us? We had at all events come to realize that the modern machine age, the European styles of architecture and the wares in the shops, all that the west has to offer in the way of external things, is not necessarily at variance with the Thousand and One Nights. Do not the desert sheiks of the Arabian oil lands ride about in cars and aeroplanes, have they not private cinemas, radios and refrigerators in their palaces, do they not dress their favourite wives in Paris gowns and do they not build themselves rococo pavilions or Hollywood villas without this affecting their Arab mentality? To the Arab, reality has always been fantastic, and compared with Aladdin's lamp or the flying carpet, radio, aeroplanes and electricity are rather commonplace phenomena. Much of that which to the superficial traveller in the orient, looks like attachment to western civilization is therefore only new shoots on the wonderful tree which the Prophet planted in the desert sand 1,300 years ago.

But if the orientals thus have a sublime capacity of misunderstanding the west, we on our side have given proof of an equally distorted attitude to the orient. It was the eighteenth century which discovered the Thousand and One Nights, spread it abroad in Galland's free translation and understood it in its drawing-room fashion. The nineteenth century was more interested in a realistic setting of the scene and regarded the work more as a cultural-historical picture book. The main reason for the European popularity of the Arabian Nights has, however, remained unchanged: the illusion that its world, despite all the exoticism, is fundamentally like our own.

It cannot be denied that there are great resemblances, as shown by the very structure of the environment. Like the caliphate in decline, Europe since the eighteenth century has been marked on the one hand by a division into innumerable greater or lesser kingdoms, an unlimited provincialism, but on the other by world-wide trading and a refined flowering of international culture. In both these worlds enterprising persons can go from one setting to another, encounter widely differing laws and customs, be dragged down to disaster by local tyrants or make their fortunes with others, in short, move about in an existence whose conventions are as relative as the rules of a game. One of the most delightful things about the Thousand and One Nights is its power to take us on an Arabian journey, a geographical experience as varied and tangible as our own but at the same time quite different. These tales transport us to Cairo and from there via the long caravan routes to Damascus and Bagdad. Far away in the north lies the Byzantium of the infidels, where the emperor sits enthroned in his well-fortified Constantinople, monks chant hymns

E

in mountain monasteries and comely Greek girls can be carried off as slaves. From Bagdad one can follow the Tigris down to the port of Basra and from there sail with Sindbad to India and the Wak Wak Islands (nowadays called Japan), or one can set off with the caravans through the high mountains where the Roc has its nest and so come at last to the mysterious China.

A still more important likeness between our existence and the Arabian is individualism. In both these motley, infinitely variable worlds the individual is the combining and vital element, it is in the individual's experiences and destiny that the world is created. In order to distinguish him from the common herd the poet likes to endow him with special gifts. In the east he is depicted as an Aladdin with a lamp, a young Hassan, so handsome that both humans and spirits fall in love with him. With us the individual whom all can identify themselves with is called Jean Jacques, who as a christening present has been given something just as wonderful as the magic lamp: genius. Or else he possesses the indomitable bravery of the Three Musketeers, the inventive talent of Captain Nemo or merely the privilege of being the hero in a book and therefore, despite perils and adventures, pre-destined by persistent luck to reach the last page of the novel. In this way the praise of individual optimism is sung just as whole-heartedly by Scheherazade as by Rousseau, Jules Verne and the modern autobiographical proletarian authors.

The similarities must not, however, blind us to the gulf between oriental and western individualism, which are as essentially different as the Mohammedan and Christian religions.

The Arabian individualism allows everything to depend on God and nothing on man himself: it is enough if Aladdin finds the lamp, whose genie serves anyone at all; wealth, social position, courage, education are external gifts. The sole quality which, for the Mohammedan, belongs inseparably to the individual is a greater or lesser measure of virtue: the genie of the flask can be used for good or evil, in obedience to or in defiance of the Koran's commandments. As a result of this conception of humanity, we meet countless individuals in the Arabian Nights but no personalities: all these young men and lovely girls are really cast in the same mould and merely assume various guises and qualities as if they were dressing up in different costumes. In obvious contrast to this, we in the west look for personal character and initiative in the individual: one must be as brave and strong as Achilles or as intelligent as Odysseus to gain success; material and spiritual heritage, character, idiosyncrasies are of vital importance. Personality is what matters here.

The Arab's distrust of his own capacity may cramp his personality, but it does give him numerous virtues which are rather difficult for us to acquire. The first is the deep sense of brotherhood which binds him to his fellow-believer, because he knows that nobody can take any credit for anything he may achieve. The rich man, the potentate or the skilful craftsman has only Allah to thank for his position; both he himself and those who are worse off take this for granted, and as a result their mutual relations are harmonious. The story of the rich Sindbad the Sailor and the poor Sindbad the Carrier – one of the most truly democratic stories in the world's literature – has its equivalent today, when the wealthy Arab stops his car in the poor quarter to ask the way and an amicable conversation ensues, to the amazement of the foreigner who is used to the social conflicts of the west.

Islam, as we know, means 'surrender' or 'resignation'. One of the explanations of this religion's untold strength is that it so directly and simply solves the contrast between our will and feelings on the one hand and the external, overwhelming reality on the other. Consequently, there is the opportunity for inner spiritual training, for self-education to which all can apply themselves and which influences people more generally than Christianity with its complex demands is able to do. One seldom meets an adult Mohammedan who has not acquired a certain amount of *el hilm*, that sublime calm of the soul, that equanimity in the face of life's vicissitudes, which comes from surrender to an almighty God.

Harmony with one's fellow-believers and with oneself are thus two typical Mohammedan virtues, but a third and perhaps more important one is harmony with the outside world. Here lies the greatest difference between the orientals and the westerners. With us, existence is something we like to influence by conscientiously studying its laws, applying our reason and collaborating with other people. The result has become a kind of tug of war between man and reality, a battle full of spurring victories but also of crushing defeats. Our reality, such as it appears through society, science and economic factors, is often stifling, and it is as a reaction to this pressure that western romanticism produced modern individualism. Our novels and films, in which a hero creates history, in which science merges into fantasy, the individual defies society and passions or will-power triumph over all mercenary considerations, reveal the tension existing between us and reality.

In the Thousand and One Nights reality can no more be understood or influenced by man than Allah can; it may only be loved as His creation. This world is formless, full of magic, spirits and miracles; not even time or space obey any certain laws. You go down a staircase into the earth and pass through a door into another world, or you dip your head for a few seconds in the bath water and in that short time live through an entire life in another place. The thought of social progress has no place here, for the world completely fulfils its purpose such as it is: to manifest Allah's omnipotence and to test the individual's virtue. This brings about a harmony between man and the world which is almost inconceivable to us, a capacity to revel in sensuous pleasure, natural beauty, luxury and honour, but to bear adversity with resignation. The Mohammedan has a proximity to life which we lack, he is friends with joy and with all fleeting splendour because he is not afraid of losing them.

After these reflections let us return to the point from which we started – Cairo of today. Here, in the capital of modern Egypt, more easily than anywhere else one can understand why the western outlook on life, despite Islam's greatness, will inexorably triumph: because of Islam's negative attitude to social problems. Formerly, under the conditions of which one could aptly say: 'Plus ça change, plus c'est la même chose,' acceptance of life's evil side was not only justified but actually desirable. In our day, industrialism, communications and a rapidly increasing population have upset the balance of the old oriental society at the same time as they have opened up undreamt-of possibilities of overcoming the difficulties of everyday life. The orientals, like the occidentals, are faced with the alternative of either being suffocated by the nightmare of unbridled industrialism or of seriously getting to grips with social questions.

68

The necessity of changing external reality that religion and tradition have told them to accept, means that the Mohammedans must reconsider their entire attitude to life; this must be very difficult and will take a long time. Instead of striving for individual virtue and happiness they must now learn to set the happiness and progress of the community first. Instead of putting up with the community's shortcomings they are taught to put up with their own, because the westerners, in their new-fangled social righteousness, have lapsed into a kind of personality fatalism which is diametrically opposed to the fatalism of the Mohammedans. We are furious if anyone in word or deed offends against our notion of democracy, but we dare not bring up our children properly for fear of injuring their individuality. We are indignant if a train is late but find it natural that people behave with no outward dignity or inward harmony.

Nothing could be farther from the truth than the idea that the Egyptian people are merely waiting to enjoy the advantages of modern civilization. Words such as welfare state, democracy and revolution mean very little, if anything, to the Arabian Nights people, used as they are to conquest, usurpation and rebellion turn and turn about with the despotic rule of just or unjust tyrants. To a great extent the future development depends on the men who at present have usurped the power in Egypt: are they capable of transforming their country in the same way as Kemal Ataturk recreated Turkey, or will their work result in new forms of fatalistically borne suffering for the people before the time is ripe for Arabian Egypt to be consigned definitely to the past?

So far, in this ancient land we can study, with both admiration and criticism, how much Islam has done for human beings and how little for society.

But beyond the Arabic world's fair and gleaming, if oddly weightless, reality – weightless perhaps because it is so meek and compliant – two other Egyptian worlds shimmer: the short Coptic-Hellenistic era and the endless ancient Egyptian.

For us here in Cairo, the first of these remained merely an art-historical experience; in order to get to know the living Copts and their problems one must visit Upper Egypt. It is in towns such as Asyut, Sohag and Quena and in the surrounding countryside, where the pressure from Arabic Cairo has been less, that the Copts have best been able to survive and preserve their individuality during 1,300 years of Mohammedan supremacy. Although there are many Coptic families – often very wealthy – in the capital, they are tolerated aliens more than anything else, almost on a par with the Jews (before the present war) and the Greeks, while in Upper Egypt there are Coptic fellah villages whose population differs very little from the Mohammedan fellahs, either in appearance, habits or material resources.

Coptic art, on the other hand, is best studied in the rich, and as an institution singularly charming, Coptic Museum in Old Cairo. Its cool and silent rooms, half severe, half idyllic, and courtyards are seeped in that atmosphere of something lost and intangible that emanates from everything in Egypt which is Old Coptic. Many are the questions arising from this strange hybrid art and chief among them what relationship it bears to the three correlative factors: Christianity, Greek culture, ancient Egyptian heritage.

For us, used to drawing a sharp line between Graeco-Roman antiquity and Christianity, it is strange here in Egypt to see them inextricably grown together into a common late-antique phenomenon. But a glance at history explains why: Egypt knew neither the early blooming of Greek culture nor the later development of Christianity, only the Roman Hellenism, which in the great city of Alexandria was coloured by ineradicable oriental mysticism. It was from Alexandria that the teachings of the cross spread across the land of the Nile as an enemy to the old gods and it therefore arrayed itself in the foreign guise of Hellenism: Corinthian columns, acanthus leaves, grapes and cupids adorned the churches and the Orphic and riotous god Dionysus represented the god of the gospels. So interwoven are Hellenism and Christianity in Egypt that we cannot say for certain which of the unforgettable dead in the portraits from Faiyum's burial-grounds are Christian: here the Roman legionary literally meets the sanctity of the east and his eyes are opened – deep-set, preternaturally large they see a reality that is unattainable for the people on ordinary Roman portraits. It is Coptic art's greatest fascination that despite Hellenism and Syrian Christianity it is so mysteriously influenced by the death-world of Old Egypt.

70

Indeed, how could it be otherwise in the ancient land of the Pharaohs? Even for us, who have a perspective that is two thousand years longer, this background is equally dominating. The various layers of culture lie one behind the other in Egypt like scenery in the theatre of time. Right at the front the modern western society, the easiest to see but also to overlook, farther away the light décor of the Arabic era and then the Coptic-Hellenistic age of transition, in which the world metropolis Alexandria and the first Christian anchorites are curious antipodes. But beyond and above these layers rise the Pyramids and temples with a majesty which makes everything else sink into insignificance. So overwhelming and present is this oldest past that the tourist is apt to stare blindly at the Pharaohs' Egypt and conceive the whole country as a gigantic mummy, the forgotten shell of a life that has long since fled.

This impression is in many ways unfair. Face to face with the sterile deserts of Mesopotamia, even with impoverished Greece, there is some justification for speaking of countries transformed into ruins, but hardly with Egypt – verdant, densely populated and seething with work. Yet there is no denying that the country is still dominated in some strange way by the past, perhaps because the living present, regulated by the river's yearly rhythm, by the course of the sun in the cloudless sky and by the eternal repetition of agricultural life, has an atmosphere of timelessness which has found its final expression in the old Egyptian monuments.

The vigour with which the Egypt of the Pharaohs lives on and the many glimpses into the country's past given by archaeological finds, have resulted in an interest in ancient Egyptian life which not only siezes on its external, visible aspects, but also seeks to show a psychological understanding of those who created this kingdom. This understanding is based on the belief that people are fundamentally unchanged through the ages. The historical novel, in our day supplemented by the historical film, is a kind of fancy-dress ball; men and women, dressed up in unassailably correct costumes – the result of painstaking research – and placed in a 'real' setting, strive for power, riches and love in the same way as people of today. How many Egyptian novels and films based on this principle have not been produced and how many more will there not be! Yet a careful study of the Egyptian monuments in particular is the very thing to upset a belief in unchanging human problems and in our ability to understand an unfamiliar form of culture.

That we have something in common with the ancient Egyptian, just as he has with the caveman of 40,000 years ago, is not to be denied. Certain animal needs, as well as the physical space in which we live, are indisputable constants. But I think one must distinguish between two sides of the psyche: the innate sphere of sensory experience and instinct, which we presumably share with the animals – they see the same space as we and their needs are repeated in us – and the world of ideas which man builds up for himself. These ideas – pictorial images and verbal structures – are not born in accordance with any hard and fast rules of nature, which would make them identical in all people in all ages and in all places. They are created by man himself and acquire totally different forms in different spheres of culture – in fact, if we look carefully, we find that they are different in each human being. It is the similarities and dissimilarities in these ideas which link and separate people into coteries, nations, religious sects and civilizations. And as man's life is dominated more by these ideas than by the animal instincts common to us all, the chances of 'understanding' between the various groups grows less the more foreign to each other these ideas are.

If we measure with this yardstick, we must admit that there is very little chance of even a superficial understanding between us and the ancient Egyptians. We may translate their hieroglyphics quite faultlessly in relation to the physical world we have in common – 'man' as 'man' and 'river' as 'river' – yet the meaning behind the words 'man' and 'river' is utterly different and the result of the translation reveals more about ourselves than about those who once wrote the original text. In some ways, our attempts to interpret the lives and thoughts of the ancient Egyptians are about as realistic as animal fables – in both cases there is a common plane, that of pleasure, suffering and the struggle for life. For children and primitive people these fairy-tales about controversies between the fox and the bear or about the carefree cricket are naively true, for us they are human satire in amiable disguise. It would perhaps be salutary if in the same way we learnt to regard our attempts to understand the Egyptians as disclosures chiefly about the disclosers themselves.

A practical means of applying this principle is to study what has been said in different ages about the Pyramids, these ancient monuments which were misunderstood even thousands of years ago and which have meant something new to each generation. A doctor's thesis could be written on all the views expressed about them; I shall content myself with giving four examples, chosen to represent four different epochs and mentalities.

The first is Herodotus' famous description of the Pyramids, long accepted uncritically as an objective testimony by a man who himself saw ancient Egypt before it died and who heard from the priests' lips the Egyptians' own conception of their culture. That 'the father of history' probably never came into contact with cultured Egyptians during his short journey but only with the common people and with many of the Greeks living in the country, who interpreted the flights of fancy and the verbiage of the temple guards and the tourist dragomans for him, is a truth heeded only of recent times. Herodotus' account of how and why the Pyramids were built at the very most reflects the fanciful notions in the heads of the Egyptian people at this late date and to an even greater extent a purely Greek mentality. Archaeology has thus quashed the theory that the building blocks were raised from the ground and put in position by wooden machinery – in actual fact, long, gently sloping earth ramps were used and subsequently removed. Still more distorted is the explanation of the motives behind these gigantic enterprises. The builder of the Great Pyramid, Cheops, is presented as a tyrant, whose actions were dictated by ambition: by leaving an insurpassable monument behind him he wanted to establish his fame through the ages. 'Cheops forced all Egyptians to work for him,' Herodotus writes, going on to relate how the king, when his monetary assets dwindled, let his own daughter prostitute herself in order to scrape together sufficient means to continue the work. That Pharaoh was a god in ancient Egypt and could not think or feel like a Greek tyrant, that the Pyramids were sanctuaries of still more collective importance to the community than our medieval cathedrals, that the Egyptians at this period had no conception of private interests and rights which they could be forced to give

73

up in order to work for Pharaoh, and finally, that the economic life of the age neither was based on money as a means of payment nor tolerated private fortunes which could accrue to the king through some form of entertainment tax – all these are truths of which Herodotus was blissfully unaware.

The Arabs' attitude to the Pyramids is as clearly related to their conception of humanity as Herodotus' is to that of the Greeks: when the story-teller who collected the motley contents of the Thousand and One Nights wanted to speak of the awe-inspiring edifices outside Cairo, he saw them not as the victory token of ruthless individualism but as proof of man's impotence in a world where Allah alone is great. 'O man, you who trust in the ephemeral! Stop and reflect: Where are the creators of the Pyramids? Their works still stand, but they themselves are but flotsam on the stream of time.' And we listen to the story of Mamun, the son of Harun al Raschid, who wanted to pull down the mighty monuments and, being unable to, tried to seize the vast treasures hidden inside them: 'precious stones, golden coins, splendid statues, all kinds of instruments and excellent weapons covered with the water of wisdom, which protects them against rust until doomsday, as well as glass which will bend without breaking and many wonderful medicines.' So, to the Arabs, the Pyramids are concrete evidence of what they wish to believe in: the inexhaustible, magic resources of reality, treasures which exist even if Allah does not permit one to find them.

Again the centuries pass, until a rather portly man with drooping moustache comes riding along in the company of dragomans who are clamouring for tips. 'About half-past three we reach the edge of the desert, where the three Pyramids rise up. Unable to control myself any longer, I spur my horse to a gallop. It is a furious assault. Involuntarily I utter loud cries and we ride up to the Sphinx in a cloud of whirling sand. The sight of the Sphinx Abu el Hul – the Father of Terror. The sand, the Pyramids, the Sphinx, quite grey and steeped in a strong tinge of rose. The sky is deep-blue, the eagles wheel round the tops of the Pyramids. We stop in front of the Sphinx, it regards us with a frightful look; I am afraid of growing dizzy and try to control my emotion. We ride on as though possessed, surrounded by flying stones, and gallop round the Pyramids.' This is Flaubert's reaction to the old monuments – a romantic meeting between the individual and the riddle of life, a seizure of life with the help of understanding and feeling.

If, finally, I am to quote a modern conception of the Pyramids, the choice is not easy. The mental perplexity of our age is clearly seen in the comments passed on these edifices, each of them different according to the individual. One could mention the 'Pyramid specialist' J. P. Lauer's view of the Pyramids as celestial steps on which the dead Pharaoh mounted to the gods. One might also quote one of the many occult treatises in which the Pyramids are regarded as models of the world; if you know the secret unit of measure corresponding to a year you can read the whole history and future of humanity in the different passages of the building. I shall merely cite the view of a matter-of-fact American, J. H. Breasted: 'The Great Pyramid is the earliest and most impressive witness surviving from the ancient world to the final emergence of organized society from pre-historic chaos and local conflict, thus coming for the first time completely under the power of a far-reaching and comprehensive centralization effected by one controlling mind.' If this acceptance of the ideals of organization and the spirit of enterprise is not a personal confession bound to its own age rather than an understanding of those who once built the Pyramids, I do not know what it is.

With all our access through the art of printing to direct experiences and exact research of countless people, with all our concrete knowledge of Egypt's history, religion, geography and social conditions, we have in plain fact not come one step farther than Herodotus as regards understanding the mentality of the Pyramid builders: we too link the Pyramids to our world, while deluding ourselves that we are making our way back to theirs.

In this respect history is a false science which can never fulfil its programme of determining '*wie es eigentlich gewesen*'. But fables about the past can never cease to fascinate us; ever interpreted anew, they will follow man along the road his new ideas open up to him. And the most imposing images of dead ideas, such as Egypt's pyramids, will always have a new meaning.

Much has changed in Egypt since Flaubert came riding up to the Sphinx – among other things, a fine asphalt highway has been built from the Nile up to the desert plateau at Giza. Borne by our faithful Lambretta, we threaded our way between buses, cars and a swarm of harassed pedestrians, and rode out through the dreary suburbs that have grown up on the once verdant plain west of Cairo. On the edge of the desert, near the famous hotel Mena House, a long line of camels with gorgeous trappings await the tourist buses. The dragomans swoop down on their victims like vultures, the tourist is hoisted into the saddle and swayingly conveyed the short distance to the Sphinx, where a fresh working group in Giza's well-organized tourist industry stands ready – the photographers who immortalize the proud camel-rider with the Father of Terror as a background. Then on to the ticket-office, the mysteriously exhibited mummy in one of the tombs, the description of the Pyramids' dimensions in metres and feet, estimation of the blocks' weight in kilos and pounds. At the base of the Pyramids is a sign in three languages stating that ascent without an authorized guide is forbidden and not far from the genuine relics is a pasteboard temple erected by Cecil B. De Mille in which his latest Pharaoh film was produced with the co-operation of countless willing extras.

Even so, the experience is overwhelming: all modern officiousness vanishes in the presence of the stern grandeur, the frightening majesty which speaks from these volumes of stone. The course of sun and shadow, the clouds across the endless desert, are the only fellow-actors worthy to rank with the Pyramids, while the tourist fair at their feet fades into insignificance. Equally as impressive as the exterior is the Great Pyramid's interior, where you crawl along through sloping passages in stifling heat to the innermost burial chamber: here you have a physical sense of the Egyptian conception of space, which haunts you like an enigmatic dream.

On our second visit to Giza we had the good luck to witness an unusual ceremony which stirred the imagination: in the presence of about a hundred specially invited persons, including diplomats and members of the government, the first stone was lifted from the roof of the tomb where one of the newly-discovered so-called 'sun boats' lay. The background to the event was as follows: the Egyptians have not only woken up politically to nationalistic self-awareness, in archaeology, too, they have high-flying ambitions and would like as soon as possible to surpass

Carter's feat in finding Tutankhamon's tomb. When a young Egyptian archaeologist, Kamal el Mallakh, chanced on two boat tombs at the foot of the Cheops Pyramid and a peep-hole between the blocks of stone was opened to make sure that a boat was really lying there, the news was blazed abroad. The journalists were not slow to enlarge the sensation and newspapers the world over outdid each other in wild surmise: according to one, the Sun God's own votive boat had been found laden with jewels and papyrus rolls, according to another the tomb just discovered was connected by an underground passage to Cheops' real, but as yet untouched and unknown, burial chamber deep down under the Pyramid.

The ceremony at which we had the honour to be present was very well staged. One of the huge limestone blocks above the long, narrow boat tomb had, in advance, been fastened by strong ropes to two hand-worked jacks, and after the youthful minister of education had said a few well-turned phrases about the revolution's achievements in all spheres, a dozen or so workers began to haul on the chain rings. All group work in Egypt is accompanied by unison singing and the droning hymn with its regular beats, rising from these men's throats while they were urged on by a fat, slavedriver type in a caftan, was far and away the most effective part of the tomb-opening ceremony. Nearly five thousand years had passed since this stone was laid in place, but the singing and the brawny, broad-shouldered workers were no doubt as unchanged as the mighty triangle of the Pyramid above our heads. When the stone block was out of the way, electric spotlights were installed and we were all allowed one by one to approach the opening and look down into the shaft. At last it was Mona's and my turn: sure enough, an enormous boat lay there, not unlike the famous Viking ships in Oslo. Half-mouldering ropes had been laid over the railing in neat coils, we caught a glimpse of a steering oar, a decorated prow, and out of the tomb rose a strange perfume. But of treasures, statues, papyrus rolls and sacred emblems there was not a sign. It was a boat, a utility craft which must have once floated on the Nile: evidently Cheops had it put into the tomb with him in the same way as other necessities – corn, furniture, weapons, servants, everything that his eternal soul, his *ka*, might need in the after life. At all events, it was certainly not a sun boat, a symbolic cult object. This does not mean, of course, that the discovery is un-important: it has given us a well-preserved sample of the craft that were used in Egypt during the Old Kingdom. But Kamal el Mallakh and his Egyptian colleagues must go on trying: Mariette, Carter and one or two other foreigners still hold the record in the annals of Egyptology.

The Pyramids at Giza have, for various reasons, become the best known of Egypt's pyramids and they are often the only ones that the rushed tourist visits. But we should remember that these monuments were once numbered by the hundred and that about sixty of them are still known in Central Egypt. Both to the north and south of Giza other pyramids can be glimpsed on the horizon and for two days after we left Cairo we kept seeing new pyramid silhouettes on the edge of the desert as we sailed up the Nile. The unique position given to the Cheops Pyramid even during antiquity, when it was regarded as one of the seven wonders of the world, was due not so much to its being the largest of them all (479 feet high), as to the fact that it was also the most carefully and solidly built. For our age, too, it has an interest with which only one other pyramid can compete – the Pharaoh Zoser's Step Pyramid. This curious monument is to be found at Sakkara, a place with such a wealth of remarkable sights that a visit to it cannot be missed.

The way to Sakkara is a simple village road which follows a tree-lined canal from Giza. We skimmed along it on our faithful Lambretta one early morning, amazed at not meeting any cars, stimulated by the clear, pure air, by the sun which was dispersing the morning mists away across the river and by the fresh greenery in the fields around us. Suddenly we spied something on the road ahead of us: a curious astonishing column was approaching in a cloud of dust. First two soldiers on roaring motor bicycles. They waved to us commandingly to draw into the side and shouted hoarsely: 'Ramses! Ramses!' Then came two open cars with officers and several men in mufti, all standing with faces to the rear. Hot on their heels came a motorized monster, the largest lorry I have ever seen, coupled to a trailer with twenty axle-trees and on this a mountain, a stone colossus – Ramses II in person. The ground trembled and sagged as this procession thundered past, and we stood gaping by the roadside, unaware that the Egyptian newspapers for weeks past had been talking of this transport of a giant statue which for thousands of years had been lying on its back in a palm grove at Mitrahine, on the site of ancient Memphis. The men of the new régime had decided that this statue of Ramses II was to be moved to Cairo as a symbol of the new birth. The cautious objections of the archeologists had fallen on deaf ears. The spirited initiators were not interested in the fact that the statue would lose its monumental proportions by being placed in a setting with quite a different scale and that it would be just as forlorn as the obelisk in the Place de la Concorde or Cleopatra's Needle on the Thames Embankment. So Ramses is now standing in the glare of the neon lights in the railway square in Cairo.

Fortunately, there had been two recumbent colossi in the palm grove at Memphis and we could visit the one that was left, as it lay smiling and encircled by the whispering trees like one of the giant Buddhas of India. A white alabaster sphinx also lies huddled in the oasis landscape as a reminder of the vanished city. A swarm of village urchins set upon us to sell doubtful antiques. When the price of the scarabs fell below any conceivable cost of manufacture we optimistically bought a few in the hope that one of them might be real.

Sakkara itself lies up on the sterile desert plateau in a desolate but magnificent landscape. It is impossible to give a detailed account here of even the most important of Sakkara's sights, but four monuments must be briefly mentioned: the Step Pyramid, the Serapeum, Ti's tomb and the newly-found pyramid.

First, the Pharaoh Zoser's pyramid. It is mainly thanks to the French archaeologist J. P. Lauer that this monument was forced to yield its secret about the origin of the pyramids through a gradually made change of the older, block-like mastaba tomb's form, probably as the result of the work of a brilliant architect and pioneer, Imhotep. As we see it now, it is the first and most interesting of all the pyramids, a monument which combines a long past and anticipates the future, a final product of the old wood and mud-brick architecture, a starting-point for the stone building style. Its step form also reveals what was probably the religious significance of the pyramids: they were celestial staircases, a means of communication between heaven and earth.

Fascinating in a more dramatic way is the Serapeum, the burial catacombs of the sacred Apis bulls. They were rediscovered in 1851 by the French archaeologist Mariette, the founder of the Cairo Museum. One can imagine his feelings when, after deductions worthy of a detective and months-long excavations of a sphinx avenue which showed him the way, he penetrated into this underground world, where passages extending for miles are lined with niches for the bulls' sarcophagi – all made of a single syenite block as large as a modern locomotive.

Here in the Serapeum one cannot help thinking of the vast amount of labour man has expended in past ages on objects which in our eyes are absurd. What has the laying out of these tombs cost in the way of toil and sacrifice, how many human lives have been wasted in order to hollow out the inside of the earth, prepare the sarcophagi and transport them from the distant Assuan and finally embalm these bulls, which chance had furnished with the prescribed sacred signs of Apis: black hair with a white triangle on the brow and the outline of an eagle on the back. Can one imagine any more unnecessary and useless work? This question can be answered with another: are we ourselves so much more sensible than the Egyptians, do we in our community use labour and human lives in a less absurd way? Our notion – seldom openly admitted but all the more indirectly alleged – that the aim of life is security, comfort and individual freedom for all, is contradicted in the most odd way by our real actions. Is not a large part of our community's resources sacrificed to armaments, which are needs we ourselves create, and do we not in our private lives stubbornly strive for the useless and the irrational, that which implies a deviation from comfort and freedom? The social revolution which is extending all over the world under the watch-word 'Access for all to the bare necessities of life!' means in practice that more and more people have access to the un-necessary, to the privileges of insecurity and unreason. That which is apparently most unnecessary seems to be what is most essential to humans. If we acknowledge this and admit that we all sacrifice ourselves for things which are beyond reason, our superciliousness in regard to the Apis tombs at Sakkara vanishes. Our skyscrapers, bombers, television sets, athletics records are

General Hassan Ragab visits Daphne *in Cairo*

With the Lambretta on the Giza road

(*Left*)
The earth cracks when
the Nile flooding
subsides

(*Below*)
A typical fellah village
by the Nile with dove-
cotes in the background
and huts of maize
stalks

no less absurd than the Apis tombs – nor are they more so, for each age ruthlessly serves its ideas.

From the Serapeum it is not far to the most splendid of Sakkara's tombs of the nobility. Ti, a magnate who lived during the Fifth Dynasty and among his titles could enumerate *Pharaoh's chosen friend, steward of his master's secrets in all his residences, steward of all the king's works, administrator of the pyramids of the kings Nefererka and Neusera,* was buried in a so-called mastaba, which, like the Serapeum, was buried in its turn by the desert sands and was therefore preserved for us. As one trudges down to its doorway through the billowing sea of sand, which within a few decades would once more bury what the archaeologists have wrested from it, if the newly-formed drifts of sand were not constantly shovelled away, one wonders how many monuments still remain to be discovered at Sakkara. It seems certain that new tombs will come to light, but it is also fairly certain to say that they will not add anything essentially new to our knowledge of Egypt, as all these tombs of great men are alike, the only difference being that the pictorial adornment, which in the best tombs, such as Ti's, is perfect in form and richly varied, has been confined in others to the bare essentials.

What impressed me most deeply in Ti's tomb was the magical feeling of *the present* in the reliefs. Here is the miracle which the tomb's creator once strove to bring about; time and mortality are vanquished, we pass unsuspectingly across the vast chasm of thousands of years and witness as the immediate present scenes from Ti's life after death. We see sacrificial bulls killed, servants bearing necessities to the dead man, we see boats from the South drifting downstream and those from the North moving swiftly upstream with bellying sails, we see fishermen hauling nets heavy with fish, crocodiles and rhinoceroses attacked by hunters, cattle making their way across a ford while the cowherd goes ahead carrying a newborn calf which moos for its anxious mother. They are not pictures which an artist has caught from reality and presents with a nostalgic 'This was', or wishful depictions which say 'This is as it should be.' Nor are they, as so often in our western art, pictures which say 'This is somewhere else', but scenes filled to the brim with the deep and calm assurance 'This *is* here on the wall, now at this moment and for all eternity.'

F

Apart from this strange 'presence,' the reliefs in Ti's tomb had another aspect which surprised me: their artistic perfection, unsurpassed during the subsequent thousands of years. In Egypt we have a case – which almost shocks us with our belief in evolution and all our set ideas – of a nation which appears at a certain moment of its history to have had a veritable revelation of its culture's primitive forms – of the principles of religion, science, written signs, architecture and pictorial reproduction. The whole of Egypt's known history can to some extent be regarded as an application of principles, as variations and repetitions of what the Old Kingdom created. Or is it due to coincidence, to the loss of preserved evidence from a time of preparation which lasted for many thousands of years, that we see the Egyptian culture leap out of nothing like this in its completed form, and then slowly be drained of its strength during the three thousand years that followed? If we want to save the thought of evolution by a supposition such as this, we must admit that all we know of this culture is its decline.

One of the most interesting monuments at Sakkara is the newly-discovered pyramid. It seems incredible that in this age, and at a place so well known to archaeologists as this, an entirely new, hitherto unknown pyramid can be found. The Egyptian archaeologist Zakaria Ghoneim has, however, performed this miracle, thereby stepping straight into the adventure book of the great archaeological discoveries. The find was not due to a fluke but to a series of deductions which he made after moving to the place in 1951 as newly-appointed inspector of the Sakkara region's antiquities. No one had previously asked himself how a huge rectangular terrace several hundred yards from Zoser's pyramid had come into existence and why so many stone splinters were to be seen there of an unusual and light-coloured type of limestone. One or two trial excavations exposed parts of an enormous building and since then Ghoneim has dug out not only the imposing lower portions of a step pyramid but also a wall of fine limestone blocks built around the temple precincts – an architectural repetition of the Zoser pyramid's curious wall. The fact that the pyramid had remained unfinished could easily be explained: the builder – in all likelihood Zoser's successor – had died before the work had progressed any further and his remains had merely been deposited in the burial chamber which as a rule lies under the base of the pyramid.

This, at all events, was Zakaria Ghoneim's firm conviction. We had the luck to find him at home in his house on the edge of the desert and the still greater luck to go with him to the fenced-off excavation area to survey the day's progress. In this way we got to know this unique man. On the one hand he was mildness and complaisance personified. Extremely scientific and cautious in his reasoning, he gave a somewhat impersonal, not to say schoolmasterish, impression. On the other hand, he was full of complexes and irrelevant criticism with regard to the European archaeologists who, if we were to believe him, had done such bad work in Egypt that they must either be totally forbidden to excavate there or be strictly supervised by the expert, self-sacrificing and conscientious Egyptian archaeologists. He was especially critical of the French archaeologists 'with their wild flights of fancy and literary encumbrances'. It was indeed dampening to hear such nonsense on the very scene of Mariette's, Maspero's and Lauer's devoted work, but when we reached the pyramid and Ghoneim began to show us his find, the little cloud of annoyance vanished. We saw that it is not easy for the sons of a young nation, which until yesterday was backward and un-developed, to take over the guardianship after the representatives of the civilized countries of Europe. Zakaria Ghoneim is one of those who have the qualifications to do so, not least because he is far from being as void of unscientific fantasy and literary encum-brance as he likes to make out. For what is one to say of his reaction to the disappointment he suffered in the pyramid's interior? He had sought systematically and long for the entrance to the pyramid until, sure enough, he found a sloping passage which led through several sealed doors and corridors full of stone to an inner room. Here, after three years' work, he was met by the sight he had hoped for all the time: a large, sealed, alabaster sarcophagus, untouched by plunderers. In the presence of a chosen group of archaeologists, leading lights of culture and politicians, the coffin was opened with solemn ceremony – and was found to be empty. This had happened shortly before we met Ghoneim and we were cruel enough to ask him how the matter could be explained. Had thieves got at the mummy after all? Had

83

Pharaoh perhaps been murdered and his body lost but the funeral and interment of the sarcophagus carried out in order to mislead the uninitiated? Zakaria Ghoneim's eyes grew dreamy but determined:

'No,' he said. 'The mummy is here in the pyramid. The sarcophagus we opened is the wrong one, perhaps it has some special significance which we don't know of. But somewhere in another underground room is the right sarcophagus and I am going to find it.'

Seek, Zakaria Ghoneim, seek with all your might, for it does happen that our wishes take on material form through our will. It was not through scientific method that Schliemann found Troy, Carter Tutankhamon's treasures and you your pyramid: you have all created this out of your faith and given it to mankind. Scientific exactitude is the mould of our time in which fantasy must be cast, it is the condition which must be fulfilled, but the essential thing is still the dream.

Our two day-long visits to Sakkara undoubtedly taught us more than anything else during our stay in Cairo about the Egypt of the Pharaohs. But the impressions received in Sakkara were supplemented by almost daily visits to Cairo's magnificent Egyptian Museum. This museum not only excels the Egyptian collections of all other countries in the matter of wealth and variety but it also contains – for those who believe in the unity of art through all ages and spheres of culture – some of the most remarkable creations in the world's art. But this very question of the affinity of works of art and the radical difference in various cultures thrusts itself to the fore in the rooms of the Cairo Museum.

It is said that one should not visit Egypt and Greece on the same journey: they are two irreconcilable worlds which cast a shadow over each other. From my own experience I can affirm that whoever has once stood on the Acropolis will never find the air in Egypt's temples and tombs easy to breathe, but also that an encounter with the world of the Pharaohs mercilessly exposes the Greeks as a frivolous, adventurous and, with all their beguiling charm, an unreliable race.

Now it is perhaps a personal matter of temperament whether we prefer to side whole-heartedly with the Egyptians or the

Greeks, or whether we think we gain a greater understanding of both through a comparison – think, in fact, that we can come to grips with the universal problem of life by confronting our western tradition with a world of culture, utterly foreign in its essence, such as the Egyptian. It is in any case a comparison which changes much of what we regard as the very framework of our existence into a variable pattern. The outer world becomes, to an undreamt-of degree, a raw material for man's almost unlimited creative power, and our respect for the mind's potentialities grows when we see how decisive the ideas and the mental tools are that we ourselves shape.

One of the spheres in which we are in obvious need of relative values in order to gain an insight into it, is art. It has become usual to regard art as a basic phenomenon in human existence as unchanging and taken as much for granted as the faculty of speech or the air we breathe. Authors of 'the world history of art' have, without blinking, put together pictorial, spatial and musical compositions, from cave-drawings and pyramids to advertisements and jazz, in the firm conviction that they all have a common kernel. 'What is art?' they have then asked, seeking a formula to fit all these objects and forms of behaviour, which, by historic coincidence, have come to be lumped together under one heading. It is not my intention altogether to deny the possibility of such a combination: I believe there is a definite aesthetic attitude which modern man can adopt to all these phenomena. On the other hand, it strikes me as pure invention when one presupposes, even in distant times, a similar attitude in the makers and users of those objects and forms we happen to call works of art. In this respect the Egyptian images and the interpretations to which they have been subjected are very illuminating.

In just the same way as the Cheops Pyramid has called forth differing opinions in different ages, Egypt's images have called forth in strangers a series of interpretations which have much more to do with the interpreters than with their makers, dead long since. The root of the error can be traced to Herodotus, who thought that the Egyptian statues were similar to those which adorned the public squares of the Greek cities. When, in modern times, Europeans began to travel in Egypt they took it just as much for granted that the series of pictures on temples and tombs were 'decorations' and 'reproductions' of the same kind as the frescoes and pictures in the churches and palaces of Europe. The fabrication of modern 'artistic strivings' in the ancient Egyptians has continued since then in such detail that it is possible to trace the entire development of modern art in the changing attitude to Egyptian iconography. Archaeologists and tourists, brought up on genre-painting and naturalistic portraiture, stood enraptured in front of the Egyptians' 'head portraits that have caught the very essence of character' and 'astoundingly true to life' portrayals of cattle being slaughtered, of harvest, fishing and women busy at their toilet. The next step was the romantic admiration of the so-called Amarna art, sculptures and paintings from the time of the Pharaohs Ikhnaton and Tutankhamon – why, they were almost 'impressionistic'. The 'incorrect drawing' and the deviations from 'the natural perspective' in many Egyptian paintings were first of all regarded as a regrettable lack of skill and afterwards – when modern art also began to allow itself certain liberties – as a conscious, anti-naturalistic system of reproduction.

I will not deny that I myself came to Egypt with the problems of modern art fresh in my mind, prepared to measure everything with a ready-made yardstick. In fact, I had already done the measuring with the aid of the illustrations and books I had studied before leaving home. It seemed quite obvious that Egyptian art at present has very little to give us. Compared with the invasion of primitive old, and individualistic modern, art, it seemed to me far too restrained, academic, objective. And in relation to Greek art I found it classical without being humanistic – that is, foreign to us in another way. But preconceived opinions seldom hold good. The very first visit to the Cairo Museum was enough to upset my apple-cart of reservations. The inner authority and ultimate sense of form which spoke to me out of the best works were so great that all sculptures I had previously seen appeared as improvisations and superficial fancies by comparison. The wooden sculptures from the Old Kingdom made a particularly deep impression: I don't think I have ever seen such a perfect statue as the so-called *Sheik el beled*. If I had come to the museum with the intention of measuring what I saw with my rule, it was the exhibits which led me in their direction instead.

One demand which the objects in the Egyptian Museum seemed to make at the outset was not to be regarded as works of art. This is in any case impossible for practical reasons: where can you draw such a line in this storehouse chock-full with finds? Statues and mummies, real and reproduced household utensils, papyrus scrolls and 5,000-year-old grains of corn lie cheek by jowl in a lifeless jumble. The collection in the Egyptian Museum is rather like an aeroplane which has crashed in the jungle and has been taken to pieces down to the last screw by natives who know nothing whatever about flying and think everything they pick up is an ornament. The aeroplane, the living whole to which the objects in the Cairo Museum belong, has to be reconstructed by means of what is told us by those who helped to take it apart.

In a handsome book, recently published, about Egyptian painting I had read a maxim by the vizier Ptahhotep, who lived during the Old Kingdom. 'Art has no limit and no artist possesses perfection.' This 4,000-year-old piece of wisdom, still true today, is astounding – until the problem of translation comes to mind. The translation of hieroglyphics into modern languages naturally involves unavoidable corruptions, seeing that the very mechanism of thought – let alone the derivations and associations of the words – is so utterly different. But a translation like this must almost be regarded as a forgery, for where the translator writes *art* there is a sign representing a stone-drill, and the word *artist* did not exist at all in Egyptian. The word *life-giver* was written to indicate a sculptor and *writer of outlines* a man who did paintings and reliefs. Also, it should be remembered that the Egyptians had no special word for beauty: *nefer* can be translated as both beautiful, good and pleasant. The conclusion of all this is that the Egyptian attitude to pictorial reproduction in at least two respects differs from ours: first, picture and writing – both the work of a writer – were not separate, but two sides of the same thing; second, the picture – gifted with life – was not a picture as we mean it, but a kind of magic reality.

Even a superficial view reveals how inextricably picture and writing are joined together in Egypt: the hieroglyphics consist largely of pictures which have acquired the value of letters, and in most of the pictorial reliefs and paintings, texts are organically interfused in the composition. One thinks also of the curious and fairly common rebuses, in which the letter signs have hands and feet and express a thought by their action: one notices, too, the conventionally sign-like purpose of, for instance, the different kinds of headgear and emblems worn by the painted figures – true epithets and definitions. But the interplay does not stop here. Champollion, the interpreter of the hieroglyphics, was the first to see that the Egyptian pictures in their entirety, and even the architecture, is a kind of gigantic writing, the object of which is to express ideas. Far from trying to create religious moods, evoke an awareness of beauty, reproduce reality, depict feelings or call forth a sympathetic echo between creator and beholder, these many-faceted entities are intended to give shape to reality and to articulate the ideas behind funeral ceremonies, religion and the maintenance of a court. This also explains the curious Egyptian reproduction style with its heads and extremities in profile placed on trunks standing *en face:* it aims at grammatical clarity. Each essential joint, the limbs and movements of the human form or the animal body, the characteristic form of each object, all must be presented in their most distinct shape in a manner approved by convention, so that the picture can easily be read. As a result, stereotyped repetition and mechanical formalization are always lurking just out of sight, even influencing certain sides of the Egyptians' pictorial art: water, for example, is always depicted quite conventionally by zig-zag lines. The way in which the Egyptians conceived their pictures as ideas and language is particularly apparent in their innumerable divine monsters, composed of human bodies, animal heads and various attributes. They are never organic, called up by an immediate vision of horror, but logically put together, rather as we combine words such as bulldog, harelip, foxglove. On the whole, it is noteworthy that neither gods, people nor even the big, historic battle scenes on the Ramses temples are optically and palpably seen in the space we call reality. The whole of the Egyptian world of pictures seems to us to float on an abstract, symbolic plane, it has no physical weight, breath of reality or tangibility.

Yet this writing, these symbols, are more real to the Egyptians than all immediate sensory experiences. This is the second main angle from which to view Egyptian images: they replace reality. It is not merely the earliest sculptures and reliefs which in pre-historic times arose out of the need for magic substitutes – the picture of the god worshipped as himself. In principle, the attitude to pictures remained magic throughout Egypt's history. An over-simplification would be this: when the oldest rulers were placed in their tombs, an entire royal household – dignitaries, wives, soldiers, slaves – was put to death to keep the dead man company in the underworld and large quantities of household goods and other necessities were placed in the tomb for his use. On the other hand, no clear distinction was made between an object (or a living being) and its image (or name): people believed themselves capable of injuring a person by injuring his image, and knowledge of the gods' secret names gave the initiated power over them. It was therefore natural at funerals, instead of real attendants and necessities, to furnish the dead man with pictures of them; his name was written in the tomb in order to bind him there, and the incantations normally uttered beside the tomb or during the burial service were made permanent by being formulated in writing. An especially important part was allotted to the sculptures, which were often walled into small, sealed burial chambers and were intended – in the same way as the mummy – to serve as a dwelling for the departed man's soul. The Egyptians' belief regarding the dead man's life in the tomb had nothing to do with modern ghost stories about walking and talking corpses, it was purely conceptual, but as the symbols were the most important reality, the symbolic life in the forms of the mummies' and images' forms was what really mattered. It was not the statue which was transformed by a magical illusion into a living human being, but all living beings consisted in essence of a picture: Tutankhamon is called literally 'the living statue of the god Amon'. To depict a dead man as Osiris *made* him into a risen Osiris, and to destroy a picture also killed the soul of the man depicted. Everything points to the fact that all Egyptian statues were such dwellings for souls, just as all paintings 'made real' what they represented.

The big difference between the Egyptians and ourselves has really a very small cause: a fateful idea which the Greeks got into their heads. It was they who conceived the subtle thought that one reality (for example, a picture) can depict another without there being any essential link between them. Modern man, having been brought up with this idea, takes it for granted; it has become a kind of secondary reaction which corrects our spontaneous identification – necessary to all understanding of pictures, all speech – of picture and subject, word and object. Without going into the psychological and cultural results of separating the symbols from the reality, we find that it is only through this that the primary condition for what we call art is fulfilled. The Greeks were the first to create pictures which were intended solely to be conceived as pictures, as symbols which depicted something instead of representing it. This new outlook gave rise to entirely new problems. Plato and Aristotle now began to philosophize over the relationship of the copy to reality, the artist emerged as a human type and the changing history of the function of depictive art in society was begun.

Yet the old notions were not quite dead. The great iconoclast battle of the eighth and ninth centuries, fought with special frenzy in the learned, Christian Alexandria, shows that it was not a question of intelligence versus stupidity, evolution versus primitivism, but of two divergent lines of thought. The Christian imagery of the Middle Ages, with its sacred icons and living symbols, once more shattered the western conception of art, until the Renaissance brought back the Greek outlook. Oddly enough, it seems as if we in these latter days are to return to the Egyptians. The theory of art's conceptual function, allied to language, which Susanne Langer has put forward with such perspicacity in her much-discussed work *Feeling and Form*, would not have surprised Ptahhotep, and in modern art the reproduction principle has gradually been replaced by immediately present pictorial symbols. The impressionists still painted pictures which said 'This is somewhere else,' Picasso's, Klee's and Mondrian's paintings say 'This is,' and demand that we take an interest in that which exists only on the canvas. What became of reality – the sunlit, reliable, Greek reality? It is not only the painters who have lost their blind faith in it: for the rest of us, too, it is resolving itself into laws, formulas and thought structures. We have only pictures left and can do nothing but create new ones.

Perhaps it is this secret affinity of spirit which makes the modern man's pilgrimage among the temples and tombs of Egypt such a moving experience?

CHAPTER IV

Sailing on the Nile

From our moorings at the Cairo Yacht Club we could see, half a mile upstream, the long Abbas bridge, over which a constant stream of cars and pedestrians flowed. Twice every day, at 10 a.m. and 4 p.m., the traffic stopped and a huge bascule was raised. Sometimes a cluster of sailing-boats passed through but sometimes nothing at all, as the motor barges, which are the commonest users of the Nile in Cairo, go under the bridge unimpeded. But orders are orders and the bridge is opened whether anyone wants to go through or not. For us, this ceremony was almost an invitation, it seemed to beckon us daily to pass through. There, beyond the open gateway, the river lay free for a stretch of 250 miles to the next bridge and dam. During all our museum visits, strolls in the city and contacts with different environments, the gateway through the bridge was our secret joy and stimulus.

At last, on November 28th, we were ready to leave. Our new travelling companion, Edries, signed on, our friends waved good-bye and we headed upstream by engine in good time to get to the bridge by ten o'clock. I have often reflected over the feeling of happiness which fills one at such moments. Up to a point, I suppose, it is the relief from rush and divided interests, the excitement at the thought of all the unknown that lies ahead. But there is another explanation which I think is the most important. To steer and to respond at the same time, to collect one's anxieties and thoughts round a boat's reactions, capacities and successful voyage, to experience everything through it and in return to find meaning and content in one's journey – all this is the same thing one experiences in a happy love relationship with a human being, it is an allegory of love. *Daphne* has always allowed me to take the initiative, through her I have learnt that it is more important to love than to be loved. At times I have sighed or complained loudly when her whims and peculiarities have upset my plans – when her sluggishness on the tack has delayed me or the engine has refused to start at the very moment it was most needed – but in some form or other that kind of thing is part of every boat trip.

THE SUN BOAT

Having passed the Abbas bridge, we noticed that the handspike of the capstan was missing, and feeling rather as a husband does who has to stop the car outside a chemist's because his wife has left her lipstick at home, I steered in towards the bank of the suburb we had now reached. The whole of the paved slope was strewn with the contents of dustbins and latrines and as Edries and I picked our way up to the street, rats the size of sucking-pigs bared their teeth at us. In a teeming, smelly bazaar street we found a smithy and in half an hour got a new handspike. We could then continue towards more welcoming shores.

Unfortunately there was not a breath of wind and sailing was out of the question. About six miles from the bridge the suburbs come to an end and a palm grove extends on the west bank where old Memphis lay. Opposite is the Maadi Yacht Club which, unlike the Cairo club, boasts of a clubhouse on shore. The white, newly-painted sailing-dinghies, the shady park and the peaceful, rustic atmosphere enticed us to tie up at the club pontoon to have our lunch in peace, without having to think of navigation. After this pastoral interlude, we headed on up the wide river, which reflected a sky so clear that it reminded us of autumn and a palm-fringed bank with not a sign of the great city which had lain there for thousands of years.

We had agreed with the General that if possible we would settle each day's 'march' in advance so that police guards could be arranged at our mooring-places and this first day, on Edries' advice, we had chosen Farouk's villa at Heluan. Like all the king's former domains, this was most beautifully situated by a palm grove and surrounded by a little park. We tied up by some stone steps, greeted by one or two armed guards who had been ordered to receive us in state, and before the sun went down we had time to look over the newly-built and relatively small villa, the impersonal quasi-elegance of which suggested a luxury hotel in Paris rather than a private house. The villa's function was also quite apparent without the grinning comments of the officer on duty: Farouk had come here for intimate little supper parties with his many lady loves.

We sat under a thousand-year-old tree with an incredible number of branches and watched the sun go down behind the palm grove and the Dachschur pyramids on the other side of the river. Large sailing-boats, with tall, pointed sails, moved past right against the terrace, gliding through the dusk like dark archangels, soundless except for the slight splash from the bows. Other boats, often laden with hay or straw so that they looked like floating temple pylons, came drifting with the current, and when two boats drew near each other shouts which we did not understand were heard through the darkness – it was the angels warning each other not to come too close.

When the last flush of sunset had vanished and only a crescent moon was left, we sat down to dinner in *Daphne*'s cabin and Edries said expectantly:

'Now tell me about your people!'

Edries' interest in European conditions was unbounded, his knowledge of English quite good and his intellect developed to such a degree that for long stretches we forgot how youthfully naïve and restricted by narrow traditions he really was. The authorities in which he had implicit faith were many, first and foremost of course the Koran, which with an inimitable inflexion he called 'our book' – there was repudiation and fellowship of belief in the words. But he also had two other key expressions which recurred in the conversation in different contexts. When we asked why the population did or did not do something which aroused our surprise, he gave as an explanation 'They are accustomed to it,' or 'It is forbidden' – two equally undeniable reasons. For me, this matter-of-fact belief in authority in an unusually independent young Egyptian was a reminder of how unique our European mental liberty is, how revolutionary the Greek outlook on life must have been at first and how few countries there are as yet which in this respect have become western. Edries' interest in social development and technical progress was only a seeming witness to inner liberation. Like the modernism I have seen in the Soviet, it was rather a question of a new form of belief in authority.

This very first evening he confided to us his future plans: he wanted to learn a lot and visit many countries so that he in his turn could 'teach his people'. 'His people' turned out to be the village of Toma up in Nubia, where he had lived until he was eleven. He would live there for a few months each year and by talking to the young men of the village he would inculcate in them the new ideas, tell them about democracy, prosperity through industrialization, hospitals, schools, education. Added to this distant ideal was strict self-discipline in his daily life. That Edries abstained from alcohol was understandable from a religious viewpoint – even if during our journey we met many Moslems who, although the Prophet had forbidden wine, were grateful for the fact that he said nothing about beer, whisky or brandy. But Edries would neither smoke, drink coffee nor sit on soft kapok cushions. In the presence of this idealist we began to feel rather depraved and destitute of higher thoughts – we who neither said our prayers nor contented ourselves with hard wooden seats. Sitting there over dinner in *Daphne*'s cabin and seeing the large black eyes gravely and attentively turned on us – 'Now tell me about your people!' – we realized that we were Representatives of the white man (admired to excess and at the same time too harshly judged in disappointment) who has changed life for the coloured man – black, yellow and red – in his own part of the world. We saw how easily this admiration bursts into blossom when, after having been with us for four days, Edries told us that he had now chosen a new career: he was going to be an author and travel about from country to country in a boat and then write books about what he had seen.

It was cold, grey and raw when the alarm clock woke us at six in the morning, but the Spartan Edries took a cold shower in Farouk's servants' wing before we started. While the sun slowly dispersed the mists and the banks began to reflect themselves in the continuously glassy water, we headed cautiously upstream by engine against the current according to the navigation we had learnt during the Delta trip. Groundings could not be altogether avoided despite our constant use of the lead and sometimes it was critical, as when we had to force a veritable rapids where our seven knots availed us very little against the torrent. On the whole, however, we managed very well, thanks to the engine. How it is possible to go upstream without one seemed incredible to us, but we saw dozens of boats which, for lack of a sailing wind, were pushed along with the help of long poles or towed with ropes from the bank by tattered figures so wretched that Repin's well-known 'Volga Boatmen' seemed prosperous aristocrats by comparison.

Owing to our many groundings, we did not reach our appointed stop for the night, Girza, thirty-four miles from Heluan, until about five in the afternoon. The entire village, a couple of thousand souls, plus a few soldiers and caftan-clad village police, had collected at the landing-stage. Could this crowd have any connection with us? The minute we had tied up on the outer side of a barge the mob started to bawl something in an inarticulate chorus. We could only make out the syllables 'ABD – UL – NAS – SER' and didn't know whether it was a demonstration of sympathy or hatred, especially as the police and gaffirs began to drive the people away with cuts and blows. Edries assured us, however, that it was all pure friendliness and that Girza's fellahs had shouted:

'Welcome all men who are friends of Abdul Nasser and the revolution!'

A solitary evening walk such as we had been able to take in the Delta was clearly out of the question, we had not only got the desired police guard for *Daphne* but had ourselves been transformed into semi-official guests. A police officer had stopped his jeep on the bank and asked if we would like to go for a drive. Why not make the best of the situation? From the river we had glimpsed in the distance the peculiar Aztec silhouette of the Meidum pyramid, three staircase terraces which rose above the desert. Could we go there? Of course! Mona, Edries and I, plus five other persons, squeezed into the jeep, which was driven by a gay giant of a soldier, and off we went at a dizzy speed along the roads which run on top of the high embankments. Soon we reached the asphalted highroad and a barrier where a score of cars stood waiting. We learnt with some surprise that the roads are so unsafe that no car may drive into Cairo by itself after dark. The cars are collected into convoys, which then drive to the city under military escort. At the village of Saft a new policeman was hauled into the overfull jeep and on the outskirts of the village yet another beturbaned country policeman and his blunderbuss. There were eleven of us in the jeep when it headed out from the edge of the desert on to the roadless sea of sand, where the pyramid was outlined against a flaming sunset sky.

Unfortunately, it was almost dark by the time we got there and the entrance to the burial chamber was closed, but we climbed up on to the terrace with a bodyguard eight strong, deeply impressed by this man-made mountain. When we reached the first 'landing' I shone my torch into a hole, which may have been dug by a treasure-hunter in his search for the entrance to the pyramid. Instantly, a large, hairy animal rushed out between my legs so swiftly that I had not even time to be scared. The soldiers, who also caught sight of it and took it to be a jackal, started firing but did not hit it. The shots had, instead, another effect. The chief of police away at Saft thought a skirmish was going on and when we came down from the pyramid we were met by a relief expedition armed to the teeth.

We all laughed heartily at the misunderstanding and returned to Saft, where the police officer invited us to have a cup of tea. He was a gay lad with a head as round as a ball, bright eyes and immaculate uniform. He had just been posted to this godforsaken village from Alexandria and was finding it hard to live without cinema, cafes or company of his own age.

'In short, there is only one thing for me to do,' he confided to us. 'I shall have to get married so as to have something to do in the evenings.'

Upon asking what was the commonest kind of crime in the neighbourhood, we were told that it was manslaughter during a quarrel. Behind the fellah's phlegmatic exterior is hidden a hot-blooded recklessness which breaks out during a fight over the canal waters or a theft from the fields. So great is the poverty and lawlessness that the peasants must guard their crops day and night; when the cotton is ripe the owners dare not leave the fields until dawn, when the dew has fallen and the cotton can no longer be picked. They therefore arm themselves, the traditional weapon being a wooden stick with a core of iron, which will easily fell an opponent; in connection with the war, rifles became common. It is a point of honour for a man to have a rifle, even if it is useless and he has no ammunition. The government had, shortly before, issued an ultimatum to the population to hand in all private firearms to the police stations before 1st January, but the officer at Saft told us that the result up to then had been very meagre: most of the peasants preferred to bury their rifles in safe places.

The two officers we met that evening were typical products of

A Mecca pilgrim's house at Nag Hammadi

The village painter, Mohammed el Alaili Hassan, at Nag Hammadi

The dovecotes at Tell el Amarna

The Pharaoh Ikhnaton's summer palace at Tell el Amarna, and our escort

the working conditions of the Egyptian police force: its members are constantly being transferred so that they will have no time to take root or be bound by ties of friendship to the population. All the more bound to his environment is the second wielder of power in the Egyptian countryside – the village chieftain, the *omda*. When we returned to Girza after nightfall, the police jeep drove us straight to the omda's house – it was unthinkable not to pay a visit to this potentate. A man of seventy or so, used to giving orders and as hard as flint, he gave us audience in the reception room that every omda's house contains and where you sit in a row on benches lining the walls. The refreshment consisted of mandarins and a pale-red liquid flavoured with essence of roses; this did not prevent us from hesitating a second before swallowing this water, which without any doubt had been taken straight out of the Nile. The entertainment was provided partly by the omda's many male grand-children, who came in and bowed, partly by a live turkey and lamb which had been brought in. We played for a while with the children and the animals while Edries, respectfully but eloquently, conversed with our host – he loved to boast about us, our fine connections, our boat, our journeys, and he was very apt to pile it all on out of his imagination. When at last we felt we could take our leave with many compliments and came down to *Daphne* in the pitch dark, we found we were followed by two men carrying the turkey and the lamb: gifts to the government's friends! Mona's dismay was understandable. We could not take these animals with us alive, nor had we the heart to kill them; we had neither the facilities for cooking such large steaks nor the wolf's appetite with which to eat them.

A disturbed night followed; not only did the two old guards cough incessantly outside in the cold, but the lamb bleated heart-rendingly despite our having taken it into the cabin. Was it strange that we connected these two sounds, the persistent coughing from consumptive chests and the lamb's lament? Was it not out-and-out justice if we passed the rich and tyrannical omda's gift on to two of the poorest villagers? Before we cast off at sunrise, Edries made the gaffirs promise to keep the matter dark, to avoid hurting the omda's feelings, and when we headed out into the morning mist on the river we saw two figures flitting happily home with the animals under their wide caftans.

THE SUN BOAT

As on the two previous days, there was no wind and again we had to curb our eagerness to try sailing up the river. The Nile otherwise is the classic home of sailing, according to archaeologists the place where the art of sailing was first discovered. At all events the canoes which glide along under palm-leaf sails on 6,000-year-old earthenware vases from Negadieh are the oldest known reproductions of sailing craft, and the 'sun boat' which we caught a glimpse of at the stone-lifting ceremony at Giza has no rival as the oldest preserved boat. The reasons for this early development are not far to seek: in no other place has nature created conditions which so strongly urge man to make use of sails as on the Nile. For the greater part of the year the river flows calmly without any rapids from Assuan right down to the sea and in this country, with the most stable climate in the world, there is only one predominating wind – the north breeze, often stiff but never violent, which helps the boats upstream just as surely as the current bears them down. Scudding or drifting – that is the commonest method of transport in Egypt today just as it was six thousand years ago, at least if one counts the number of boats, for in the matter of volume of transport the big motor barges have been an increasing factor of recent years.

The great crux of Nile sailing is the days without wind. When time was of no account the Nile skippers could wait a day or a week for the wind to return, and as long as there was an unlimited supply of patient, expendable labour they could use men who towed the boats, jumped into the water when they went aground and strained at the oars when the current was too strong. All this is still done, but less and less: even in Egypt engines have begun to take over man's drudgery.

Nowadays it is mostly the long-distance transportation which goes by motor-barge, while the local traffic is carried on by rowing-boats of the kind called *feluccas* and by larger sailing-boats to which Europeans often mistakenly give this name but which are really called *aiasas*. We see how greatly the types of boat on the Nile have changed during these thousands of years when we compare the soaring prows and sterns of the old Egyptian craft with the present-day broad, snub-nosed boats. The actual method of navigation has also altered: Herodotus describes how in his time the boats drifted downstream with a drag-anchor at the stern and a kind of drift-anchor at the bows, while the aiasas nowadays drift backwards with only one drag-anchor at the bows. One thing, however, has remained the same: the sounding stick with which the depth is measured in shallow channels, as indispensable to the modern motor craft as to Pharaoh's royal barge. This is due to the constantly-shifting sandbanks; no boat can navigate safely on the Nile and the only way to avoid running aground is literally to feel your way along.

Well-meaning persons in Cairo had urged us to employ a pilot for our voyage and I will not deny that this would have made things much easier. River navigation calls for specialists: every year, every day, the channel alters, and only those who have moved up and down the river for years on end know when, where and how to avoid the snags. Also, the skippers – *raies* as they are called – help each other: when they tie up for the night, and at every lock, they exchange their latest experiences and when they pass each other on the river they call out advice. It was out of the question for us to sail with a *raies*; not only is it hard to get hold of a competent one – they are all employed on the barges – but *Daphne* is far too small for any but intimate friends to live on board. In any case, the whole charm of our journey was, to our minds, this responsibility. We had not sailed *Daphne* down from the far North in order to cruise on the Nile as passengers.

Since our return home from Egypt I have read several books about the nineteenth-century tourist trips on the Nile, accounts which in many respects reminded me of our own experiences. Up to a point our journey was a renewal of that excellent way of getting to know Egypt which the trips with the specially-built sailing houseboats, the so-called *dahabias*, afforded. On the other hand, our adventure was very different from the placid existence of the gentlemen who kept diaries and painted water-colours, and of the ladies shaded by their parasols and shocked by the nudity of the fellahs, on the dahabia's sun-deck. Everything which for us was risk, hard work and immediate contact with people in the villages, was for them freedom from responsibility, comfort and aesthetic distance. In those days the traveller signed a contract in Cairo with some Coptic or Armenian businessman who owned a floating *Sesotris* or *Lotus* and then moved on board with migraine-afflicted wife, demure daughters, governess and hounds for the

two or three months' trip to Upper Egypt. They were so homely,
these boats, with their cabins furnished with oriental rugs, their
saloons with pipe-rack and stove, their attentive servants, their
friendly, smiling cook and their strong, brown-skinned crew of
ten. Then the picturesque voyage began. Palm-fringed shores,
peasant women with water pitchers on their heads, temples and
tombs glided past and in the evenings there were the sunsets –
those Egyptian sunsets which the diaries never weary of describing. The stench, the excrements, the flies glued round the children's eyes like black-rimmed glasses and the many human
tragedies were as remote as the difficulties of navigation. The
skipper's breach of contract in refusing to stop at enticing places
of interest when the favourable tail wind was blowing, and the
rhythmical singing of the crew as they strained and sweated to get
the boat off a sandbank, were the only contact the passengers had
with the practical side of sailing. And when, towards the end of
the nineteenth century, the dahabias became far too slow and
costly a means of transport for new categories of tourists, who
began instead to use paddle-steamers for quick trips up and down
the river, gone too was the relationship with nature which sailing
involves. The next step was our modern way of 'doing' Egypt in
a week or ten days with the aid of a night-train or aeroplane.

After leaving Girza we had rather a troublesome morning. But
just as we had succeeded in wriggling off our fifth sandbank two
motor barges approached in the channel behind us. Wisdom bade
us steer in their wake – as a rule, the fully-laden barges went a
fraction more slowly than our engine allowed us to do, so we had
every chance of following them at a suitable distance. After a
while one of the men on the rear barge waved a rope at us and we
were not slow in accepting the offer. It was extremely pleasant to
be towed along without the noise of the engine and we stretched
out luxuriously on deck. But *Daphne*'s zig-zag course without
anyone at the tiller evidently gave the barge's helmsman more
work; it slowed down and the raies told us to make fast alongside
if we wanted to be towed any farther. Lashed to the barge fore and
aft, and with fenders in between, all went swimmingly, but our
peaceful seclusion was at an end: there was a lively conversation
with the raies and the crew, who were invited on board *Daphne*;
we returned the visit; we admired the barge's new American

engine; we even shared a meal with the crew, at which their staple diet, a porridge-like mixture of meal, peas and potatoes, was eaten out of a large common bowl. The comparatively young raies, a handsome man with moustache, poker-straight back and blue eyes (perhaps a reminder of Napoleon's campaign?), was at first rather reserved, but Edries' stories soon made him thaw and our friendship was assured when he was invited to take a look through our big Zeiss binoculars. He had never looked through field glasses before and his amazement was extreme.

'Can't you twist them so as to see all the way to Cairo?' he asked hopefully.

In the late afternoon, as we approached our appointed stop for the night, the town of Beni Suef, we were astonished to see five policemen presenting arms on a stone embankment a mile or so before the town. Full of misgivings, *Daphne*'s skipper shaved at express speed and changed his trousers, after which we took a cordial farewell of our barge-hosts, cast off and started the engine, and made for Beni Suef straight across the river, at this point half a mile wide. Sure enough: at some stone steps, which we later found out were 'the government's landing-stage', stood a flock of officers, a gentleman who said he was the governor's representative, the headmaster of the boys' school, and several others. It would have been quite pointless trying to explain to these people that there must be some mistake, that we were not V.I.Ps. or official guests, but three adventurous travellers who felt very embarrassed at this reception and would rather have seen Egypt from its anonymous, everyday side. Moreover, we had no idea what the General had said about us to the Home Secretary and what the latter had told the authorities along our route. For all we knew, this kind of reception may have been quite normal for strangers in the Egyptian provinces. Could we do aught but put a good face on it and persuade ourselves that we were really very lucky? For what would we have seen on our journey if we had not been able to leave *Daphne* in the safekeeping of the police wherever we went and been kindly driven round to see the sights and visit hospitable people?

The headmaster invited us to get into his little car to attend 'a show in a girls' school' – that was all we were told. Off we went through the narrow, teeming streets lined with wide-open shops as in all Egyptian country towns. The car stopped in front of a barrack-like building, we were ushered in to a large reception room, where the governor of the province, the chief of police, a high-ranking officer and a few others welcomed us, and then we all trooped into a large open courtyard, where several hundred people were seated in front of a makeshift stage. Everyone stood up, the orchestra played the national anthem and we sat down in the front row, Mona beside the governor.

By degrees it dawned on us that we were watching a spectacle in honour of the Prophet's birthday, arranged by the pupils at the Beni Suef women's training college. The chance of suddenly seeing a hundred or so young Egyptian girls, aged between fourteen and eighteen, appear in modern freedom was not to be missed in this country where a pair of large dark eyes between headdress and veil are usually all that a stranger sees of the fair sex. The programme began with a chanted declamation out of the Koran, executed with surprising passion by a girl with long plaits. Then came dances, songs and short plays, some of them charged with propaganda for Nasser and the revolution, some of them historic and dealing with Islam's first martyrs. The girls had themselves written all the scenes and acted with impressive ardour and sweeping gestures, especially when, dressed in false beards and bedouin dress, they represented men. It was interesting for a westerner to see that these plays had neither beginning, climax nor end: they seemed to start in the middle and go on until they petered out. They were like the Arabic music, which in the same way gives snatches of eternity, or the architecture which, eschewing any kind of massiveness, screens off unbounded space. The governor, a Cairo lawyer who had recently been appointed to his post and made polite conversation to Mona in French, was anxious the whole time lest we should not like the performance, but we could quite sincerely convince him of the contrary.

After the school show we were invited by the headmaster and his wife to visit their home. We realized later that their intention was partly to let us see the refrigerator, the coloured photographs and the bedroom furniture complete with canopy of which they were so proud and which of course we were not slow to praise. It was midnight before we were back on board, feeling rather queasy after all the coffee and oriental sweetmeats.

But not a minute later than half-past six next morning the headmaster and the chief of police were down at the quay to take us to the town's grammar school, 'a sight not to be missed'. We were slightly startled to find that the pupils began their school day with rifle drill in the schoolyard.

'We didn't think it would be so easy to come to an arrangement with the English about the evacuation,' the headmsater explained. 'And now we've got the Jews to think of . . .'

We were not spared one of the cold, dreary classrooms, we were shown the electrical apparatus and chemistry experiment bench in the laboratory, the 'hobby section's' lampshades on pine-cone feet and the teacher's pride, the 'national' landscape paintings, which were not done in oils but with coloured tufts of cotton stuck on to cardboard. When at last, carrying a large bunch of flowers, we got back to *Daphne* and could start, Mona said:

'Whatever happens, you must promise me never to be president.'

The day was overcast and cold – it was one of the very rare times we ever had bad weather in Egypt. For nearly two hours we went by engine in the wake of a big barge, but without asking for towage. Suddenly, at a place marked Kafr Mansur on the map, our guide pulled in beside four other barges which had moored by the bank; out on the river lay a dozen grounded aiasas dotted over a stretch of half a mile. We didn't give the matter a thought but went on optimistically by ourselves – only to run aground time and time again whenever we tried to pass. The governor at Beni Suef had sent a pilot and two policemen to the spot by road to help us; they waved to us from the bank to attract our attention, and with our crew thus reinforced we tried again, with the same bad results. They told us that the passage was one of the most ticklish on the Nile, the river here was shallow all the way across and sometimes only boats with a draught of three feet could pass. The day before, barges with the same draught as *Daphne* (five feet three inches) had got through, but now the threshold had suddenly banked up again. What was to be done? The answer was disheartening: wait. The previous year traffic had been cut off for over a fortnight before the current carved out a new channel; no one knew how long it might take this time.

We made fast to the barges, among which we found the one that had towed us the previous day. We were all pleased to see each other. The raies with the blue eyes came aboard *Daphne* and after a short conference he brought with him three other barge-skippers. We then started off with all these experts to try out another arm of the river behind some low-lying islands. The big barges were far too clumsy for such reconnaissance, but *Daphne*'s shape and good engine allowed us to maneouvre more easily among the sandbanks. First, we nosed our way downstream, then pushed up into the other arm, passed the line where the barges lay, thought we had got through – but came to a dead stop a little higher up. We returned the same tedious, roundabout way and after two hours we were back where we started. Two barges heavily laden with bales of cotton now came heading down the river. They had evidently summed up the situation and decided to force the bar: on they came, borne by the current, with the crews yelling at the top of their voices and the two helmsmen working the huge wheels like madmen. Time and again the boats were checked by the sandbanks and lay almost still, but at last they glided out into deep water and a roar of delight went up from all the barges. One of those that were waiting now started off and managed to press through the ploughed-up furrow. Our friends also started and we followed them. The keel scraped bottom nearly all the time, but we got through. The barges stayed behind to help the aiasas and we went on alone in a rather thoughtful frame of mind. What would the passage be like when we returned after a month or two and the Nile had sunk still further? According to the blue-eyed raies there was no need to worry: the water keeps digging out a new channel which is often deeper when the river gets narrower. But was it so certain?

Apart from one or two 'normal' groundings we had no difficulty in reaching our goal for the night, which lay not far from the village of El Fashn. One or two police officers were waiting at the landing-stage, but we declined, as gracefully as we could, a visit to the police station and the omda – our tired senses longed for a quiet, much-needed evening at home. After the various adventures by day in the hot sun and open air, the long, dark winter evenings in *Daphne*'s cabin were soothing to mind and body. After dinner we would sit around the paraffin lamp, which gave us both light and warmth, writing letters and log-book, reading books about

Egypt, listening to the radio and talking over our experiences – until suddenly, about nine o'clock, we would discover that it was 'dreadfully late' and turn in, to rise at dawn, rested and eager for what the new day would bring us. Often we would light the little methylated spirit lamp that hung from the ceiling – Edries despised such molly-coddling and made do with the warmth of his sleeping-bag in the cold after-saloon.

The morning at El Fashn dawned bright and was memorable because the longed-for wind at last arrived, thereafter favouring us almost every day. Here, about 250 miles from Rosetta, we could sail on the Nile for the first time. It was a great moment for us when, undisturbed by the hum of the engine, we could once more listen to the splash of the bow-wave and feel *Daphne* move with the almost sensuous pleasure which only the interplay of wind and water can give to a boat. The wind was dead astern so we put the booms wing and wing on either side, but did not set the spinnaker, well aware that we would have to strike all sails every time we went aground. Compared with the aiasas, *Daphne* has many drawbacks as a Nile sailer and if we previously had cause to bemoan our keel, we now saw that our sails too were anything but ideal. While the bellying sails of the Nile boats pulled them before the wind like docile sprites of the air and the sky-high rough bars allowed them to catch the breeze above the embankments, we were often left lying becalmed and, even worse, at every twist of the channel had the trouble of changing over the booms and always balancing on the verge of gybing. But our speed was good, as there were no waves to hinder us. With the bow-wave rippling on either side we sailed happily upstream, watching the palm-fringed banks glide past. This was sailing with a difference.

The landscape itself seemed to us to have changed; the villages were less over-populated, more idyllic than nearer Cairo, and we made out the first small Coptic churches which alternated with unassuming mosques. Although on this first stretch there were a number of pyramids, temple ruins, tombs and churches we could have stopped to look at, our time was limited by the ambition to sail as far as possible and we therefore sifted the guide book's many monuments rather ruthlessly.

This first day's sail gave us an unexpectedly good result: despite our having lost nearly an hour at the village of Matai with a troublesome grounding, we managed to cover forty-six miles before sunset. On the landing-stage at Samalut, where we were to moor, stood a reception committee so many-headed that in panic we told the chief of police we intended to spend the night on the other side of the river. He agreed rather reluctantly, on condition that we took two policemen with us as night watchmen. Relieved and happy, we steered across to the little village of Beni Halid which lay glorified in the sunset beneath the canyon wall of the Arabian plateau.

The east bank of the Nile up as far as Nag Hammadi is the poorer and more sparsely populated, as the desert plateau here leaves only a thin strip – which sometimes vanishes completely – of arable land between cliff and river, while on the west side fields stretch for miles, far beyond the ancient canal Bar Yusuf, which may be an earlier Nile bed. The highroad and the railway both run on the western side, where nearly all the towns in Central Egypt are situated. On the east bank one comes across poverty-stricken small villages, a population which is more intermixed with the desert bedouins than the easy-going fellahs to the west, and endless burial grounds – both ancient tombs carved out of the rock and modern cemeteries for the earth-grudging villages and towns to the west. Beni Halid, where we sought shelter this night, was a peaceful spot with rustling palms and reminded us of an oasis, lying hard-pressed as it was by arid desert. A cluster of sailing-boats and one or two motor barges laden with sacks of cotton seed lay by the bank and we found an excellent moorage on the outer side of a derigged aiasa.

When you have been sitting for twelve hours at a stretch on a small boat you long to move about, to stroll into the landscape you have been looking at all day. We explained at once to the village sheik who met us – head of the gaffirs and subordinate to the omda – that we wanted to go for a walk, and a few minutes later the astonished villagers could see a curious procession: first came two Europeans who tried to behave as if they were saunter-ing quite alone, five paces behind came the sheik with a talkative negro dressed up as a scout and, bringing up the rear, eight gaffirs armed with rifles and walking in single file, for the village lanes and the paths between the patches of garden were very narrow. When we stopped, all the others stopped; when we turned round, they all tripped over each other. In this manner we came by degrees out into the desert, where the last houses of the living imperceptibly gave place to dwellings for the dead.

For in Egypt the ancient custom still survives that on fixed festival days families go to the burial grounds to live with their dead. These burial grounds, therefore, often look like a continuation of the village or as towns complete with streets and dwelling-houses, in which neither bedroom, kitchen nor privy is missing. This form of burial is not absolutely essential, it is only the well-to-do families who indulge in it, while the poor ones have to make do with a simple hollow in the sterile desert earth – though always covered over with flagstones so that the jackals will not dig up the corpses. The house-like tombs are not the only primitive heritage in the fellah's conception of death and burial. Few things moved us so greatly during our Nile journey as the meeting, a few days after our visit to Beni Halid, with a funeral procession on the river, a dead person who in this time-honoured way was borne over 'to the other side', while a group of women set up that unceasing lament, that conventional wail which has nothing to do with spontaneous grief but which has been handed down for thousands of years straight from the Egyptian realm of the dead. It is known that man is most conservative in the face of death – perhaps because at the thought of the ultimate peril we fall back on what is most deeply and securely anchored in the world of our imagination. Far down under all personal memories, the association with childhood and with what is first learnt at one's mother's knee, which may make the Soviet soldier cross himself before death, are the primitive memories, ceremonies and habits of the human race which we repeat without being able to account for their meaning. To these belong the three scoops of earth at a funeral service, and the coin which, all over Europe and well into the Middle Ages, was given to the dead in the grave so that they could pay the ferryman. This ferryman, this river of death which we meet in Greek mythology, in Dante and in our own legends, are nothing other than memories from the funerals in ancient Egypt.

Dusk was falling and a large moon hung over the desert as we turned back towards Beni Halid. Had it not been so ridiculous – and also irritating – to stroll dreamily about like this in the moonlight with an armed escort ten strong, we would have taken a much longer walk. Instead, we landed up at a betrothal party at the house of the village sheik, whose daughter was to marry a policeman from Beni Suef. The fiancée was not present, nor was his intended bride. She was sitting in an upper room to which only women were admitted, while the men crowded into the ground-floor room and made short work of the refreshments. We had already learnt that oriental courtesy by no means includes a western host's obligation to make polite conversation to his guests, and after we had been shown to a place of honour in the room, not another word was said to us. Instead, we began to ask Edries about betrothals and weddings: how did young people get to know each other, how could there be any mutual attraction between them under such strict circumstances? The question was more than a little naïve. There is no question of any attraction or acquaintanceship. When a boy comes of marriageable age, his parents look round for a suitable girl, negotiate with her parents and the wedding takes place. But we were insistent: in a small village the young people must nevertheless know each other, first as playmates, then at school and in everyday life. School, hm . . . many fathers do not even let their daughters go to school, and if they do go, it is only when they are very small; after puberty it is unthinkable. Sometimes the boys try to watch their chance near their intended's home to see what she looks like, but the mothers keep a sharp eye open and as a rule a boy has to be content with asking his own mother or sister: is she pretty, fat, gay, what sort of eyes has she got? I soon found out for myself that the system by no means excludes romance and infatuation, for Mona, who was curious about the fiancée, asked permission through Edries to go up and see her. She was at once conducted to the upper storey. When she returned half an hour later she was full of what she had seen. The girl had been sitting on a rug in an unfurnished room, surrounded by the old women of the village and with a shower of coins in her lap – the collection from the invited guests. She was not a day over fifteen, had a pair of green cat's eyes, a small, pouting mouth, black locks that hung down over her shoulders and was full of giggling coquettishness . . . When Mona had been describing her for a while I felt more in love with the young beauty than if I had seen her myself.

We had seen on the map that near Beni Halid lay something which was called 'Rock Temple of Hathor'. Early the following morning the omda put his lorry at our disposal; Mona and I climbed up beside the driver and Edries behind with a heavy armed escort, and away we went across trackless desert. The lorry stopped at the wall of a canyon where an old Egyptian quarry lay: the rock-face itself was cut out in zig-zag levels and in front of it a curious monument had been left free from the rock – more than anything else it resembled a modern abstract sculpture on feet that narrowed towards the bottom, only that it was as large as a three-storeyed house. It seemed inconceivable that this was a temple, but it was equally improbable that it should be merely a product of the stone-cutter's fantasy. A disturbing, puzzling monument, which leaves the field free for speculations and is no doubt the result of a long series of events, of both human and natural agency, which we cannot reconstruct.

On the way home to *Daphne* we were surprised by a show of goodwill on the part of the people of Beni Halid; it began when the wife of one of the gaffirs came out of her house and gave us some round cakes of hard bread baked from maize, the commonest kind of bread in the villages. The women in the other houses were not to be outdone and hard cakes of bread began to rain down on us from all sides. We received so many that they lasted us for the next two months; they had a peculiar smoky taste which we got to like and which no doubt came from the dried cakes of cow-dung used by the fellahs as fuel.

We ran before the wind all day, sometimes in the wake of large aiasas, but they kept leaving us behind and we had to choose new guides. At one or two points where the channel crooked round low sandbanks, huge clouds of dust swirled up and we were smothered in miniature sandstorms, but for the most part we advanced upstream very pleasantly, surrounded on the starboard side by fertile fields and on the other by scant greenery against a background of quarries and rock tombs. We were now approaching Minya, which, with its population of seventy to eighty thousand, is the second largest town in Central Egypt. Its rows of houses and minarets had already appeared in a bend of the river when we ran aground and had to strike all sails before we got floated with the help of the engine. We were uncertain as to where we were to put in, and kept an anxious look-out for The Egyptian Ginning Company's factory and for a villa which might belong to the works manager, Mr. Sidney Carver. While still in Cairo we had received an extremely kind letter from him; he had read in the newspapers of our intention to sail up the Nile and, although we were strangers to him, had invited us to be his guests when we got to Minya. In a little backwater just before the town we did discover both a factory, a villa and, what was more, one or two eagerly waving people down by the landing-stage. It was Minya's mamour, Mr Carver and one or two others.

Never have we been so spontaneously received as old friends as we were by Mr and Mrs Carver at Minya, or come into such immediate contact with people whom, up to that moment, we knew only by name. Both of them belonged to that category of Englishmen who have been living in Egypt for several generations, but have always sent their children to be educated in England before they in their turn take up an appointment in the Nile country. Entirely English in their way of life and mentality, they were at the same time deeply concerned with Egypt's problems and had a much more sympathetic attitude to the country than the foreigners we had met in Cairo. They had built themselves a very comfortable and homely villa in modern European style with a view over the Nile, and they liked living in Minya. We strong-mindedly resisted the temptation to move into a guest room which might have been in an English country-house – for me it is a matter of loyalty to *Daphne*, as after an interlude of this kind there is always the risk that our cabin seems cramped and uncomfort-able. But we did accept a much-needed bath – Edries, however, in the servant's wing, as we could not force upon our hosts a freedom from prejudice which was foreign to them. This was rather letting Edries down – during our visit to the Carvers he had to keep below stairs with his Nubian countrymen – but on the other hand we needed a short relaxation from the strain of being Representatives and enjoyed talking to Europeans in a European way and breathing the atmosphere of this cultured home. Edries, too, often had a similar need of a change from his friendship with us. When we lay moored to a barge he would disappear from *Daphne* and spend his time with the Egyptian crew, whose meals and prayers he shared. When he came back we could feel how the solidarity with us, recently so complete, had loosened.

In the afternoon the Carvers took Mona and me, together with two English week-end guests from Alexandria, to a party at the house of a wealthy Coptic family by the name of Wissa. 'The whole of Minya' had collected – all the foreign engineers and industrialists, all the big Coptic landowners and business men for miles around. Our joy at meeting people we could talk to – not only as regards language but also mentality – gave us a measure of the gulf which, despite all the good will on both sides, divides Christians and Mohammedans.

It was a sensation for us to change for dinner with the Carvers, to eat roast beef and discuss duck-shooting, until, at a rather un-Continental hour, our eyes would not stay open and we made our way to our little floating home through the chill night mists by the river bank. During the afternoon Edries had filled the water tanks and fetched naphtha from the Shell depot, so that we were all set to start early in the morning. To our surprise, many of the guests from the previous day's party had been curious enough to get up at that early hour to come and have a look at *Daphne*. We therefore had to begin the day with a little party of our own, at which Mona was undoubtedly the chief attraction: to the small Coptic wives, used to a life of luxury, it seemed incredible that she could live on such a boat, 'with no servants, no bedroom, no dressing-table and yet be so chic!'

For us, this morning reception was a lesson which taught us which side we really had the most in common with: it was with Edries.

CHAPTER V

To the Horizon City

Our eagerness to be gone from Minya was due to the fact that ahead of us we had a stretch of the river where some of the key-points of Egyptian archaeology lie. Our first port of call was to be Beni Hasan with its painted tombs from the Middle Kingdom, a little farther away Ashmounein-Hermopolis awaited us with the famous catacombs of the ibises and the baboons, and near it the most important place in Central Egypt, the 'Horizon City' of the Pharaoh Ikhnaton at Tell el Amarna.

The visit to the first of these places was rather spoilt by the complications resulting from our undeserved presidency, a delicate and comic situation in which our main concern was not to appear ungrateful for the disproportionate care lavished on us by the authorities. It began when the *Inspecteur des antiquités* of the district came with us all the way from Minya. How this singularly ignorant young man, puffed up with his own importance, could have been appointed to such a post remained a mystery to us. Least of all would he own to the embarrassing circumstance which later in the day he let slip to Edries: that he had never been in Beni Hasan before. No sooner had we left Minya in the fine morning weather with its glassy calm than he seized my Guide Bleu and read at frantic speed – stopping only to give lofty explanations of the many errors – the description of the tombs, which he later served up to us on the spot almost word for word.

'An hour at Beni Hasan is long enough, and that will give us time to see Tell el Amarna in the afternoon,' he declared.

We saw that our most urgent problem was to get rid of him in order to visit the monuments more or less thoroughly during the next few days. After we had been gliding for an hour past palm-covered points and green bends of the river the inspector once more aired his views:

'You could see as much of Egypt in two weeks by train or car as you will now in two months. It's not very practical travelling in a boat like this.'

At that moment the day's first grounding occurred. The

112

inspector, who had not the faintest idea what a keeled boat was, thought his last hour had come when *Daphne* took on a list of forty-five degrees. He clutched the railing like grim death and for a moment I was tempted to hand him a lifebelt and advise him to swim for the shore. After half an hour's toil we were afloat again and could proceed.

The whole morning we had caught sight of police who were on the look-out for us and it gradually dawned on us that a veritable training manoeuvre for the local police force was going on with us as pretext: while little *Daphne* threaded her way laboriously upstream between sandbanks and islands, fully-manned jeeps flashed along the roads, officers on horseback and gaffirs jogging along on donkeys came out on the points and the telephone wires between the police stations in the villages were presumably buzzing with contradictory reports about our position. At the village of Matana, which we reached about noon, we were waved into the bank and four officers stepped aboard to accompany us to Beni Hasan. Mona was just getting lunch ready and asked conventionally if they would care to join us – an invitation which, to her surprise, they accepted. For the next hour she had her work cut out conjuring up a lunch for eight people and washing up in *Daphne*'s little pantry. During the whole of our journey Edries never once showed any domestic leanings and was quite content to be waited on – for him, as for the inspector and the four officers, it was natural to see a woman working. For that matter, village chieftains and policemen in the provinces did not say how-do-you-do to Mona – it is not polite to speak to another man's wife.

Two things showed that we were approaching Beni Hasan. Here in Central Egypt, as I have mentioned earlier, the east bank of the Nile is 'the side of the dead' and during the last few days we had glimpsed many tomb openings in the cliff beyond the narrow strip of arable land on the port bank. The tombs were now more frequent, forming at last an even line along a ledge half-way up a somewhat higher hill, whose crumbling, curiously-shaped sandstone crown reminded us of the great Sphinx's neck. The second sign that we were nearing our goal was the police, who were standing so close together that each could notify the next man in the chain with his whistle of our arrival. At a small inlet between two stone dams the reception committee was assembled, about fifteen officers and village big wigs, who had all come from the other side of the river, as the vicinity of Beni Hasan is almost uninhabited. The most handsome of the company was a tall man with an enormous scarf loosely flung across his shoulder and a monocle; he introduced himself as chief of the local Secret Police. This secret, which gave itself away with such refinement and seemed to be known to all, gave us almost a feeling of Pharaonic bureaucracy – often in the tombs one sees the title *steward of his master's secrets*.

Horses and donkeys stood saddled and waiting, we had only to choose. After sitting still for six hours in a boat, we felt the need of stretching our legs and rather diffidently said so, without reflecting on the consequences: all the officers and befezzed gentlemen had also to climb up by their own motive power to the tombs, puffing and blowing. Our retinue had been prepared for a 'normal' visit to Beni Hasan, such as that paid by the respectable ministers of public works, generals of infantry or famous film stars whom they had previously accompanied. We on our part wanted to study the hundreds of square yards of paintings in the tombs. The result was that both sides had to make a sacrifice. We tore ourselves away from one burial chamber after the other far sooner than we had wished and the officers – sighing, yawning, shuffling their feet and clearing their throats – fought their deadly boredom and impatience. The only one of our hosts who did not tire was our *Inspecteur des antiquités*: he was as eager as we were to get to know these fantastic tombs.

Beni Hasan is remarkable for being the place where the culture of the Middle Kingdom, otherwise so obliterated and sparsely represented, can best be studied in a dozen or so relatively well-preserved and richly painted tombs. If the vicinity of Cairo is the centre of the Old Kingdom and the Luxor area that of the New, the era of the XI and XII Dynasties lives on in this burial ground of the feudal rulers of the Gazelle-nome.

From the narrow terrace that runs in front of the entrance to the tombs there is a magnificent view over the Nile Valley: in the foreground the silver-gleaming river twists along, with here and there a backwater and a green island, in the middle distance villages are dotted about in the fields that extend for mile after mile into the background, where the Sahara quivers in the sun. At first sight the interior of the tombs is a disappointment: unlike the tombs at Sakkara, which were dug out of the sand, they have always been known and have therefore been exposed to incomparably greater vandalism. The mystery of death has been aired right out of the Beni Hasan tombs, which without a doubt were plundered of their movable contents even during antiquity. Then Christian anchorites and Mohammedan shepherds moved in and, for religious reasons, began systematically to destroy the diabolic reproductions on the walls. In the tombs where fires have been lighted the walls have been completely blackened with soot, and as they were all wide open to anyone who liked to go in until 1920, boys from the village have scratched drawings on the walls with sharp stones – not 'rude' pictures such as are inevitable in Europe, but Nile boats sailing along. It is a rather bitter thought that all this destruction, the result of sheer ignorance, is nothing compared with that carried out by persons interested in antiquity. Until well into the present century it seems to have been the accepted thing that a visiting tourist not only carved his name on the walls of the tombs but also hacked out as big a bit of the paintings as possible to take home with him as a souvenir. Here, as at Tell el Amarna, the more purposeful travellers have brought a hammer and chisel with them in order to detach real 'museum pieces'. To make matters worse the archaeologists, who at long last decided to study the paintings in earnest, took it into their heads to rub them with wax, which made them temporarily brighter and more distinct but later collected dust and dirt, so that the paintings have become as dark as old icons. This last-named damage can probably be repaired by means of washing according to modern museum methods. A surface of a square yard has been cleaned as a sample, but the experts are waiting for a decade to make sure that the colours have not been spoilt by the chemicals used.

Yet all this cannot prevent the sepulchre paintings at Beni Hasan from being a great experience. It is an art which is as far removed from the classically harmonious wall reliefs of Sakkara as from the butterfly lightness of the tomb paintings at Thebes with their swarm of dolls' figures. The Beni Hasan paintings are Picassonian in their brutal yet refined strength, in their disturbing and disharmonious portrayal of mankind. Another comparison is Etruscan art, which has the same rather clumsy love of flowers, birds and four-legged animals, the same capacity of placing athletic figures in restless movement against an empty background. The scenes of wrestling, boxing and martial exercises extend in foot-high bands above the wall-panels like illustrations in a manual on ju-jitsu; we see hunting in the desert, sieges, military campaigns, and get a strong impression that physical training and the will to fight were essential values for this harsh nobility which helped Pharaoh build up the Middle Kingdom after nearly three hundred years of impotence and decay.

When we left the last tomb after four hours, our hosts' patience was almost at breaking-point. Out of consideration to both them and ourselves we had recourse to a stratagem, which succeeded beyond our hopes: after most cordial expressions of thanks we declared that we regarded the visit as ended and would like to retire to *Daphne*. Through a chink in the curtain we watched them all – except two gaffirs who were to guard *Daphne* during the night – board a ferry which rowed them over to the west bank. Like schoolchildren playing truant we crept ashore again, taking with us one of the gaffirs, and set off along the bank to a small rock temple called Speos Artemidos which, according to our map, lay about a mile and a half to the south in a little valley. The setting sun poured a golden glow across the road, which twisted along between flowering mimosa trees in the narrow strip of arable land near the river. There was not a human being in sight, only white ibises which flew up, startled, from beside the fields. After a while we came to the ghostly ruins of quite a large village, where all the houses were roofless and sanddrifts had piled up in the deserted streets. The gaffir told us that robbers had lived in the village and that the king's soldiers had come one day and said:

'In an hour's time we're going to set fire to all the houses. Those of you who don't clear out will be shot.'

Which king's soldiers? The gaffir didn't rightly know, only that it was before Farouk's time. But the robber tradition does not seem to have died out in the neighbourhood despite the severe punishment. Mr Carver at Minya had told us that the cotton barges had, until quite recently, been boarded regularly by river pirates in these parts and had been forced to pay tribute; the new régime was the first to tackle the problem in earnest and has, for the present at least, made river traffic safe.

It was easy to find Speos Artemidos, which turned out to be a rock hall in the steep southern slope of the little valley. It was built by Queen Hatshepsut and is decorated with reliefs representing the goddess Pakhit with a lion's head. We discovered something else, however, which interested us even more. Not far from the rock temple we saw the entrance to a very much more modest cave and farther up the valley still others. Some were obviously ancient Egyptian burial chambers, but under projecting rock walls and between huge boulders we also saw primitive walls which divided off small rooms. Above them all, as at the entrances to the tombs, small crosses were carved. This explained it all: we were in a valley which at one time had housed a colony of anchorites. During the summer, when we sailed to Istanbul, I had been reading Jacob Burckhardt's brilliant book about Constantine the Great, in which a long chapter is devoted to the origin of monasticism in Egypt, so I knew a little more than I would otherwise have done about this strange period in the country's history. Burckhardt traces monasticism back partly to the peculiar heathen *reclusi* – ascetics, walled up in single cells and dead to the world, who lived within the precincts of the Serapis temple at Memphis, but he connects it chiefly with the pious Christian Egyptians who, in order to flee the evils of this world, went to live among snakes and hyenas in the desert. They acquired such a name for holiness that they soon found themselves surrounded by whole colonies of successors and disciples. For several hundreds of years, from the third century onwards, Upper Egypt, with its population decimated by war and famine, with its ruins of the great city of Thebes, with its opened and plundered tombs and with temples the mural reliefs of which were blackened by the camp-fires of robber bands, was one of God's chosen provinces on the earth. Thebais, as the country was called, became renowned for centuries as the wonderland of long-bearded hermits, where the lions of the desert slept docilely at the holy men's feet, but where diabolic temptations could also assail them, as fiercely hot and stifling as the *khamsin*, the desert wind. Antonius, you who became the most famous of Egypt's anchorites, did you live for a time during your wanderings in this little valley at Beni Hasan? Did your well-known temptations descend on you in Pakhit's rock temple, where the cat goddess still incarnates all that is dangerous in woman's being, where Thoth with baboon body and ibis head represents the heathen wisdom?

Like other cross-valleys to the Nile, this one had been formed millions of years ago, when tropical rains emptied their deluge over the plateau and countless tributaries cut their way down to the great river. Now it formed only a kind of road down from the hills for the desert's wild animals when they came to drink. We saw curious tracks down in the soft soil where the valley opened out on the shore, but were far too ignorant to know if they were other than those of the common jackal. In the time of the hermits, at any rate, considerably more dangerous and timid animals must have slunk past their huts and caves. We made our way farther up the valley beyond the last scraggy bushes – and there met a stern world of cliffs and hard shadows, more remote from Life than any other setting. In the midst of this desolation I came upon a cavity which could be nothing else but a grave; the supposition was confirmed by three crosses which had been carved at the head. The grave was empty, as one might expect after 1,500 years; empty except for a tiny, bright object in the bottom layer of sand and dust. Picking it up, I found a flawless, white human tooth. Was it the irony of fate that this symbol of the animal in man was the only thing left of a hermit who had sacrificed all to raise himself above the demands of this earthly life?

A good breeze gave us a fine sail the following morning. By nine o'clock we had reached the ruins of Antinoe, where, as appreciative readers of Marguerite Yourcenar's *Memories of the Emperor Hadrian*, we had thought of stopping for the greater part of the day in order to examine this city, founded in memory of the emperor's favourite, the beautiful youth Antinous, who was drowned here. The Coptic textiles from Antinoe which we had seen in Cairo further whetted our interest in the place. Unfortunately, very little of the once flourishing city remains. Great piles of burnt and unburnt bricks, scattered blocks of stone and a few shapeless remnants of buildings were all that we could discover. When we continued our journey after an hour we saw a steep part of the bank strewn with human bones and skulls – the river had evidently eaten into an old burial ground. Even up to the beginning of the nineteenth century Antinoe is said to have had considerable ruins, but they met a fate which has befallen countless other ancient monuments in Egypt: when the sugar factory at Roda on the other side of the river was to be built, stones were taken from here. It was about the same time that Mohammed Ali was seriously thinking of using the Great Pyramids at Giza to build the Delta dam.

When we reached the town of Mallawi about noon and moored at the landing-stage something unheard-of happened: no police officers, no car, no reception committee awaited us. If we had previously complained of excessive attention, we were now given a useful lesson. What were we to do, how could we go to Hermopolis? Neither the crew of the adjacent aiasas nor the swarthy individuals on the bank had the reassuring look that would have disposed us to leave *Daphne* unguarded at the landing-stage. There are degrees of destitution which excuse both theft and plundering, even if they are a poor consolation for the victims. Nor did the wretched road leading to the town a mile and a half away tempt us to lift the Lambretta ashore; it would scarcely have nosed its way through the crowd. The only solution was to send Edries off to the police station. After an hour he returned proudly with the mamour himself and soldiers of various kinds: they had been waiting for us at the neighbouring town of Roda.

The Hare-nome's capital, Khmounou, which during the Hellenistic era was given the name of Hermopolis, Hermes' city, must be quite old, as according to legend it was here that the primary god created the world. It must also have been a good-sized city, as its few remaining ruins are so scattered: it is about three and a half miles from the river to the village of Ashmounein, where the great Thoth temple lay, and from there about seven miles to Tounah el Gebel, which was the city's burial ground during the Hellenistic and Roman eras, while the ancient Egyptian burial ground lies on the east bank of the Nile. In order to show us all this the mamour of Mallawi had made arrangements with the car-owning omda in one of the villages we would pass – the police force itself had only jeeps and lorries at its disposal. This omda, who had recently succeeded his father in the office, was about thirty and was afire with eagerness to attract the notice of the central authorities of the province – hence his willingness to act as chauffeur to 'the government's guests'. He was a splendid example of the fact that social position, far more than geographical environment, creates human types: a more typical rich man's son and blasé snob than this omda, in red fez, silk galabia and pince-nez, could not be imagined. With a monumental disregard for all he met, he drove his shining new Peugeot at breakneck speed along the narrow roads. There were many narrow escapes and both fowls and cats met with a violent end, but our omda did not slow down even when a young pregnant woman with two small children in front of her came riding along on a donkey. Cars are seldom seen on these narrow village roads and the animal turned and bolted ahead of us along the edge of the road; one by one the riders fell off as we tore past, but neither the omda nor the officer sitting with us in the car had a thought of stopping to see if they were all right. At the level crossing in Mallawi we saw an incredible and comic sight: a car, 1920 model, held together with bits of wire and a few boards as in a funny drawing, stood waiting for one of the dozen passengers on the roof to climb down; inside the car sat as many again and one or two more were hanging on outside. I asked to get out for a moment to photograph the miracle car, but hardly had the omda pulled up before all the sardine-packed passengers vanished into thin air, except the driver. Our police officer got out, abuse rained down and the driving-licence, which the wretched man produced to order, was used to slap his face with and was then confiscated.

'It is forbidden to drive with more than five passengers in a car like that', the policeman explained rather apologetically.

And our life-and-death drive continued. On we rushed, raised above humdrum human life and its misery like gods, who do not even notice whom they crush beneath their chariot wheels. If we were not such gods in our own eyes, we were at least in the eyes of those who respectfully flung themselves out of the way at our approach.

The day was sultry and great clouds of sand were blowing in across the valley – it was the notorious, hot, sandstorm wind, *khamsin*, tuning up for one of its lesser overtures. Even in this mild form it was very unpleasant, as we found when we came out into the desert. Banks of powdery, shifting sand like snowdrifts on our northern roads, lay across the tracks left by previous cars. Visibility was only a few hundred yards, nose and throat were filled with fine sand and we wondered what would happen if the wheel tracks that we were following became quite obliterated. The omda's light car stuck time and again in the sand but we were helped by an escorting police car and so escaped being shipwrecked on the suffocating ocean of sand.

After two hours or more an oasis appeared: palms swaying in the wind, the derrick of a subsoil water pump, a few huts for the workers and archaeologists. Farther away we caught sight of part of the ancient burial town encircled by sand dunes. For twenty-five years Tounah el Gebel has been the object of loving care by the Egyptian archaeologists: the Cairo University has, under Professor Sami Gabra's supervision, excavated several hundred late antiquity houses of the type, still common, that we had seen outside Beni Halid – tombs to which families go at special festivals to live for several days with their dead. It is the transition between Egyptian tradition and the intrusive Hellenistic culture which makes Tounah el Gebel's architecture, reliefs and paintings interesting. Especially worth seeing is Petosiris' little burial temple from the fourth century B.C., for it shows an attempt to blend the Greek and Egyptian style. After one or two unsuccessful experiments of this kind it was seen that the combination was unfruitful: from then on buildings were either entirely Hellenistic, as in Alexandria, or purely ancient-Egyptian, like the huge temples of the Roman emperors in the Nile valley.

Herodotus relates of the ancient Egyptians' animal cult that the priests from the temples where a certain species of animal – cats, snakes, fish, etc. – were sacred, collected all the dead ones of this species in the whole country in order to embalm and bury them in the endless catacombs of their temple. The caves at Samoun, a day's journey north of Asyut, filled with millions of crocodile mummies mixed with one or two human mummies, were not missed by any nineteenth-century tourist, and Flaubert, among others, has given a macabre description of them. Nowadays a visit is more often paid to the ibis and baboon catacombs at Tounah el Gebel, where we too decended into some of the labyrinthine passages that run for miles. Day in, day out, for hundreds of years, a specially trained body of workers wrapped up embalmed ibises in small, neat mummy parcels, which have been stacked like wood in one rock chamber after the other, where they lie packed up to the roof. The baboon mummies are much more rare, as they must have been in real life. Why the moon-god Thoth, the god of writing – and of science and art, which were connected with it – incarnated himself in both the ibis and the baboon will no doubt be a mystery for ever; most likely it is due to a historic chance – two totem animals and a primitive myth of creation may have been assigned this special place in a larger religious system. But one cannot help wondering what deeper resemblances may associate art and science with, of all things, the teachable monkey with its profound gaze, and the dazzling white ibis, whose head, wing-tips and legs are black.

On the way back from Tounah el Gebel we stopped at Ash-mounein to look at some gigantic statues of the Thoth baboon which had recently been discovered and were then being erected. But our omda hurried us on: supper was awaiting us at his home and we drove to his village in the quickly falling dusk. It was a community of about 4,000 inhabitants, but there were only two buildings of any size. One was a sugar factory which belonged to the omda and the other was his private house with a small garden in front of the neo-classic façade. His own electricity plant provided a flood of light which made the house stand out among all the low, dark hovels. We were ushered into a dining-room on the first floor, where a table groaned under all the food that was laid out. A European never ceases to be astonished at the lack of taste and the general confusion which the increasingly dominant western way of life brings with it into oriental homes. Here, a sideboard – German 1880s by the look of it – was adorned by female papier-maché figures holding candelabra aloft, gilt chairs stood ranged along the walls and in a special glass case was a ghastly collection of painted coffee-cups and insipid china figurines. No woman appeared and the waiting was done by the omda's two younger brothers.

'We have grown poor in Egypt,' our host sighed. 'My father had a Packard and I have to make do with a Peugeot.'

'A gifted young man who will go far,' the police officer commented on the way home. 'He understands the new democratic age.'

The day's experiences did not end with the dinner at the omda's. As we drove through Mallawi we saw a brightly lighted tent and heard wild, inciting music: a circus was visiting the town. Eagerly we asked the officer if we could look in at the performance for a moment – quite unaware that the tent was full to overflowing. He hesitated for a second and then gave an order to his men. When we – without being allowed to buy tickets – went in, we found a whole box at our disposal: the police had simply emptied it by force. The audience consisted of two completely different elements: on one side of the arena the inhabitants of Mallawi, dressed in semi-European clothes, blasé, sophisticated and with the ready intellect that befits townspeople; on the other side the rustic fellahs in galabias and turbans, simple village folk with genuine reactions. Not one woman was to be seen among the audience, but as against that many among the performers. We had the impression that this was a far more interesting and attractive part of the programme than all the horses and performing monkeys: the woman animal, on show in the most diaphanous of veils or dressed à la filmstar in décolleté western evening gowns. Now that almahs and ordinary prostitutes have practically disappeared from provincial towns in modern Egypt and the chances of enjoying feminine beauty outside the family circle – for that is what it amounts to in a polygamous country – have become increasingly few, films, illustrated weeklies and the touring variety shows have a gigantic mission to fulfil. The fellahs in particular were in ecstasy at the sight of singing-girls and shimmy-dancers; several of them grew quite delirious and had to be forcibly held down in their seats by their companions. The applause after each number was the most enthusiastic I have ever heard or seen. The Mallawi section of the audience was much more restrained – the town has a cinema where much stronger meat is offered every evening – but it appreciated the more intellectual points, the clowns, the political skits and the conjuring tricks.

Tell el Amarna, Aketaton, Ikhnaton . . . There is no alchemy stranger than that of names, no mixture of the material and immaterial which is more complete. We hear a name: its colour, its rhythm, its unconscious associations give us an advance conception of the person, the place or the thing it denotes. But once we have got to know them, the indefinable sum of our experiences takes up its abode in the name. Tell el Amarna, Aketaton, Ikhnaton . . . Surely they must mean something translucent, fleeting, light and young? There was nothing vague about our expectation as we glided out at sunrise from the landing-stage at Mallawi on to the mother-of-pearl mirror in which silhouettes, Chinese in their delicacy, came drifting towards us in the faint mist. Tell el Amarna, it could not be the first, rather mean, drearily straggling village we passed, nor the massive houses on the next point. But there on the port side: suddenly the crumbling cliff, riddled with the openings of tombs, drew back and a wide, triangular plain opened up; against this airy expanse, quivering in the sun, a village with light-coloured houses was outlined under the tall flags of the date-palms, a village which was a fortunate oasis surrounded by the barren, empty desert.

After two hours' navigation from Mallawi without any disturbing shoals we made fast to an empty barge in the middle of Tell el Amarna, welcomed by one or two grinning gaffirs. The village police officer and his colleague from the neighbouring village Wadi Quandil, who came down to the bank before long with a dozen white, unusually fine saddle-donkeys, may not have been so very different from their fellow-police in other villages we had visited, but at Tell el Amarna everything was gayer, more friendly and care-free. This impression was not only due to the light and the beautiful location. The opportunities of earning a little extra, which the archaeological excavations had given the population time and again during the past generation or two, had evidently made possible the slightly better living conditions which had changed the village into a happy community. Laughing women and children peeped after us through doors and from roof-terraces as we rode past on the white donkeys through the labyrinth of lanes. In front of us rode the officers, after us came the gaffirs and beside us ran the donkeys' owners, which was all to the good, as the animals were saddled only with a blanket and had neither bridle nor reins – the idea being that we were to guide them with the help of small sticks.

Our ride through Tell el Amarna raised a question which we had often asked ourselves during our journey: is there a living national art in Egypt? As previously, we had to answer it in the negative. For some reason, architecture and handicrafts in the fellah villages are unusually monotonous, their form clumsy and meaningless; they invite social and psychological comments rather than assessment in terms of art. It is one of the riddles of cultural life that a people who once stood at the summit of what the human race has created in the way of varied feeling for form, can lose this sense so utterly that not even so-called national art has retained any trace of it worth mentioning. Ceramics, textiles, tools, buildings, singing and dancing – none of all this (which, according to our romantic belief in the creative power of 'the national soul', 'functional needs' and 'unintellectual genuineness', ought to be on a high level in Egypt) can, with the best will in the world, interest our artistic sense.

The almost inevitable conclusion is that the concept of national art is a myth and that neither handicraft nor the 'higher' forms of art can develop without a culturally superior stratum from which impulses find their way down and leaven the community – often with a delay of centuries. It was no doubt this delay and the changes the impulses had undergone during their long wandering which gave rise to the nineteenth century's false notions about a spontaneous national art.

We found only two spheres in which one can, nevertheless, speak of an Egyptian national art, both probably the last shoots on the withered tree of ancient Egypt. One was Hadji art, the paintings which adorn the front of the Mecca pilgrims' houses and which I shall return to later. The other is the architecture of the dovecotes. We had already caught sight of these structures at one or two other places; they are quite common in the villages and sometimes form small towns on their own with tens of thousands of winged inhabitants. The pigeons live freely in these houses, finding their own food and belonging to nobody, but they pay rent to the owners of the dovecotes in the form of manure, eggs and frequent broods of chicks, which have their heads chopped off and are eaten up just before they are fledged. The reliefs in the tombs show that pigeon-breeding was customary even in the days of the Pharaohs and it is presumably from the dovecotes of the great houses that this imaginative, often extremely pregnant architecture, varying from village to village, has come down to us.

On this morning in Tell el Amarna, on the outskirts of the

village, we saw for the first time at close quarters a large and splendid pigeon colony. It consisted of tall, windowless structures with walls leaning gently inwards, true temple pylons, but the roofs were crowned by rows of small cupolas which ended in a knob. I dismounted to take some photographs, one of the gaffirs fired a shot and the pigeons began to soar in wide circles above our heads like a huge, fluttering cloud. But the shot had frightened not only the pigeons. An old woman suddenly rushed out of one of the dovecotes and showered abuse on us, but the policemen merely laughed. If I have ever stood face to face with a real witch it was at this moment, for a more wrinkled face, more piercing eyes or a more fiery temper I have never seen. The supernatural impression was increased by about a hundred pigeons which sank down and formed a flapping bodyguard round the old crone, while others perched on her head, shoulders and arms. To ward off some awful curse over our morning ride I handed her a twenty-five-piaster coin, which instantly mollified her. Edries interpreted her assertion that she was 130 years old, that she had looked after pigeons all her life, had never eaten anything but live pigeon chicks, had every intention of living to 200 and had recently grown new teeth. This last claim was at any rate true, according to the testimony of the neighbours and of our own eyes: she had the whitest and most perfect set of teeth I have ever seen. I thought of Huxley's novel *After Many a Summer*, in which an English nobleman lives to be 200 by eating carp viscera; perhaps a lifelong diet of young birds has an equally rejuvenating and preserving effect?

Outside Tell el Amarna the fields lay like a narrow band between the river and the desert, an example of the man-made character of the Nile Valley. Not even Holland can show anything like it, for in Egypt man must water everything if it is to live and there is not one wild tree and hardly a weed. The second a fellah sees a useless growth he pulls it up and plants something which can give him food instead. The border-line between the two worlds, the arid desert and the cultivated ground, is often as sharp as a razor; it is quite easy to stand with one foot in each. We followed a narrow path along the edge of the oasis; on our right was the desert plain, shimmering in the sun and framed by distant blue mountain ridges, and on our left the lush crops beneath the light shade of the palms. Everywhere in this sea of green, in this steaming garden, white-clad people were to be seen amongst the clover and maize. The fellah families very often go out in full force to their fields in the morning and do not return until sunset. Water-buffalo, children and old people are taken along, all lend a hand with the work, and with enough bread and corn-cobs to go round, the day passes pleasantly. At the sight of the laughter, the smiles and the obvious happiness one so often encounters in the Egyptian provinces, the social zealot is seized almost with indignation: these people are happy against all the rules and because they clearly don't know any better, they must learn to realize that they are unhappy. But on this morning we let the fellahs teach us to go against the rules in the same way: we were happy in spite of being unjustly privileged and spoilt westerners.

The cool morning air – the dry, clear air of Egypt – was still intoxicatingly light and our donkeys were frisky with untried strength. The second they reached the edge of the desert they broke into a gallop across the empty plain where Ikhnaton's Horizon City once lay. It cannot be denied that the heretic Pharaoh had a good eye for the site when he founded his new capital on this virgin soil; airy, spaciously spread out from the life-giving river's shore across the desert, which has the same abstract, implacable purity as his doctrine. And because the Horizon City – obviously regarded as the unclean abode of demons – was allowed to decay and sink down undisturbed into the sand when the capital was moved back to Thebes after Ikhnaton's short reign, the place became a kind of Egyptian Pompeii, a miraculously fixed instantaneous photograph of a bygone world. The archaeologists have had a comparatively easy task: most of the city still lies beyond the arable land and the houses. When one looks down on the plain in the slanting sun of late afternoon, the old city's radiating system of streets is still plainly visible beneath the light covering of the desert sand. So far, only parts of Aketaton, as the city was called of old, have been excavated and examined, chiefly the great sun temple and Pharaoh's summer and winter palaces. It was in these latter ruins that the sensational find was made towards the end of the nineteenth century of Ikhnaton's state archives, the sort of find that historians dream of: here they could read the original letters to Egypt's Pharaoh from the kings of Mitanni, the Hittites and the Babylonians, as well as reports from border governors and complaints from allies, a correspondence which throws a new light over not only Ikhnaton but the history of the entire Near East. Another equally sensational find was made by German archaeologists shortly before the First World War, when they came across, not far from the sun temple, the court sculptor Tutmosis' workshop, full of abandoned and unfinished works; one of them was the world-famous, painted limestone bust of Queen Nefertite. The fact that such things, which we count among the most costly treasures of world art, were of so little value to the Egyptians that not even thieves removed them from the ruins, shows, if anything does, that the Egyptians had no feeling for art as such. When the practical need for which these sculptures had been created was no longer present, they were valued no more highly than an empty tin in our day.

We stopped at Ikhnaton's northern palace and from its yard-high remains, in which fragments of wall paintings are still to be found, tried to form an idea of how it once looked. It must be admitted that the ruins have very little to give the uninformed tourist. A proper understanding of them demands a thorough study of the literature about them, comparisons with archeaological ground-plans or expert guidance; otherwise they are mostly a jumble of walls and stones. The reward is all the greater for the trouble of visiting the tombs, which are carved out of the rock round the city. Most of them are unlikely ever to have been used, as their builders – court dignitaries and government officials – moved back to Thebes after Ikhnaton's premature death. In an almost incredible manner these burial chambers have compensated the archaeologists for the havoc time has made of the palaces and temples built of perishable material – sun-dried bricks and wood – in the city itself. For the reliefs in the tombs not only depict festival and working-day in the Horizon City but also give regular ground-plans of the public bulidings, so that with their help it has been possible to dig out and interpret every single room and even find holes filled with rich soil for the ornamental trees and flower-beds of the palace gardens.

The day was a sore but fatalistically borne trial for our escort, who had to wait for hours while we, armed with lamps, descended through the darkness of the tombs to the days long past when Ikhnaton lived in his city. We managed to visit three different groups of tombs, separated by rides of several hours, but the king's own burial chamber, which lies in a ravine about seven-and-a-half miles from the river, is rigidly closed to tourists and in any case plundered of the rich pictorial adornment that was still here when the tomb was discovered a generation ago. Everything indicates that the mysterious heretic Pharaoh really was interred here when his hectic reign came to an end after barely twenty years, but the mummy is sure to have been violated, just as his name was obliterated from all monuments when the reaction set in under Horemheb perhaps ten years after his death.

It is a paradox that to so many of us today Ikhnaton, of all people, has become the best known of Egypt's rulers, the main intermediary between the ancient land of the Nile and ourselves, for he was by far the most un-Egyptian of all the Pharaohs. Reformer in a land based on conservatism, visionary among a nation of practical realists, uncompromising in an environment which had always known how to reconcile conflicting opinions, and fiercely bent on swift, immediate results where his predecessors had built for eternity – such he was, the unique prophet of the Aton cult, and clearly it is these very traits which have made him so alive and understandable for us. But this understanding has often gone too far and there is no denying that the modern interest in Ikhnaton has allowed itself utterly untenable projections of our own mentality and our conditions on to the mysterious Pharaoh. The romanticizing knows no bounds: for some, he is (thanks to the famous Hymn to the Sun) a forerunner of St Francis, if not of Jesus Christ himself; others regard him as a kind of champion of democracy who recognized the worth of even the most humble of his fellow-beings and took into his service the gifted sons of the people. The many relief pictures of Ikhnaton with the lovely Queen Nefertite and the small princesses are taken to be a profession of sentimental family life and to those persons brought up to admire realism in art, the style introduced by Ikhnaton stands as a precursor of the realistic reproduction of the Greeks and the Renaissance.

In point of fact, there is a gulf fixed between Ikhnaton and all these modern phenomena. The Amarna art is no more realistic than the tomb-reliefs of the Old Kingdom, as a style it is reminiscent more of Chinese than of Greek art and its best feature is a refined mannerism and a broadening of the formerly common motif circle. As for Ikhnaton's marriage, it can hardly have been the bourgeois idyll one has imagined, as he probably took over Nefertite from his father's harem and himself kept up a large household of women, which can be seen in his excavated palace; it also seems that Nefertite, soon after her husband's death, wrote to the King of the Hittites asking him to send her by return one of his sons as a new husband. Finally, concerning the suspicions that Ikhnaton was a democrat, one need only see the bent backs on all the ceremonious reliefs and read the fawning, servile funerary texts to dismiss the thought as absurd.

Yet there is no getting away from the fact that Ikhnaton, with all that we sense in him of abnormity, visionary fixation and final tragedy, when the house of cards he had built collapsed, is closer to us than any other pre-Greek person. Breasted calls him the first individual in history, and he is right in the sense that here, for the first time, we meet a man who seems to have an idealistic attitude foreign to the social order around him, a personal philosophy of life. It is Ikhnaton's loneliness which makes him our kindred soul. At the same time we should remember that this first cleavage of an individual out of the tribal fellowship called for just as exceptional powers as the splitting of the atom in our time. Ikhnaton was not driven by private opinions in the ordinary sense when he broke with the traditional faith of the Amon priests and founded his own religion. He did so because the sun-god Aton had appeared to him and because he himself, as Pharaoh, was a god to whom all subjects must bow down. These mighty factors gave his personal whim its enormous power and the result was this strange forestalling of the individualistic drama which became a common occurrence only when the strength of the collective body had gradually been expended. The way is long from Ikhnaton to Rousseau, but it exists: that is why he is at once so close to us and so inconceivably remote.

The shadows cast by our patient donkeys across the desert sands had already grown into curious giraffes and the sun was nearing the Horizon City's western abode of light as, tired after our day-long ride, we turned homewards. When we reached the first palms darkness had already fallen, but the moon rose and the stars were lighted. This homecoming through the oasis in company with the last belated fellahs made a deep impression on us. Everything was equally moving: the peace that met us here in the world of men, the water gleaming in the small canals by the roadside, the shadows of the palms across the ground and the village burial-houses which merged imperceptibly into the houses of the living. Between the tree-trunks lay horizontal ribbons of smoke in floating spirals and in front of the houses were flickering fires round which white-clad figures crouched in a ring at their supper. We went on through the dark, silent village streets, where only an occasional door stood open into a lighted room. As we passed we caught glimpses of these incredibly simple homes: a few primitive vessels of pottery, a hearth in one corner, a strip of matting unrolled as a bed on the earthen floor comprised the entire furniture. At last we came to the Nile, across whose broad stream the moon threw a glittering bridge. A cluster of aiasas outlined their bows and curved mainmast yards against the starry sky, but in their midst we instantly made out two straight masts: *Daphne*, guarded by two sleeping gaffirs, had been waiting for us faithfully and now opened her bright and cosy cabin.

We could hardly sit down after our long and unaccustomed ride, but asked our companions to bring the donkeys back at sunrise, as the Horizon City still had many secrets for us.

CHAPTER VI

The Fellah's Egypt

Nineteenth-century travellers in Egypt differ from us in one vital respect: they were already hardened to social injustice from conditions at home and could regard the life of the people along the banks of the Nile with greater composure than we, who have grown up in Europe after the great democratic equalization. The tightly-corseted young ladies and the gentlemen in stiff collars did feel sympathy for the simple fellah during their walks up to the temples, but conditions in the picturesquely backward orient at that time seemed beyond help in quite a different way from now. There is an air of light-hearted indifference about the old travel journals; what the writers witnessed in towns and villages was a motley and entertaining spectacle for which they themselves were not responsible. Moreover, they had a special reason for valuing the strange religious beliefs and customs, for these helped to place in their right perspective the conventions still surviving in Europe. Morals, etiquette, beauty, piety, happiness and wisdom can also look like this, the travellers seemed anxious to point out if we read between the lines; our Victorian attitude to all this has no absolute value.

This tearing-down phase in the development of European culture, when the ruins of the old were to be cleared away for a new social structure, is today completed. It is the building-up problems which now engage us, both socially and ethically. The gestures and doctrines of an unfamiliar religion are no longer a picturesque illustration of the relativity in man's world of thought, but a creative act in a direction which follows or opposes our own striving. The community, the social and economic conditions, have in the same way become something for which, directly or indirectly, people feel an increasing responsibility.

Egypt's future, too, is in the melting-pot, bound up with ideological and economic questions which concern us all, unstable because here it is so very much a matter of possibilities and planned reforms rather than results already attained. It was therefore unavoidable that on our journey we were continually coming up against the country's social problems.

On only two occasions did we completely forget this viewpoint and light-heartedly accept things as they were: during our three days at Tell el Amarna and during the weeks in Nubia, of which I shall have more to say in a later chapter.

Our last morning in Ikhnaton's city was devoted to the winter palace and the sun temple; we were then accompanied to the bank by the village sheik, the gaffirs and the white donkeys, all of whom were now our fast friends. On the previous day we had already selected, more or less at random, the village of El Quseir as our next port of call and the police at Tell el Amarna had notified their colleagues there of our arrival. Our late start and the poor wind meant that we had to go by engine all the afternoon in order to arrive before nightfall.

Towards five o'clock El Quseir hove into sight on the fertile west bank, quite a large but in no way remarkable village. Perhaps for that very reason, and because we chanced to stop here on both the up and the down journey, it became for us the epitome of a typical fellah village before all reforms and improvements. Our first visit had a more 'official' tone and therefore gave us a somewhat touched-up picture of the community. The provincial governor had ordered the headmaster of the grammar school in the adjacent town of Qusiya to be present so that we should have an English-speaking person to receive us. He was now standing together with the village schoolteacher and a covey of gaffirs on the steep bank which was deeply hollowed out by the river.

Their eagerness to show us hospitality scarcely allowed us to make the boat fast before being conducted to the omda's house. It was the same as all the other houses in the village, except that the doorway was flanked by two plaster lions, more curious than beautiful, executed by some village artist. This house, like the entire edge of the village, threatened to be swallowed up by the Nile within a few years – three or four, according to the omda's own estimation of the river's encroachment during the past ten years. It may have been this 'sentence' in conjunction with an unusually modest holding – seven acres as against the hundred or two hundred an ordinary omda has – that made El Quseir's ruler so unassuming and human. He came straight from work in the field and welcomed us in the inevitable reception room on the ground floor. Its raw, damp air, the sparse furniture and the walls damaged by water to breast height surprised us until we understood the reason: every year when the flooding comes the streets of El Quseir are turned into canals and the inhabitants move up to the top storeys of the houses, taking with them for safety their stores and domestic animals. For three or four weeks there is nothing to do but wait, visit each other by boat and hope that the river will spare houses and fields.

Egyptian hospitality is intended for visitors who have seen their fill of the villages and who have walked or ridden until they are ready to drop. The guests are therefore shut into dark rooms where they are often left alone for hours on end. For us, who had been sitting still all day and were burning with exploratory zeal these visits to omdas and chiefs of police were a trial which we did everything in our power to shorten. Our announcement that we wanted to look round always caused undisguised amazement – whatever was there to see in an ordinary village? We therefore had ready an explanation which, moreover, was by no means a mere pretext: we said that we were interested in the paintings that adorned the houses of the Mecca pilgrims and asked if we could see the more beautiful of them. In this way we could both walk round the villages – even go inside the pilgrims' homes – and above all make the acquaintance of a genuine national art ignored or despised by educated Egyptians.

As is well known, it is one of the Mohammedan's elementary duties if possible to make a pilgrimage to the holy Kaaba in Mecca some time during his life. This pilgrimage has always been both difficult and expensive, an undertaking which only the very rich or the very self-sacrificing can carry out. The fact that since time immemorial this pilgrim's duty has been ruthlessly exploited for monetary gain by Mecca's emirs, inn-keepers and other inhabitants may seem outrageous to westerners, who would no doubt long ago have arranged cheap and easy conducted tours to Mecca. But the Arab takes the wise view that the only things of value are those that are hard to get; an Egyptian fellah who wishes to acquire the coveted title of *Hàdji* must leave his home for at least two or three months and on his departure deposit about £150 (£300 if he takes his wife with him). In a country where a factory worker earns fifteen piasters (about three shillings) a day, one can understand what £150 is worth – and is amazed that in most villages there are nevertheless people, perhaps one in a thousand, who have made the pilgrimage.

It is understandable too that the Hadji wishes to commemorate his feat in a visible manner. This is where art steps in to bolster up social self-justification – one of its missions ever since the tattooing of the stone age to present-day managing directors' homes with -*ism* pictures. Shortly before the pilgrim comes home his family commissions a village painter to adorn the entire front of the Hadji's house. The motifs are very largely recurrent: river boats, trains, buses, aeroplanes – the various means of conveyance used by the pilgrim – the Prophet's tomb, the mosque at Mecca, preferably the pilgrim himself, his family, police, lions, fish, scorpions, birds, flowers and other subjects thought up by the painter. The arrangement of the paintings is quite individual and one never sees two alike. The ground is always white and the material ordinary water colours with the addition of egg, but as rain is very rare in Upper Egypt the paintings remain fresh for about five years and last in faded form for twice as long – in other words, for just about as long as the pilgrimage can be expected to have any current interest.

This art does not become common until south of Cairo and it ceases altogether as one approaches Nubian territory at Assuan. Its range is therefore the same as that within which ancient Egyptian paintings have been preserved, a fact which is hardly a coincidence. It would be interesting to try to single out different schools and influencing groups, but our cursory examination showed rather that the artists work by themselves and in accordance with their personal taste. A problem which I did not quite manage to solve is how the Moslem faith, hostile to pictures, has been able to take these reproductions, especially the pictures of humans, into its service. At a guess, it seems as if during previous centuries Hadji art restricted itself to the motifs that the Sunnite Mohammedans can accept – flowers, half moons, arabesques and calligraphic inscriptions. With many Hadji painters these elements still predominate, but new motifs – animals, boats, mosques – have evidently been introduced gradually until the various products of modern reproduction technique have blunted the taboo and the human figure too has been included. This notion is confirmed by the fact that the human figures comprise the most clumsy and worst executed motif in the Hadji paintings, while the ornamental elements are often beautifully depicted with a sure hand.

During our trip I photographed as many Hadji houses as I could, both in colour and in black and white, and in this way collected quite comprehensive material. Many of the paintings, however, are so unskilfully done that their artistic value is practically nil. Two circumstances seem to determine the quality. The first is, of course, the painter, an ordinary fellah, who does the work as extra income but whose artistic talents vary considerably. The other is the financial resources of the village: the more pilgrims, the more orders and the better the chances of perfecting Hadji art.

At El Quseir we photographed five Hadji houses during our evening walk with the headmaster of the grammar school, the omda, the village schoolteacher and a dozen gaffirs. The schoolteacher was very young and had just recently arrived in the village straight from the training college. Evidently he felt an urgent need to show off in front of the El Quseir inhabitants, for in the winding caravan that our company formed, respectfully gaped at through doors and windows, he insisted not only on walking beside me, although paths and gateways made single file the natural procedure, but on taking my arm the whole time. I soon began to feel like a pretty girl being courted by an over-fiery cavalier. It was of no avail to stop and turn round to the others or to point around me to free my arm. At last I saw no other way out but to lead the procession towards a narrow plank across a deep ditch – which luckily was dried-up, as he fell headlong into it.

In the evening four police officers arrived from the nearest town – one of them in plain clothes: he was 'secret police'. The omda had invited us to 'a very simple dinner', which we found consisted of six courses, among them a large roast turkey. We sat with the officers in the reception room, waited on by the omda himself; 'the secret policeman', who was stalwart and brawny, tore the turkey to pieces with muscular, hairy arms and handed round the bits.

'Anyone would think you had got hold of a criminal', his colleagues joked.

The conversation otherwise was one long paean to Nasser and the revolution. Within the space of a few years everything in the country had been completely transformed; all abuses had been corrected, hospitals and schools had been built everywhere, illiteracy overcome, officials been made incorruptible, and so on. I will not deny that one can be a completely idealistic supporter of Nasser's régime and that the disinterested Egyptian patriot may even have many reasons to be one, but there is a way of praising which betrays flattery and scheming. It suddenly dawned on us that these officers thought we had personal connections with the revolutionary men and could give them a favourable report... The omda, who must have had the same idea, said nothing, he remained gentle, dignified, a little sad. We liked him.

The one who reacted most strongly to the officers' blatant flattery and smooth song of praise was Edries – perhaps because he was the only one present who had really taken the cause and programme of the revolution to heart. His passion for honesty as a scout gave him additional courage to speak his mind. He related what we had seen with our own eyes: that the *courbasch* whip was still used unstintingly in the villages, that the police officers behaved with overweening arrogance to the population and willingly let their hands be kissed by the fellahs and that several of the schools we had looked at were beneath criticism – dark and cramped, like stables, so out of date that the pupils had to copy from the blackboard the more important passages from the one and only textbook in the village. What was the revolution in these villages, where nothing had changed? A hope and a promise, at most.

The officers would not hear of any objections, however, and said something in Arabic to Edries, who afterwards translated for us:

'We're not talking to you who know the country, but to our guests.'

We did not find out how burning these questions were, in El Quseir particularly, until two and a half months later, when we chanced once more to shelter for the night in the village. On that occasion nobody had been notified of our arrival and no officers or detectives met us. Only the gentle omda welcomed us, and on our return to the village after an evening stroll he besought us to come into his reception room: there was something very important we must hear. Without warning we found ourselves in the presence of a kind of hastily summoned village council, consisting of the magistrate, the sheik of the gaffirs, one or two of the elder fellahs and the schoolteacher – the only one of those present who could write. All came up and greeted us, but we noticed that the magistrate and the elder fellahs shook hands through the cloth of their turbans, which they had hanging over their shoulders like a scarf. When we later asked Edries the reason, he admitted with a laugh that it was fear of contamination with something unclean: strangers haven't the vaguest idea of hygiene and moreover we might have been in contact with pork and other repulsive things . . .

'The elders of Quseir wish in all humility through you to call the government's attention to their village . . .' This was the sum of the appeal the omda directed to us.

'But what can we do? We have no authority and it's not our business to interfere in such questions,' we tried to explain through Edries.

No evasions helped. In order that the problems would stand out more clearly the schoolteacher had put down the salient points in black and white. The first wish was for a new school. El Quseir, with its 7,000 inhabitants, is joined on to the village of Deir el Quseir, which has 6,000 – in practice the two villages form one community. El Quseir has no school at all; the children have to make do with Deir el Quseir's little school with room for 225 pupils, who sit packed into five classrooms ten feet by twelve. This means that only very few of the village children – because of the low average length of life they comprise the majority of the population – have a chance of going to school, where, moreover, the tuition is so sketchy, owing to the lack of textbooks, that the pupils soon forget the little they have learnt.

The second need was a road. It is three miles to the nearest car road, over rough paths, even though room for a road had been left between the fields. This question is part and parcel of the third wish: better medical care. The doctors will not come to the village when there is no road for a car, or rather, they must be paid a fee of £10 plus cost of journey before they will stir themselves. In practice this means that the villagers have to manage with their old wise women and with the barber who performs minor operations. A fourth wish is pure water, now that there is all this talk about the Nile water being dangerous, and a fifth, stone embankments against the river, which every year devours new parts of the village. In addition, a little more arable land is needed. Of Deir el Quseir's 600 or so acres, 400 belong to three wealthy families, while the rest of the population owns what is left . . .

'That's a lot of wants all at once, when there are thousands of villages the government has to think of,' we said after listening to this sorry tale.

'We never gave it a thought before,' the magistrate answered. 'It was as it had always been, but now there's a revolution and everything must be better. If only you will tell the government about conditions here, they are sure to help us.'

Could we do anything else but promise to pass on El Quseir's hopes to the best of our ability? – a promise which I am now keeping.

From El Quseir we scudded on beneath the steep, towering cliffs of Gebel Abu Feidan, which rise sheer out of the Nile on its east side. Countless eagles and hawks breed in the rocky clefts and we saw them wheeling high above us. A flotilla of aiasas lay at the foot of the cliff loading stone, which small naked men armed with hammers and chisels were prizing loose from narrow ledges above the abyss – a sight which cannot have altered much since the time of the Pharaohs, when slaves extracted building stones for temples and pyramids from the same rock.

We were now approaching the largest town in Upper Egypt – Asyut—where a dam is built across the river and the banks are joined by a bridge, the first since Cairo. It is often a blessing to be unaware of the troubles that lie ahead; ignorance lends an optimistic vigour which the well-informed lacks. We had been following a motor barge until, just before sunset, we reached a sharp bend and saw the minarets of Asyut and the broad wall of the dam a mile or two away. Glad to have arrived before nightfall we were already wondering where we would moor in the town when our guide slowed down and moved into the bank, where four other barges were already lying. We were left out in midstream with our engine running, quite at a loss: should we spend the night here too? The men called out that there were sandbanks below the dam, no one could get through at present. Sure enough, we saw five or six grounded aiasas and two big barges stuck fast among the eddies below the dam. But our goal was within sight, beckoning us; we were expecting letters and according to the guide book the town boasted a Greek restaurant . . . We headed recklessly up towards the dam in the gathering dusk.

Edries stood as usual in the bows, taking soundings with our plumbline. For practical reasons we had agreed on a sign-language to signal the results of the plumbing: when Edries stretched out the palm of his hand, the water was deep more or less everywhere, two fingers meant 2 fathoms, two crooked fingers $1\frac{1}{2}$ fathoms, one finger 1 fathom. After that no more signs were needed. I could myself feel if the keel grounded. We picked out quite a different way from that marked by the grounded barges and aiasas, a way which was evidently not the usual one, as people on the bank started to shout in warning and point in another direction. But I noticed that the main strength of the current was coming obliquely from the starboard bank; that surely denoted that the river was deepest there? Mona, wise from experience, had stowed away everything movable in the kitchen regions and was trying to read the message of the eddies as intently as I. At first everything went swimmingly: Edries, grinning from ear to ear, stretched out his whole palm. Then the water swiftly got shallower, from two fingers Edries changed straight to one, we slowed down and hunted desperately about for a deep channel. One fathom, one fathom, one fathom, slight scraping of the keel, one fathom, one fathom . . . Slowly we pressed our way up until we sighted a low spit of sand to starboard. The river here was over a mile wide, the night was closing in and above the wall of the dam a necklace of lamps were lighted. We should not have seen the stranded barges at all if the crews had not been cooking their supper over open fires on deck. It was now definitely too shallow straight ahead and by literally feeling our way along – the current helped us to get afloat every time we went aground – we edged nearer to the barges on the port side. At first we tried to force our way past above them; it proved to be impossible. Our arrival seemed to be causing a sensation and all the men climbed up on the cotton bales to get a better view of our progress. As we got within earshot they shouted that we should try to get past astern of them: on the other side it was deeper. Our engine hummed, full of purpose and persistence; *Daphne* jogged and lurched on the sandbanks but we never stuck fast; and before we quite knew what had happened we had passed behind the barges into a deeper channel.

It was now dark, but we took our bearings from the west abutment of the dam. When there was no doubt that we had successfully crossed the threshold, Edries threw down the plumb-line and came aft to shake my hand as enthusiastically as if I had just won an Olympic gold medal for Egypt. Poor Edries, as a scout he felt the need of looking up to a leader and his boyish mind asked nothing better than to have an object of admiration, but *Daphne's* skipper is not cut out for such a part and Edries had learnt to make do with comradeship on an equal footing. Now at last he thought he saw his chance.

'Yes', I answered. 'Sometimes one's luck is in.'

I little knew how right I was until I heard in Asyut that no boat had got through to the dam for a whole week; this threshold was known of old as the most awkward in the Egyptian Nile.

A welcoming group stood waiting as usual at the lock, a police major came aboard and despite the late hour the bridge was lifted and the lock was opened specially for us, so that the very same evening we could moor beside Asyut's tree-lined street a mile or so above the dam. Notwithstanding its 100,000 inhabitants, the town was hardly a metropolis. The police major had told us that there was a skyscraper with a lift up to the elegant Windsor Restaurant, and we hopefully decked ourselves out in our fine feathers. We were a trifle crestfallen to find that the skyscraper was only six storeys high and the restaurant – utterly void of any other guests – was very much simpler than a factory canteen in Sweden. The Greek proprietor had, however, a bottle of resin wine, which enabled us with due ceremony to toast the day's journey and the important news we had received: owing to necessary repairs, the Asyut lock was to be closed down two weeks later and would not be opened until February. This meant that we were shut in on the Upper Nile until then – a welcome excuse to spend the winter in Egypt and include Nubia in our programme.

Asyut, which was once the capital of the Jackal-nome, has little more than a few vandalized rock tombs to show the tourist and the bazaar streets of the modern town have no interest for those who have seen a dozen other Egyptian provincial towns. The best thing about our stop here was that we could fill our water tanks with pure water from the mains and take in stores – in the Egyptian countryside hens' eggs and vegetables were about all we could get. After only a day we continued our journey.

As is natural above a dam, the river was comparatively deep south of Asyut and we had very few groundings the first two days as we ran upstream before a fresh wind. At times the tension was almost unbearable as Edries from the bows signalled $1\frac{1}{2}$, 1, 1, 1, $1\frac{1}{2}$ fathoms and *Daphne*, with all sails set wing and wing, skimmed along with foaming bow-wave: to hit a shoal at that speed meant not only the bother of striking the sails and laboriously getting afloat with the aid of engine and kedge, but a risk for the whole rigging. In addition, the river bends and the twisting channel kept us constantly at sail drill – the balloon had to be changed over from one side to the other, the booms must be swung across when there was imminent danger of gybing and the sheets had to be adjusted the whole time. At times we sped past so close to the bank that we could have jumped ashore into the lush clover and the village children raced ahead shouting with glee; at times we glided along between low, treacherous sand-banks in midstream, anxiously on the look-out for guiding aiasas.

Near the town of Sohag the channel became so difficult that we longer dared to sail. Here we were faced by an enormous bridge which was not marked on the map: it was the Achmim Bridge, completed a few months previously. Its bascule was opened as we drew near and a whole swarm of aiasas, which had been held up since morning, saw their chance and slipped through with *Daphne*. A row of ramshackle houses appeared up on the high embankment and on a houseboat we saw a group of officers waving eagerly: the mamour of Sohag with his men, who had looked out a suitable landing-place for us. The houseboat belonged to the State and was inhabited by officials – a practical and common way of solving the fluctuating need of homes for civil servants in different parts of the country. While we were still getting straight on board, a large American car pulled up on the quay and Mr Harder, who was to dominate our Sohag visit, appeared on the scene.

Mr Harder, who was an Englishman and manager of the ginning factory in Sohag, had been told of our arrival by the Carvers at Minya. He personally was an extremely nice man who showed us great kindness, but through him we had an insight into certain sides of Egyptian industrial life which, I cannot deny, made our blood boil. First of all, however, I must tell of the positive aspects of our acquaintanceship. Mr Harder took such complete and authoritative charge of us that for the first time since our arrival in Egypt we deserted *Daphne* as regards quarters for the night. Bath, guestroom, food, car and not least himself – all this Mr Harder put at our disposal with a cordiality to which we could not help responding. Up to a point, Mr Harder's kindness was probably due to loneliness and boredom. To live as a bachelor in the factory-owned house, which was as impersonal as a hospital and smelt of linoleum, and to be surrounded by an Egyptian township with no other Europeans, must have been a torment to such a non-introspective person as Mr Harder.

He first expressed his pent-up kindness by driving us to the famous White Monastery on the edge of the desert, about an hour's drive from Sohag. This cubic, desolately monumental building like a fortress, erected in the 4th century A.D. out of blocks of stone from ancient temples, supplemented our impressions from the valley of the hermits at Beni Hasan: it represents the second stage in the development that changed the free anchorites' 'non-worldly' colonies into organized monastic communities. The White Monastery, which once housed more than a thousand monks within its protective walls and even up to the beginning of the 19th century was a gold mine for European scientists on the hunt for Coptic manuscripts, has nowadays been transformed into a kind of fortified village, where several relatively well-to-do Coptic clerical families have built themselves fine houses on the site of the collapsed nave of the basilica, while the chancel still serves as a Christian church for the local peasants.

Besides Mr Harder, we were accompanied by the district chief of police and a few officials from Sohag. For these Moslems, including Edries, the visit to a Christian church was an unusual and interesting experience. Three Coptic priests in black cassocks received us in a very kindly manner. The eldest was a little gnome with scared and gentle eyes, the youngest was a pronounced negroid type, such as one often sees in Upper Egypt, while the third, obviously the leader, made a hard and fanatical, but at the same time cringing, impression – from him one could see what 1,300 years as a downtrodden, capriciously treated minority has meant for the Copts. As the priests could not speak a word of English and the Mohammedan guests showed such a benevolent interest in the monastery, the visit soon took on the form of a showing of the church's peculiarities to the sons of the Prophet. In the dark chancel two doddering fellahs were busy intoning prayers from a large book: it was a kind of divine service which goes on uninterruptedly, with reliefs, from Saturday afternoon to Monday morning and which was plainly regarded as just part of the day's work, for our hosts made no bones about talking in loud voices, leading us up to the chancel to show us some damaged frescoes and even offering us coffee in front of the high altar – it was served by a small boy who came along carrying a tray.

'And here is the sacrament', one of the priests explained, pointing to the altar. 'It is bread and wine changed into the flesh and blood of Christ: all Christians eat and drink of them in order to partake of the divine grace.'

Edries' furrowed brow told us how strange, barbaric and foolish this god-eating seemed to him. Slightly ashamed, we answered evasively when he asked if we too believed in this. He already knew all about baptism and described to the astonished mamour how infants are dipped into the font while the priests say incantations. This meeting between educated, well-dressed Egyptians brought up in sober Mohammedanism and poor, uncultured representatives of an ancient, ousted dogma was to us a curious experience which turned our old, customary ideas upside down. We quite well understood the reaction of the Prophet's sons to the saint's images of the murky church and the piled-up *ex votoes* on the walls, shapeless wax images of feet, kidneys and female breasts hung there by sick people who had recovered.

And we could not help thinking of the sober mosques, free of all idols and images, clean, peaceful and full of light. When we got outside, our companions drew a deep breath of fresh air with a look of liberation and the mamour sent his servant to the car for a bundle of newspapers, which were spread out on the filthy village street in front of the monastery. They became five small prayer-mats on which our companions, with sublime indifference to their Coptic environment and without risk to their well-creased trousers, could say their evening prayers under the open sky.

The Christian population of the village were no different from the Moslem fellahs either in appearance, dress, housing and working habits, education or cleanliness. Only the crosses, painted on the houses and tattooed on the foreheads or hands of the inhabitants, indicated their faith. The educated Copts like to make out that they represent the pure, unmixed Egyptian race, while the Mohammedans have blended their blood with Arabs and other fellow-believers. There may be some justification for this assertion in the towns, but in the country districts the fellahs of both creeds have remained almost equally unaffected by foreign racial elements.

In the evening, at Mr Harder's, we met the entire European colony: apart from our host, a retired English officer, Mr Stanley, who was employed at the factory as 'second man', and his pretty Czech-born wife. 'The third man' was also present, he was an Egyptian and had joined the factory under the pressure of the new regulations controlling foreign business concerns in Egypt. In practice he was a mere lay figure, handsomely paid to support the company in relation to the authorities and treated with all the deference that sensitive self-esteem could desire. We noticed that we made a gaffe when we spoke ironically of the taste with which King Farouk had furnished his palaces and villas: 'the third man' thought them wonderfully beautiful and the Englishmen chimed in. There was no end to the eulogy on Egypt in general and its present leaders in particular, who were more or less dragged into the conversation – but only as long as 'the third man' was present. We had the feeling that the western business men stick at nothing to retain their hold on a market which is very lucrative. They know that this will not be possible for much longer: just as the

Europeans in the sugar industry are being replaced all along the line by local labour, the cotton trade will soon be taken over, more or less by force, by the Egyptians. In the long run this is probably all to the good: the westerners need not then stand as the accused in the conflict that the awakening of the Egyptian working class will bring with it.

During the talk over a glass of whisky 'between us Europeans' which rounded off the evening, Messrs Harder and Stanley did maintain that no danger of Communism existed at present – the workers still think of themselves as fellahs. But what of the future? Our hosts preferred not to touch on this unpleasant subject. Good Lord, as long as we can go on like this for another few years and as long as we can get our money out of the country, we'll always manage somehow. This getting the money out of the country seems to be the great crux for the westerners in Egypt, while the government's problem is to see that foreign exploitation finally ceases and the country itself benefits by its own resources.

'But don't get the idea that the people are unhappy,' our hosts declared with conviction. 'On the contrary, our workers are very satisfied with their chances of earning money and no reforms are contemplated. You will see for yourselves tomorrow at the factory . . .'

The inspection of the loading yard, the ginning halls, the drying-room, the packing-rooms and the room where sacks were filled with seed, that we made together with Mr Harder, made a very deep impression on us – but not in the way our host had thought. The most frightening of all was that the factory was shown to us with pride and not with shame. I am quite well aware that someone from the Scandinavian welfare states with their good working conditions is not the right person to judge an Egyptian factory, but Edries, who had grown up in Cairo, was just as indignant as we at the sight of the almost naked men handling the bales, the young children struggling with heavy baskets or feeding the sorting machines in a choking cloud of dust. The rate of working was doubled everywhere as Mr Harder approached and the many overseers in particular were well on their mettle. They strode proudly into the range of my camera, brandishing their tool, the *courbasch*.

'Don't be afraid,' Mr Harder reassured us, as we stared in

horror at these long leather whips and heard their sharp cracks. 'They don't lash the workers, they only crack the whips to keep them on their toes.'

We were also told that work goes on in shifts all round the clock, so that there are always between three and four hundred men kept busy. Wages had recently been raised and were fifteen piasters (about 3s.) a day for the adults and ten for the children. These had all forged certificates showing that they had reached the age stipulated by law – sixteen years.

'Don't our workers look healthy and happy?'

Reluctantly we had to admit that they did – like the Egyptian fellah population in general. Along the whole of the Nile valley we had seen these stalwart, well-developed athletic bodies and smiling white teeth, which tried to make us believe that they were among the world's healthiest and happiest people. But we had also realized that this seemingly good health has a dark reverse side. We had learnt about the fellah's real living conditions, his material circumstances and intellectual possibilities from a book which I had bought in Cairo, H. C. Ayrout's *Fellahs d'Egypte*, translated from the Arabic. The fact that it had been allowed to appear under the prevailing censorship and that despite its anything but cheerful contents six editions had been printed in two years, says quite a lot about its objectivity and current interest. From this book we had gleaned that the average length of life of the Egyptians is twenty-eight years as against ours of over sixty in Scandinavia, due partly to the heavy infant mortality, partly to the national diseases which are so rife – dysentry, hereditary syphilis, malaria and the worm disease, bilharziasis, spread by the slime of the Nile. As the fellah has developed no further mentally than a child, it is obvious that he is happy. A more disturbing question is whether the fellah is so healthy just because he has so many diseases. How is the race affected if, for thousands of years, all the weaklings are ruthlessly weeded out and only the very sound individuals reproduce themselves? What is a community like where only those whom disease cannot get the better of are left and only one child in five may live? One thing is certain: as a physical race the Egyptians do not resemble the old and degenerate civilized peoples but rather a vigorous and healthy negro tribe.

This brings us to the key question: is physical health and happiness the goal for which society should strive? In that case Mr Harder is right, conditions in Egypt are quite satisfactory. If, on the other hand, one considers that mental qualities are more important than physical ones and that it is just as wrong to make happiness an object in life as to make enjoyment its highest value, the problem is seen in another light. One can then answer Mr Harder that it is not enough if his workers look healthy and happy: it would be better if the intelligent and frail ones also had a chance to live and it would be preferable if they were unhappy because they would have learnt to expect more of life. It would have been absurd, of course, to accuse Mr Harder personally of conditions which are more or less normal in Egypt today. We put forward our principles and he his practical view of the problem as we rolled along in his car in front of a large cloud of dust on the way to Abydos. Mr Harder had persuaded us to make the trip to this old holy city from Sohag instead of from Balyana as we had planned. Although the road was longer, the chance of seeing a little more of the Egyptian 'inland' tempted us – besides, it was so difficult to say no to our profusely kind and sociable host.

The Egypt we saw from the road, coated with dust, shady, shut in by dense greenery and crowded villages, was something quite different from our bright, open and airy river-Egypt. We drove along beside glassy, tree-lined canals, where primitive ferries made of two or four petrol drums served as transport, we crawled at snail's pace behind flocks of sheep or jog-trotting camels and bounced over water pipes which the peasants had illegally laid from the canals to get extra irrigation for their fields. With some astonishment we learnt that this was the main road from Cairo to Luxor and Assuan, but on the other hand it is of no great importance as both goods and people are mostly conveyed by river or railway. Outside one village we passed a dazzlingly white, newly-built hospital, which had a curiously forlorn air. It appeared that this, in common with a whole series of other provincial hospitals, had been built in Farouk's time but that most of them stood empty – no doctor would work in the country districts for the monthly salary that was offered: £12, including bonus for the increased cost of living. Let us hope that the hospitals which cost so much to build do not fall to pieces before the problem has been solved.

Our eagerness to get to Abydos was great: there we would see our first Egyptian temple, or at all events the first temple of the classical Egyptian type, for the burial temples of the pyramids and the remains of Ikhnaton's sun-temple walls at Tell el Amarna were something else. But our patience was put to a severe test, which once again confirmed that one does not enjoy hospitality scot-free. Instead of the temple ruins of Abydos a town suddenly appeared at the end of the road: Balyana, where *Daphne* was to bring us. But what about Abydos? Mr Harder gave a friendly grin.

'Mustn't neglect the inner man. I rang up our agent in Balyana and asked him to get lunch for us – just a snack, you know. We can see the temple in half an hour on our way back.'

It was market day in Balyana and the teeming little town made a specially picturesque and pleasant impression, with smiling fellahs, goods being sold both in the street and the open shops, scales hung up on branches of trees in the market -place, barbers, scribes, harpists, all busy out in the open air – everything seen for only a few seconds outside the car windows as we nosed our way to the cotton agent's house. If we could not study the temple ruins we decided that we would at least have a thorough look at Balyana while lunch was being prepared. But he who reckons without his host makes a mistake. Mr Harder drove the car into a courtyard, whose gates were shut behind us and we were prisoners for the next five hours. Not that any physical violence was used against us, but we were ensnared all the more effectively by courtesy and consideration. The agent, a grey-haired, toil-worn Greek by the name of Evangelos Kondilios, was these two qualities personified, a gentle, hyper-sensitive and pathetically lonely man for whom our visit was a great event. The Greeks occupy a unique position among all the Europeans in Egypt; they are the only westerners who really live with the people, they are to be found as grocers or café proprietors in every village far into the Sudan and can hardly be called foreigners, as they have been in the country for more than 2,500 years – Herodotus came across them almost as often on his journey as we did on ours. Evangelos Kondilios' loneliness, therefore, had no national or linguistic basis like Mr Harder's but was a personal characteristic. He lived a secluded life and with endless pains had trained a simple village lad to be a perfect cook and servant. Now that his chief arrived on a visit from Sohag with European travellers the moment had come to show what this apt pupil Muhammed had learnt during years of patient tuition. Mr Kondilios and Muhammed had been in a whirl of activity ever since the telephone call in the morning, now Muhammed went on with the preparations in the kitchen alone while the host talked to us in the living-room. At the end of half an hour I ventured to suggest that we might perhaps go for a little walk before lunch was served.

'Oh, but there's nothing to see here,' our host protested. 'Anyway, lunch will be ready in five minutes . . .'

After half an hour the sound of the feverish work in the kitchen was as promising as ever, but when nothing happened except that the church bells in the adjacent Coptic church began to ring, Mona suggested that we should go and listen to the service for a while.

'No, the service is just over and they're closing the church,' Mr Kondilios said. 'Lunch will be ready in five minutes . . .'

Three hours later the doors leading in to the dining-room were thrown open by the pale but composed Muhammed and 'the snack', consisting of six main courses, three kinds of dessert, three different wines, cheese, fruit and pastries, was served. It was stiflingly hot, the conversation was mostly about cotton prices and we became more and more stupefied as the afternoon wore on, until we were in a complete state of torpor from this nightmarish surfeit of food. Far away in our mind's eye we saw the ruins of Abydos bathed in the transfigured afternoon light and street noises forced their way in through the window as greetings from an unattainable liberty – we very nearly broke down from impotence, despair and suppressed rage. At the same time our host's pride was so touching, his pleasure at our strained compliments so great and Muhammed's relief, as the test approached its happy end, so manifest that we heroically accepted yet another half chicken, yet another piece of confection, yet another glass of soporific wine.

Mr Harder had reserved half an hour for the visit to Abydos.

The gathering dusk and our apathetic state, however, made the time seem almost too long. Having confirmed that there really was a large temple adorned with coloured reliefs here, we set off for home. Ramses II's temple, the great and small Osiris temple, the sacred lake and a closer study of Abydos in general would have to wait, for we had long since realized that we must make another visit by ourselves from Balyana, as we had originally planned.

We left Sohag the following morning at seven o'clock. At the cotton factory's jetty we took on board Mrs Stanley, 'the second man's' pretty young wife, who was coming with us for one day. She said that in her humdrum life as the sole European woman in the place she had been so excited by our invitation that she had not had a wink of sleep all night. The morning was fine but rather chilly; at first there was a dead calm, then a faint head wind, so that we had to start the engine. Our guest lay on the foredeck sun-bathing, Mona read, Edries steered and the skipper busied' himself by turns with navigation and writing up the log-book. At about two o'clock we passed the former provincial capital of Girga, which is being slowly devoured by the Nile and has already been abandoned by the governor, who has moved to Sohag. Half an hour later we came to a reach of the river which, judging by the strong current, was evidently very shallow.

A small passenger motorboat which saw us hesitate waved to us to follow, but it drew less water than we did: suddenly we stuck fast while it went gaily on. We began to take soundings and managed with great difficulty to force our way upstream between the sandbanks for another half mile. But by then it was shallow everywhere. A rowing-boat with a party of duck-shooters came near. Upon our asking where the channel was, all the men pointed in different directions – they looked like a many-armed Indian Buddha. There was nothing for it but to turn back and try another part of the river closer to the west bank, where we had seen boats passing. Easier said than done. We went aground again and again, and each time the strong current flung us sideways. Sometimes we spun right round, utterly helpless, before our powerful engine got us off. At last our good luck ran out. Before we could regain steerage-way after a near-grounding we drifted down towards a large invisible sandbank, on to which *Daphne* was forced up. There she lay, with her covering-board under water. We were not in danger of our lives, but I saw at once how hopeless it would be to get floated by our own effort. Edries and I did everything we could, however; we rowed out the main anchor with the dinghy and winched in the chain – but the anchor dragged through the sand. We put the engine into reverse and strained it to the utmost. *Daphne* merely settled down into the sand. The sun went down, the heartless crews of passing aiasas merely jeered at us in answer to our appeals. When darkness fell we had to give up and Mona, despite the heavy list, cooked some delicious ravioli for dinner.

At about nine o'clock a rescue party turned up from Girga, sent out by the worried Mr Stanley, who had driven there to meet his wife. It was an enormous motorboat with about sixty shouting people on board – officers, police, soldiers and fellahs. Scenes of utter confusion followed; everyone bellowed orders at the same time and the boat, borne by the swift current, came alongside *Daphne* with a violent collision. At first, recourse was had to the ancient method of getting anything done in Egypt: the fellahs plunged into the cold water, which reached to their chests, and shoved to the accompaniment of rhythmical song. Then the motorboat, with equally poor result, tried to pull us off and while this was going on another rescue expedition arrived from Balyana, where certain rumour had it that *Daphne* had been wrecked and two persons had been drowned. Despite my protests more and more officials stepped aboard *Daphne*, which was weighted down still further, and by degrees the whole thing turned into a farce, the climax of which was reached when half a dozen police officers stripped stark naked. *Daphne* was dressed over all with uniforms, shirts and underpants, and the six men leapt into the water to lend a hand. How could they dream of succeeding when forty hefty fellahs and two motorboats had had to give up? The officers' staggering zeal was prosaically explained on the following day when the valiant six asked me to write a certificate for them so that they could bring themselves to the gracious notice of the governor.

Obviously, only a big barge could pull *Daphne* off and the motorboats went home, but the officers insisted that two soldiers remain on board as guards against possible plunderers. The Nile racing past and the rustling of the sand allowed us very little sleep that night. When we looked out at dawn, we saw the two soldiers pacing up and down on a large sandy island which the current had formed in the lee of the boat. Edries suggested that it should be called Daphne Island and that we should plant a few palms here on our way downstream in two months' time, when the river had sunk still further. At ten o'clock we saw a curious sight on the arid strip of ground a stone's throw from where we had gone aground: two or three fellahs came along dragging, Allah alone knows where from, some gilt armchairs, which were placed as the front row of the stalls, and a little later a bevy of dignitaries appeared and solemnly took their seats. Then a big barge hove into sight with Girga's befezzed mamour on deck. It nosed its way cautiously past Daphne Island, anchored, and three men rowed a wire on board. After that it was child's play to pull *Daphne* off the bank with the winch. We went alongside the barge to thank the crew and ask what we owed them. Nothing! The governor at Sohag sent his greetings and wished us better luck during the rest of the voyage.

We had had a narrow escape: if help had not come in time, *Daphne* would soon have been embedded for ever in the sand of the Nile. Luckily, this was the only time on our way upstream that we needed outside assistance to get floated; we managed to work loose ourselves from the other shoals we encountered. As for Daphne Island, we were very disappointed on our way down two months later when we passed the spot and could not see a sign of it: evidently the same current which had formed it in the lee of *Daphne*'s hull had swept it away again when the boat was no longer there.

CHAPTER VII

The Death God's City
and the Love Goddess's Temple

In three hours we reached Balyana without further mishap and moored at a small pontoon bridge. Now that the tension was over we felt that the adventure at Daphne Island, the sleepless night and the physical exertion had left their mark. We longed to sleep, but *Daphne* was smothered in Nile slime from all the helpers' feet, one or two rail stanchions were broken and the taffrail was cracked. Not until we had cleaned and tidied up the whole boat, overhauled the engine and got hold of a village carpenter to repair the damage to the wood did we give in and tumble into bed – to be awakened in the evening after a good sleep by Evangelos Kondilios, our host of two days before, who diffidently wondered if he and Muhammed might ask us to dinner.

Good, kind, tender-hearted Evangelos, if you unintentionally tried our patience during the first visit to Balyana, you were our guardian angel during the second. A hot bath, an excellent dinner and a pleasant talk about your home island of Mytilene, which we had visited with *Daphne*, were the best relaxation we could have wished on this evening. Even Edries, who otherwise was always critical of foreigners living in Egypt, was quite won over by your gentle nature and did not judge you for the somewhat immodest bathing-beauty hanging above your bachelor's bed.

Evangelos went so far as to confide in Mona:

'I've turned fifty and I have scraped a little money together. Now I am going to write to my father's cousin, who is a priest in Mytilene, and ask him to find a pretty and capable girl for me . . .'

Evangelos had the use of a small car, in which he drove about buying up cotton from the peasants. He offered to take the day off on the morrow and drive us to Abydos, and we accepted gratefully.

Abydos stands on the edge of the desert a mere half-hour's drive by car from Balyana, but we very nearly missed the temple this time too, as on the way there we landed up in the middle of a wedding. Shrill notes from a flute and the inciting beat of drums sounded from a house round which people were flocking, we stopped and were asked to come forward and see *the bride's furniture being carried into the house.* Evangelos told us that an Egyptian fiancé, when he gets engaged, deposits a sum of money with the girl's parents – a relic from the days when the bride was bought – and that this money is used for buying household goods. On the wedding-day they are all loaded on to as many camels and carts as possible to make a striking impression as they are carried in triumph through the village and into the new home to the accompaniment of music and dancing. How old is this ceremony? Has it, like the trills of joy and the death wails, the hair-plaiting, the water-raising shadoof, the village architecture and so many other things, come down to us from the ancient Egyptians? There is at all events good reason not to hurry too blindly past the fellah world of today to the dead ruins if one wants to get to know the vanished kingdom of the Pharaohs. For a moment we were tempted to accept the bridegroom's invitation to stay for the whole of the wedding, but when we heard that the next item on the programme was a gargantuan meal our courage failed us and we discreetly withdrew.

To call the old Abydos a sacred city is not very significant as all Egyptian cities were more or less sacred and, through their temples, were consecrated to mighty gods. The great sacredness of Abydos was due to the unique position of the city's god: Osiris, the dead and resurrected god, the central figure in the Egyptians' conception of a life after death, the saviour god who, to a greater degree than the state gods Re and Amon, awakened a spontaneous piety. Even during predynastic times the Death God had a temple here which subsequently grew, changed, put out new shoots and scattered seeds to other places in that strange, vegetative way which is a basic feature of Egyptian architecture. The Egyptians lacked our reverence for old buildings as such, and it was one of the Pharaoh's duties to renew the temples of the kingdom as far as possible. At the beginning of this century Flinders Petrie excavated traces of about a dozen Osiris temples one above the other at Abydos, but the resemblance to a living plant is here carried so far that the temple definitely seems to have withered and died away when the Egyptian culture met its winter during the Roman era. In our day the vast temple area lies desolate and empty inside its high, massive mud-brick walls, the ground is mutilated by archaeologists' spades, which have exposed one or two stone foundations, and only the two sacred lakes outside the walls still reflect slender palms.

Abydos, where according to tradition Osiris himself lay buried, was for thousands of years the country's leading burial city, for not only the Pharaohs of thirty dynasties wished to have their real or symbolic tombs in the vicinity of 'him who loves silence', but also as time went on increasing numbers of their subjects. Usually they no doubt made do with a small cenotaph which was erected near the temple, but many of the Pharaohs built themselves large burial temples, of which only one, Seti I's, has been fairly well preserved to the present time. This burial temple from the heyday of the New Kingdom is the chief sight at Abydos and we studied it thoroughly, under the guidance of the young and friendly Egyptian archaeologist Abdel Moneim Akef, who lives in the little archaeologist's villa.

In the matter of Egypt's monuments, the modern traveller enjoys privileges of which he is scarcely conscious. The tourists of old, such as Plato, Herodotus and Strabo, probably had to content themselves with looking at the massive mud-brick walls of the temple precincts from outside, and the Egyptian people were allowed to see at the very most the exterior of the temples. To gain admittance even to the forecourts one had to belong to the lower priesthood, and the inner chambers, where the cult images were kept and the mysteries were portrayed in the mural reliefs, were entered only during special ceremonies by the higher priesthood – the innermost room originally by none but Pharaoh himself at rare festivals. When the old religion died and the temples were closed, they sank down into the desert sand and had their divine images destroyed and their reliefs painted over when they were transformed into Christian monasteries and emergency dwellings; the meaning of the hieroglyphics was forgotten and ancient Egypt became more invisible than ever. Now the archaeologists have patiently restored all that can be restored and invite us to acquaint ourselves with what was once so inaccessible. There is no longer anything to prevent us from passing through forecourts and halls into the holy of holies and from deciphering, with the aid of the translations in the guide-book, the secrets of the hieroglyphic texts. Unfortunately, they are secrets to which we are indifferent and privileges which have lost all value. Too late, three thousand years too late, we enter these doorways; what should have been a living contact becomes a few absent-minded reflexions – as though a gravedigger were to lay before us the whitened skull of the loved one of our youth and thereby give us what we had so passionately desired.

Seti I's temple is an important monument in the history of Egyptian art, even if the classically restrained and elegant court style which characterizes this Pharaoh's buildings appeals less directly to us than the powerful and brutal language of form used by his son Ramses II. It is, however, wise to check one's aesthetic reactions and the art historian's habits of thought if one wants to understand the Egyptian temples. These buildings have more in common with modern factories than with architectural splendour and their reliefs are a mechanical equipment rather than narrative ornaments. The product manufactured by Seti I's temple meant blessing to the country and immortality to the dead Pharaoh; production was carried out according to the well-tried and technically most developed methods of the age. The principle was to force the gods by ceremonies and incantations to deliver the desired benefits. This took place with the help of an invention which to a great degree replaced human labour: instead of perpetually praying priests and real sacrifices offered by Pharaoh, there were pictures of prayers and sacrifices. Such permanent actions of divine service were often joined together into whole batteries, twenty sacrificial pictures beside each other reinforced the action twenty times and varied it in different ways. In its day Seti I's temple must have been a technical marvel: here the seven mightiest gods – Amon, Osiris, Isis, Horus, Harmakis, Ptah and Seti – were worked on simultaneously in seven inner chambers, the pictorial equipment was extraordinarily rich and the whole vast apparatus could be managed by a small group of specially trained workers, the temple priests.

We visited the temple with the same ignorant curiosity, the same interest in the superficially queer and the same lack of understanding of essential details as if we had been seeing over a sugar factory or a paper mill. The Egyptian archaeologist tried to play the part of the demonstrating engineer, but he too was an ignorant layman: nobody knows any longer just how the divine deposits were mined.

But if the doctrines of the old religion are unknown to us and its secrets are dead letters, we can still form an opinion of its age-old problems and the perspectives common to humanity. On our way home from the Death God's City I could not help pondering on the strange fixed idea of eternity and an existence on the other side of the grave that played such a big part in ancient Egypt. On this point, as on so many others, the ancient Greeks differed radically from the Egyptians: for them, life here and now was the only thing they seriously reckoned with, while existence in Hades was an empty shadow-life with no real meaning. Can the reason be the very different external conditions of life determined by the natural features of Greece and Egypt? In Greece the landscape is so unchangeable that we can still stroll in the Homeric countryside, visit Odysseus' sheltered bays and bathe our faces in the Castalian spring. It cannot be a coincidence that there, in the clarified world of sea and mountain, which forms an inflexible frame round the existence of the individual, the Greeks' object in life was an intense acceptance of the fleeting present. They built perishable monuments and lived only for the day: from the golden age of Hellas, the centuries between Homer and the 5th century, there are very few ancient relics preserved. In Egypt, on the other hand, where the changing, unstable countryside has left no trace of the old landscape, we find monuments built for eternity. I cannot say why Egypt's transience was so palpable on this evening as we drove back to *Daphne* between the calm reflections in the canals and the green fields. Perhaps it was the superfluity of young, sprouting life in this ancient land which seemed overwhelming in the golden light of the sunset? Everything in fellah-Egypt speaks of an intense, utterly ruthless generative power: under the influence of sun and water an unbroken metamorphosis takes place of the earth's basic elements, which rise out of the fields in frequent harvests, become living cells in human beings and animals, return to the soil as manure, are changed into mud-bricks for house-building, into fuel, clothes, pitchers, sweat, love, warm human bodies, which in their turn sink back into the fields to begin the cycle anew. Women here begin bearing children at the age of fourteen and continue without a break until they drop in their tracks or become barren: the generations succeed each other as quickly as the crops in the fields. It is the excess of life which is life's enemy in Egypt; new life is for ever thrusting up and demanding room of the living.

Can this be the reason for Egypt's death cult? Perhaps the people in this land, where the individual length of life has always been meted out very grudgingly, have never had time to finish with life before being forced to leave it? The normal cycle of life, determined by the body's growth, maturity and final decay – the full life which allows the old, heavy with years, to die content – has not had a chance to exhaust the Egyptians' will to live as in the case of the Greeks and modern man. The thought of a continuation after death under more stable and reassuring conditions is therefore natural. The realm of death was the vast emigration country of the Egyptians, to which families sent their dead with costly equipment, while themselves making prudent preparation for the important journey.

If this is true, the Egyptian death cult is not a flight from reality and a morbid satiety with life, as we have been apt to think; it is one of the most passionate and strong-willed confessions of life which the human race has ever made. Who has more stubbornly protested against ultimate death and opposed the laws of mortality? The fact that the will to live has burnt most fiercely in an environment where it has constantly been threatened, that the open expanse of the desert has induced the need of being enclosed in deep, protective, rock chambers and that the collective existence in the world's first ant-heap community gave rise to the dream of everlasting seclusion in an individual mummy, has much to teach us about human nature.

It was with some trepidation next morning that we headed out on to the river from Balyana – the adventure at Daphne Island had slightly shaken our nerve. But once we had got the sails up and were scudding along before the wind, the joy of sailing took the upper hand, especially when, on passing a village, we were joined by a dozen large aiasas, which offered a fine chance of a race. For a long stretch we sounded only one fathom and sometimes less, but the aiasas around us shouted good advice and at times we merely grazed the bottom. The Arabian Hills on the east bank, which had kept in the background since Girga, now came forward to the river again. By one o'clock we had reached the Nag Hammadi dam, where a large flotilla of aiasas was waiting, but for some reason only we were allowed to enter the huge dripping lock-chamber. As we sat there, waiting, we could hear the humming, monotonous song of the workmen up on the quayside as they ran round turning the crank to open the sluice-gates. One of the lock engineers informed us that we were now 220 feet above sea level. We went on into the higher, brighter world above the dam, where shady, park-like banks were reflected in the water. About half-past three we were approaching the big bridge at Nag Hammadi which takes the railway across to the east side. Here the banks change character up to a point: the east bank becomes the fertile and well-populated side while the ground opposite is bare and arid and tombs have been hewn into the adjacent cliffs. 'To go west' in Thebes is therefore synonymous with the last journey and 'the First of the Westerners' is one of the Death God's names. A train was just crossing the bridge, after which it was opened; this was evidently the normal opening-time, as a whole swarm of aiasas went through from both sides.

Nag Hammadi is quite an important small town, which has two circumstances to thank for its origin, but also for its un-commonly wretched social conditions. In the centre of the town is a palace surrounded by a park; here one of Farouk's close relations, Prince Yusuf Kamal, resided right up to the revolution as the owner of about 70,000 acres of land. The new régime was now portioning out this land to the local fellahs, but the reform has not yet visibly affected their living conditions. The other vital factor in Nag Hammadi is the sugar factory, one of the biggest in Egypt. Here, during an annual working period of four months, sugar is produced from the harvest from the former royal domains, whose new owners are bound to cultivate the same quantity of sugar-cane as the fields previously yielded. The government's grandiose plans to create a new and prosperous Nag Hammadi are not a day too early: at present the town is a glaring example of the seamy side of the latifundia system and unbridled industrial capitalism. Tumbledown hovels, stinking streets, a population in rags, an uncommonly large number of crippled and blind and, according to the word of our usual company, the police officers, a distressing amount of crime characterize the community. In my mind's eye, I see the sum total of Nag Hammadi's misery in the picture of a shapeless black heap which lay in the street by the police station; one could have taken it for a rag-bag or a tattered covering that had fallen from a passing cart had not an arm, as gaunt and twisted as a piece of wire, been sticking up out of the cloth with the palm cupped beseechingly towards the passers-by.

In Nag Hammadi, too, there were Mecca pilgrims who had had the fronts of their houses painted, and during one of our walks we were lucky enough to meet the town's Hadji artist, the creator of the pilgrim paintings, which, judged as art, were unusually good. He was a friendly man of about forty; his name was Mohammed el Alaili Hassan and he looked like an ordinary fellah – which is what he was, apart from the few days when he carried out his painting orders. I interviewed him via Edries and found out that he had begun to paint quite spontaneously at the age of eighteen and had never had a teacher. But like other fellahs, he had seen houses with Hadji paintings since his childhood and in this way become familiar with the motifs. With each order he would add something out of his head, as the fee depended on the satisfaction of the Hadji who had commissioned the work and all wanted to have something different and superior to the paintings of former pilgrims. It took about five days to paint a whole house and the minimum fee was £3 including the material; if the Hadji liked the finished work of art he would give an extra few shillings when he came home and even the guests, who assembled in the house to hear about the wonderful journey, paid something, depending on their appreciation – a solution of the problems attending works of art painted to order which seems well-nigh ideal.

We had no wish to prolong our stay in the shadow of Nag Hammadi's sugar-factory and set off early next morning. As always above the dams the river was deeper and calmer for the first stage and without mishap we reached the village of Dendera, about thirty miles upstream. The police station lay up on a small point, or paved embankment, which stretched out into the river for about fifty feet; we found an excellent mooring-place below it.

Naguib Zaki, the village police officer, might have been an effective minor character in an Egyptian version of *Dead Souls*. At first he seemed quite normal. He glared ferociously at all who did not instantly move out of the way in respect as he approached, he bawled at the gaffirs for not understanding his orders and then invited us in honeyed tones to tea at the police station. But even at this first meeting we began to wonder: he importuned us to have dinner with him at his home, it was a point of ambition which must be carried at all costs. As we had never mixed 'privately' with police officers before and as in addition we did not take to Zaki, we declined with one or two polite excuses: we were too tired to go anywhere this evening . . . But Zaki was not the man to give in. At sunset we saw a deputation of four gaffirs approach, carrying steaming tureens: since we wished to rest, dinner was served on board *Daphne*. Edries laughed till he cried at this obstinate hospitality and our feeble efforts to defend ourselves. It was impossible to repulse such a discreet kindness, but we knew full well that it was not going to be easy to spurn Zaki's continued overtures once we had eaten out of the proffered tureens. On the following evening, when we returned from the temple visit, he invited us home to dinner and simply would not take no for an answer.

He lived in a dark, ramshackle house in the middle of the village. We were shown up to a damp, musty room on the first floor, where a table and one or two rickety chairs were the only furniture. A 500-candle-power petroleum lamp cast a murderous light and during the next hour our host expatiated in broken English on the tribulations of his profession. Dendera was, on the whole, a quiet spot, no crimes had been committed during the three months he had been there. It was very different at his previous post at Nag Hammadi, where murder, theft, kidnapping and blackmail were the order of the day – largely owing to the sprawling fields with their man-high sugar-cane which afforded shelter to all kinds of shady goings-on. Once he had been fired on from ambush, a bullet had whistled past his ear. But he had his suspicions as to the culprit, and when a pretext offered a little later Zaki could clap the man into jail and flog him every day, until unfortunately he had to be sent to hospital. Accounts of this kind followed one on top of the other and our disgust did not lessen when our host broke off the entertainment from time to time and went out into the kitchen to bellow at his wife and the family servant. The latter, he told us, was a widow with three children whom he had taken into his service out of the kindness of his heart, but she was lazy despite the handsome wage he paid her of £1 per month. At last dinner was ready: a couple of pigeons stuffed with rice were borne in by the servant. She could not have been a day over twenty, but her face was terribly ravaged; from two enormous black eyes all the world's sorrow looked out at us. Mona was so upset that she waited her chance to slip a ten shilling note into her hand, but the poor girl could not control herself and kissed Mona's hands in a flood of tears. His suspicions aroused, Zaki followed her out into the kitchen, we heard voices raised in anger and distress and after a while he returned with the fatal note in his hand.

'You may give her a tip by all means, but this is far too much. She will get a wrong idea of the value of money. Have you a 5-piaster coin?' (about 1s.).

After dinner – washed down with Nile water – the family was allowed to come in. Zaki was a modern man who did not keep his wife hidden from strangers' eyes. She could not have been over thirty and after her toil in the kitchen had put on a floral dress, but like most of the women in Egypt she had more the appearance of a suffering animal, fat and ungainly from the shut-in life, worn out by seven confinements and without even a pretence to the simplest schooling which could have lifted her above the level of livestock. Questions put to her direct via Edries she answered only after her husband in each case had given her permission and the whole time she respectfully followed his every slight change of mood, in common with four of the children, who, dressed in white and terrified, had been ordered in to say how-do-you-do to the visitors.

It appeared that the family had nothing whatever to do with anyone else in the village: Zaki never paid any calls, not even on the omda, his wife had no women friends and the children were not allowed to play with the other children.

'It is not proper to make friends with those you are to rule over. They must have respect for me,' Zaki declared with a domineering glare at the wretched servant.

We felt we had risen out of a deep grave when at last we were home again.

'It's bad, very bad,' was Edries' comment.

Mona felt a suffragette's revolutionary storm raging in her breast:

'I'll never again believe all that silly talk about oriental women being happy in spite of everything,'

My own attempts to shake off the unpleasantness followed another line of thought:

'The fellow must be crazy. I don't think the other police officers are like him.'

This opinion was based on the impression we had received of another police officer who, on the morning of this same day, had come from the adjacent provincial capital Quena to accompany us to Dendera's temple. His name was Mohammed Addimirdasch Mohammed and he was far and away the nicest officer we met during the whole journey, a man who possessed much natural authority and at the same time great humanity. His view was the opposite of Naguib Zaki's: that a police officer's duty was to make friends with the common people in the villages, and he had other ideas about his profession which are taken for granted with us but are daring and original in Egypt.

The road to Dendera's temple, which lies some little distance outside the village, winds through a landscape which reminds one in an odd way of the Roman campagna. Large stone-pines, cypress-like tamarisks, the plain with the hazy-blue mountains in the background and flocks of sheep watched by shepherds – had not palms and camels supplemented the impression I should have been on the look-out for the dome of St Peter's on the horizon. Now we were approaching instead another sacred edifice, Dendera's temple, where the ancient cult image of the Goddess of Love and Heaven, Hathor, was once kept. This image has of course long since been lost, but it would be well-known to us even without the copy hewn into the rear wall of the temple: the Hathor image was so common in ancient Egypt that it gave rise to a special column capital, the so-called Hathor capital which is to be met with frequently. This curious triangular woman's face with cow's ears and cow eyes is one of the Egyptian religion's most singular creations, a being which, far from making a grotesque impression, has a strain of smiling wisdom and biological femininity: it leads one's thoughts to both Leonardo's Mona Lisa and the female animal licking her new-born young. The Greeks identified Hathor with Aphrodite, but this merely made her commonplace: as Love Goddess, Hathor banishes her Greek sister to the realm of pin-up girls and candidates for a beauty contest.

The Dendera temple dates in its present form from Ptolemaic and Roman times, its reliefs are apt to be coarse and insensitive, and a general impression of decadence, religious conventionalism and cultural decline rests over the building. Yet it is of untold value to us for two reasons: first, its formation and adornment revert in everything essential to the older temples that have stood on this site ever since the beginning of the Egyptian era – it is a kind of sum total of the Hathor religion's traditions; second, the Dendera temple is one of the best preserved in all Egypt, a building which, in a miraculous way, has reached our age almost intact. This very possibility of seeing an interior, where both roof and walls are extant, of mounting to the upper terraces, where holy processions marched round on festival days, and of creeping down into the secret chambers where the most costly and secret things were kept, makes this visit intensely interesting. The temple guard also showed us the obligatory curiosities: the relief portraits of Cleopatra and her son by Julius Caesar, Caesarion, and the inscriptions which Napoleon's soldiers carved in the roof on that memorable day in 1799 which Vivant Denon describes so vividly. The hardened warriors, who had been pursuing the fleeing Mamelukes along the Nile valley for week after week, were so moved by the Dendera temple when they stumbled across it that they spontaneously honoured it in the best way they could: by presenting arms.

We strolled about the temple precincts for the best part of the day with our noses in the Guide Bleu, in which the functions of the various rooms and the meaning of the endless series of reliefs are summarily given. Actually, one could just as well devote a whole week to nothing else but seeing all the pictures and a whole life to an attempt to interpret them. No less time was set aside by the priests who once, at an early age, were received among the servants of the goddess and were then gradually initiated into the temple secrets. In the man of today this wealth of detail – incomprehensible when all is said and done – arouses both surfeit and fatigue. Flaubert confessed quite frankly: 'The Egyptian temples bore me!', but for us Dendera still had the charm of novelty and surprise.

There are two ways of understanding the Egyptian temples. The first – which not only dominates the Guide Bleu but recurs in most of the standard works on Egypt's cultural history – reflects a rationalistic nineteenth-century attitude. The temples were built, it is contended, in order to glorify the builder – Pharaoh – whose name cartouches, portraits and vaunting accounts of feats, real or imagined, fill halls and courtyards. The different Pharaohs strove to excel each other as regards the magnificence of new buildings and extensions to old ones (we recognize Herodotus' views on the builders of the Pyramids). As to the architectonic design, it is pointed out that the temple was not a place of public worship but was looked on as the god's house, where he was thought to live, with the priests as his personal servants. The temples therefore follow the architecture of dwelling-houses, or rather palaces, and the space is functionally designed in accordance with the practical needs: this corridor was built for the processions, this storeroom for the sacrificial gifts, in this room the properties of the cult were kept, and here the priests stole along to work the false miracles. The reliefs were regarded as a kind of adornment, and the motifs were chosen so that they would have some reference to the function of the room, rather as one nowadays paints Venus on the wall of the marriage-room in a registry office and a maritime picture in the ticket-office of a steamship company. If a lunch-room for the priests, a privy for the staff and living-quarters for the caretaker are lacking, this is not due to any fundamental impossibility, only to the fact that the architects did not happen to think of it.

One must oppose this interpretation of the temples even if one is unversed in the uncontrollable mysticism that often colours the views about Egypt's ancient monuments. In connection with our visit to Abydos I myself sketched a 'functional' interpretation of the temples which I think is much more to the point than the idea of the Pharaoh's self-assertion and the god's dwelling: the temples are power stations in the service of the community; transformers which are enlarged and modernized in accordance with the march of science. But they are also something else: they are attempts to shape and understand the world.

Champollion was the first to maintain that the Egyptian temples are a kind of writing, descriptions of the world or theological tracts. But they cannot be compared with a modern account of an observed external reality or with a model which has been built from an existing pattern. The temples are the primary thing, they are the model which thought then projects in order to grasp what is formless and universal. 'In the beginning was the Word,' says St John. In the beginning is the symbol, the temple building with its heavenly and earthly River Nile, its story of creation and its divine forms, its division of the year into thirty-six ten-day periods, its rites which aid growth and bestow prosperity, its meetings between the living god Pharaoh and the supernatural gods, who through his mediation assist the country – all this and infinitely much more has its exact form in the temple and its connection with the outer world, shown by the very care with which the building's axis are placed in relation to the position of the celestial bodies and the changing seasons. In this way the formless world acquires measure, dimension and meaning through the temple, which is the great book by means of which the priests learn to understand existence. The whole of this world-shaping side of the Egyptian temples is especially apparent at Dendera, where Hathor's role as goddess of heaven makes the astronomical and cosmic reliefs so numerous.

It cannot be denied that our Greek-influenced world has grown right away from this mentality – the Greeks made the models of the world copies instead of prototypes – but on the other hand we retain in our Christian heritage many features of pre-Greek conceptions which can help us to understand the trend of Egyptian thought. Take, for instance, the Byzantine churches, which were similar world models with distinct spheres for the Saviour, the angels, the apostles, the saints and the earthly life, or the Gothic cathedrals, in which the stained-glass windows were placed so that the sun's angles of incidence during the changing conditions of the year gave light and life to the pictures in conformity with their current interest and each symbol had manifold, truth-revealing significance. As regards the ceremonies and mysteries celebrated in the Egyptian temples, they are unlikely to have differed in a logical respect from the eucharist performed daily in Christian churches. Transubstantiation, this act which is at once a commemoration of something which happened long ago and a creative reality which gives the participants a new relationship to the world, still has for many people a living meaning which surpasses all rational truth.

When we awakened on the second morning after our arrival in Dendera, we could hardly believe our eyes: the sky was overcast and a cold wind was blowing from the north. Just as we were about to start the police officer's serving-maid stole down to see us and we had the satisfaction of once more giving her the note that her tyrannical master had taken from her. Zaki was inside the police station putting a call through to the governor in the adjacent Quena: wise from our grounding at Daphne Island, we had decided to pay a courtesy visit to the *mudir* in the new province we were now in. The shallower the river became, the more important it was to have protectors in high places. Zaki returned to say that His Excellency would expect us in an hour's time. We cast off with no regrets and left our problematic host waving on the bank; at the moment of parting he had presented us with his photograph, on which he had written a dedication.

After only forty-five minutes we landed at Quena's civil service club, where the governor's car, the chief of police and one or two others were waiting. The town itself, which lies a mile or two from the river, gave quite a neat and prosperous impression, the governor's house, shady and airy, had an unmistakably English air about it and the mudir himself, a corpulent man who might have been a Turk and comported himself with great dignity, was all amiability. We were served tea out of silver-rimmed glasses and chanced to mention during our halting conversation in English that our immediate goal was the potters' village of Ballas, not far up the river. After our visit to the mudir, Edries passed on the hint that we should also call on the town's *mamour markaz* – the district chief of police, who offered us coca cola, but spoke only Arabic. When, our duty done, we returned to *Daphne*, a mounted police came galloping from the town: the governor asked if we could receive a return visit. Without a doubt His Excellency, who drove up half an hour later in his car, had expected a more stately craft than our little *Daphne*, but with good grace he balanced his way courageously on the long plank, which sagged alarmingly under his weight. After him came two officers bearing two pitchers richly painted with gold and a Nile landscape; they were surely the ugliest in the world but were therefore unique. They were formally handed over to us by reason of our interest in Egyptian pottery.

We set off the minute the governor, tensely watched by all, had dared the gangway for the second time and safely reached the shore. The sky was still overcast and the north wind uncommonly gusty, but just because of this I was tempted to clap on all sail: at last *Daphne* was to be given the chance to sail in a wind to which she was accustomed. We had a fine but rather nerve-racking trip, as for long stretches it was shallow and Edries had to stand and take soundings, while Mona begged in vain for a quiet half-hour for lunch.

Our interest in Ballas was due to the unique position of this place among all the agricultural villages of Egypt, so alike in many respects. Even down in the Delta we had met aiasas laden to the mast-tops with peculiar melon-shaped, yellow-coloured objects; upon asking what they were we were told 'ballas!' and when we wanted to know where they came from we again received the word 'Ballas!' in reply. We put two and two together a little late when we found that the ballas is the most important vessel in a fellah home, the earthenware pitcher in which the women fetch water from the Nile; all these pitchers come from the little village of Ballas, twelve miles south of Quena, where good-quality clay, ideal for pottery, is to be found in unlimited quantities.

A cluster of aiasas by the shelving shore told us from afar where Ballas' landing-place was, but there was not a sign of the village itself; it lay nearly a mile from the river. We tied up beside an empty aiasa near a mound of neatly stacked Ballas pitchers on the bank. It was a joy to see the work of loading: along a chain of about fifty men the pitchers flew swiftly from the stacks on shore to the aiasas, which had been built out to twice their normal width by means of a frame with netting rigged out from the sides. As the boats are meant to drift down the river, not sail, they are loaded so high that they finally look like floating temple pylons with walls sloping slightly inwards.

A trifle out of humour, we strolled up towards the village in the grey, chilly weather. Such days occur so seldom that they make one aware of the miracle of the perpetual sunshine, the bright play of colours and the pleasant temperature of the other winter days, the ideal weather which in the north is the rare guest of summer. Ballas' police officer, who met us, was hardly an ornament to his profession: he had a Judas face with shifty eyes and his tone of command was not taken seriously by anybody. Edries heard in the village that he was an alcoholic, which in a totally 'dry' Mohammedan village must be as scandalous as it is difficult.

In many respects Ballas struck us as being different from the ordinary fellah villages. Not only were the houses largely built of rejected pitchers, joined together with clay, which gave them a surrealistic air, but an unusual prosperity was obvious: we saw more Hadji houses than anywhere else and moreover found the artistic level of the paintings surprisingly high. Who was the artist? The whole village was afoot because of our visit and it was not long before word reached him by way of the 'jungle telegraph'. He was a man of about thirty with a sensitive face and a shy smile. He told us his name was Sajid Ali and that he was the second of three brothers, all painters; the eldest, Amin Ali, had died a year or two before. Together they had decorated about a hundred houses and formed a real local art-school with distinctive individual traits in the common style. Their colour-scheme with bright-blue and orange as the base was unusually attractive and the motifs were executed with a fresh naïvety and ingenuity of form which would have pleased Paul Klee.

Sajid Ali himself conducted us round to the houses that he considered most worth seeing and our praise made him both happy and embarrassed; never before had any stranger taken any interest in his paintings. Edries, who translated our questions and Sajid's answers, was not slow to make it clear to the amazed inhabitants of Ballas that they had a great artist in their midst and that the photographs I took would be published in foreign papers. For my own part, I was sorry to take with me only reproductions of Sajid's art. Had he no sketches or perhaps even canvases? He shook his head regretfully. Could a more typical monumental painter be imagined? – he had never painted on anything but walls. But Mona had a brainwave:

'You can borrow coloured chalks from us and there must be paper to be had somewhere . . . '

So Edries ran to get the chalks and I bought a school exercise-book at the village stores. Sajid promised to have a Hadji painting on paper ready for us by the next morning.

'Don't forget the Prophet's tomb!' we exhorted him on parting. 'And the sphinxes! And the railway train!'

Coffee-drinking at the police station to round off the walk could not be avoided. Our host the police officer spoke hardly a word of English and stared at us in such gloomy silence that we squirmed in our chairs and began to feel like arrested criminals. On our way home at dusk we saw flashes of lightning to the north and soon a menacing rumble of thunder was heard. *Daphne*'s cabin seemed all the cosier with its paraffin lamp, dinner and nice books. Suddenly, about half-past nine, there was a clap of thunder right over our heads and heavy drops of rain began drumming on the deck. Our five guards, who had been sitting round a fire on the bank, knocked on the door and implored us to let them in, but the space in the cabin was so cramped that we could not possibly have made room for them, unless they had sat on our knees all night. Instead, they found scant shelter with the crews of the aiasas under a rowing-boat turned up on edge. For the Egyptians, including Edries, this rain was a catastrophe and sleep was out of the question for them, while we children of a northern clime turned in contentedly and fell into a deep and blissful sleep to the homeland music we had missed for so long.

Soon after two in the morning we were awakened by despairing shouts which could be heard above the beating rain and the slapping rigging: we looked out and saw that all the ready-loaded aiasas, whose high walls of ballases formed a trap for the wind, had broken loose from their moorings and drifted out into midstream. One or two managed to drop anchor and ride out the storm, while others ran aground and had part of their cargo shattered.

It was still raining at sunrise, but by eight o'clock the sky cleared and the sun appeared. We were still light of heart and merely thought that the rain had freshened up the countryside. But in Upper Egypt rain *is* a catastrophe. Not until later in the day did we hear that part of the town of Quena had been washed away by the deluge, that several people had been drowned and that the cloudburst had undermined the railway line to the town. Perhaps the rain should not be blamed entirely for the fact that a passenger-train had been left standing out on the track and had been plundered by robbers. In Ballas, too, there was confusion and lamentation. Mud ankle deep covered the roads and we could not have visited any potters' workshops if donkeys had not been put at our disposal. The Ballas pitchers are fired out in the open in large silo-like kilns, in which the pitchers are stacked day by day as soon as they are turned, until the kilns are full and can be covered over. Then a fire is kept going for four hours with dry maize stalks, and then the ballases are left to cool. The effect of the night's rain on these kilns can be imagined, both the half-filled ones and those that were still hot. Months of hard work had been wasted. But in a situation such as this the Mohammedan religion shows its strength: all resigned themselves to the disaster with admirable fortitude and in many workshops new pitchers were already taking shape on the wheels.

Owing to the storm and the general muddle we had forgotten all about the Hadji painter and our art commission. Despite the rain and thunder he must have worked all night long, as ever since the morning he had accompanied us as donkey-driver to the potters' workshops. Shame to say, we did not at once recognize him in this capacity – the westerner does not so easily distinguish all these men in turban and galabia. He, tactfully, said nothing and not until we were on our way back at noon did Mona react:

'Heavens above, it's the artist, Sajid!'

He beamed with pleasure and instantly drew the exercise-book out of his breast. It was full from cover to cover with bright pictures, smaller in size and, because of the dry chalks, not so brilliant in colour as the wall paintings, but otherwise fully the equal of these. We glanced through the book in delight and decided to set an example: the villagers could take a lesson in what art is worth! Sajid's eyes goggled when he was given £5 for the exercise-book and the bystanders were still more amazed. For them there was only one explanation: we were fabulously rich and misguided paschas who showered money around us. Suddenly they all began to beg. The potters, whose kilns had been ruined by the rain, saw a chance of compensation and sang grateful praises to Allah. The donkey-drivers, who had placed their animals at our disposal, already regarded themselves as wealthy men. A swarm of several hundred children raised a scream which rent the skies: 'Bakhshish! Bakhshish!' Threatened with a riotous assault we decided on a hasty retreat.

We flung a handful of coppers to the children and managed to escape in the ensuing tumult. It had been plain from the start that the trickiest matter of all would be settling up with the donkey-drivers, and after a short consultation we decided that Mona and Edries were to go aboard to make *Daphne* all ready to sail, while I stayed behind and pretended to take photographs. When Edries gave the word, I handed to the donkeys' masters a sum which, though on the generous side, could not of course fulfil the expectations aroused by the artist's fee. I got on board in time, however, and we cast off, but even far out in midstream the wails and curses reached us.

There are evidently risks attached to adopting a modern attitude to folk-art!

Once round the nearest bend in the river we set the sails, but the night's storm had been succeeded by almost breathless sunshine and we made very little headway. When a tug with two barges came on the scene we started the engine again and went on in their sure wake. It was already past noon and we had thought of sailing only a few miles to a village where the police had been notified of our arrival, but when the helmsman on the rear barge told us that the train intended going right on to Luxor through the darkness we decided to follow it.

Hour after hour passed, sunny and uneventful, and dusk fell. First came the hour when the shadows grow long across the scorched desert, the Nile reflects the palm-groves of the east bank in a glorified light and the rock cliffs of the west, where the dead are at peace, grow so ethereally blue that they look like a mirage. Then came the swift sunset, whose colours, thanks to the dry desert air, are so much more gorgeous than with us. The night, glittering with stars but moonless, was drawn across the sky from the east like a black curtain. By now we could hardly make out the shores we were gliding past, and kept all the closer contact with the barge train. At about seven o'clock bright pinpoints of light appeared ahead: the street-lamps and hotel windows of Luxor's strand promenade. But here in the last bend of the river the difficulties began. The tug was uncertain of the way; it stopped and the skipper shouted questions to the fellahs sitting round their brushwood fires on the starboard bank close by. Then the train went on with extreme caution. So that we would not get left behind in the dark the men on the rear barge offered us a rope. We accepted, never thinking that it might be dangerous: the train did not draw as much water as *Daphne* and we were dragged high up on to a sandbank before the tug found that it could not get through. As we lay there, stuck fast and twisted beam on by the current, the entire train came drifting back at good speed. The collision was unavoidable. I worked frantically but futilely at the helm, Edries stood nonplussed, but Mona flung out her arms desperately to ward off the crash – a hopeless measure, but a proof of courage and love for the boat which was a lesson to us men. Luckily the collision was not disastrous, only part of the bulwark was broken; *Daphne* got floated and drifted downstream with the barge-train.

We had now had enough of night manoeuvres. We anchored while the train continued to poke about among the sandbanks until at last it found a way and disappeared towards Luxor's inviting rows of light. One or two dark aiasas under towering sails glided soundlessly past us like ghosts, so we hung out a riding-light, had something to eat and turned in.

When we looked out at sunrise at the hazy morning we found we were about fifty yards from the starboard riverbank, where bent figures straining at long ropes were towing small aiasas and feluccas laden with agricultural produce, wives and children, all on their way to the market at Luxor. We weighed anchor and followed them; now that it was light, we had no difficulty in finding the way and in half an hour we reached the town, or rather village, as despite its many hotels and two and a half mile road by the river, Luxor is only a small tourist resort occupying a fraction of the city area of ancient Thebes. Not far from the river we caught sight of the mighty pylons of the Karnak temple: we followed the strand promenade with its villas and hotels, passed the Luxor temple and reached the fancy-looking building which bears on its façade the proud name of WINTER PALACE.

Could we, who did not have to pay for any expensive rooms, choose any hotel other than the finest and most famous in Luxor! We tied up at a monumental flight of stone steps below the hotel, Nubian servants came running with a gangway and we jumped ashore to greet dear friends: Juan and Astri Morales, Mona's uncle and his wife, who had flown down from Stockholm to spend Christmas with us in Luxor. It was Tuesday, 21st December. For ten days we were to forget the trials of river navigation and devote ourselves instead to carefree days with friends and to studying the ruins of ancient Thebes.

CHAPTER VIII

Christmas in Luxor

When one has seen what is left of the old Memphis – one or two huge, mutilated statues in a palm grove – one is not surprised that 'Thebes with the hundred gateways', the capital during the thousand years when Egypt was a world kingdom, has gone under so completely that at the beginning of the nineteenth century only a few poverty-stricken fellah villages were left here, built into tombs and ruins. It is tourism which has revived Thebes and drawn a settled population of about 15,000 to the surroundings of the Luxor temple. A kind of Ideal Egypt has arisen here, with nothing but well-built houses, friendly, urbane inhabitants, asphalted streets, flowering gardens and the quiet of a small country town, overshadowed by the papyrus columns of the temples, bathed in the clear winter sunshine and counter-balanced by the majestic view across the river. Even nineteenth-century tourists anchored with their dahabias below Luxor's temples, each with his country's flag fluttering from the mast-top. There were English lords, American society girls in Amazon skirts, German *Geheimrat* families and Swiss merchants; in the daytime one rode on donkeys to temples and tombs and bought genuine and counterfeit antiques – the local art industry was even then highly developed – and in the evening one arranged 'fantasias' to celebrate the completed journey: the dahabia was illuminated with hundreds of lanterns, fireworks were let off against the brilliant starry sky, champagne was drunk and lofty thoughts were sent to the far-off homeland shivering under the winter snow.

But when, at the turn of the century, the dahabias began to be replaced by more democratic paddle-steamers and the railway, which previously had stopped at Asyut, was extended to Luxor, it became necessary to build hotels. This was when they arose, these dreams in neo-Rococo or the latest fashion Modern Style. The Winter Palace is the most traditional of them, a fine allusion both to the Tsar's residence by the Neva and the fact that the tourist season in Luxor is limited to four winter months – during the rest of the year one should preferably be a mummy or a dark-

Tuition in Gourna's new school

Coptic school-children during a lesson in the school yard

Ramses II's burial temple at ancient Thebes

skinned fellah to endure the climate. The winter, on the other hand, is all the more enticing to the shivering Europeans and Americans who, during the decades before the wars, could still indulge in the luxury of spending the cold time of the year in this idyll of guaranteed sunshine. We were reminded in an amusing way of this vanished world when the police officer who met us on the bank introduced himself:

'Major Wilson!'

It appeared that Wilson was the Christian name he had been given by his parents as a result of the American president's visit to Luxor at the time of his birth.

In our day the forms of tourism have again changed – in Luxor as all over the world. Gone are 'the quality', who even had plenty of time; the watchword now is democratization and above all rationalization. Conducted tour succeeds conducted tour in Luxor and the whole thing is arranged so efficiently that in two or three days one 'does everything'. The cost of the private journey has been forced down at the same time as the volume of production has increased beyond all expectation; new groups from all levels of society now have the opportunity of seeing Egypt, while the income for the country, the hotel-owners and the dragomans swells. The result is therefore just as satisfying as the development within most other industries, but also just as unsatisfying. For experience shows that whatever becomes a cheap standard article loses both in material quality and psychological value. The sorry truth is that the memory of a modern tourist trip to Egypt lasts for only a few months – then it pales, one can no longer produce it in company and after a while it is not even fit for everyday use. But by then one has had time to acquire new travel impressions from other cheap places.

We had a good chance of studying this modern tourism from our moorings by the bank of the Nile. In the morning there was always a dead calm, and the coolness of the night lingering in the sunny air reminded us of a summer's morning in the Alps. We sat on deck drinking our morning coffee, but buses were already rolling along the riverside road, taking groups of tourists to the temples under the guidance of diploma'd art-historians from the various agencies in Paris, New York and London. Other groups took a motor-boat over to the west bank, where a vast fleet of cars was waiting to take them to the Valley of the Kings and the other sights. The Winter Palace, which clings to its distinguished traditions, has, besides its own motor-boat, sailing feluccas for tourists who are willing to pay a little extra for the picturesque. This small flotilla, which plies to and fro across the river, is worked by a dozen dark-skinned Nubians. As they lived on a little house-barge next-door to *Daphne* and as their fellow-countryman Edries could talk to them in their own language, which is quite different from Arabic, we became very friendly with them and shared their daily joys and sorrows. It was no easy work rowing the heavy feluccas through the current to the opposite bank in the dead calm of morning, but now and then it would happen that the Aga Khan or some American tourist gave them a princely tip. Their big problem was to scrape together enough money during the four months of the tourist season to be able to live at home during the rest of the year with their families in their primitive Nubian villages above Assuan. In the evenings they lighted small fires on the bank, sang and drummed – for us it was a greeting, full of atmosphere, from the dark interior of Africa, which otherwise is so remote here in the bright valley of the Nile.

Juan and Astri had a room at the Winter Palace overlooking the palm-fringed strand promenade, the majestic river and the plain where the two Memnon statues stand on guard in front of the burial cliffs – no city has had a more beautiful position than ancient Thebes. But we had unexpected guests at the Christmas table, or perhaps not altogether unexpected: at a gay dinner six months previously our friends Alvar and Elissa Aalto had promised to come down to Egypt to sail with us, but what with the burden of work resting on a world-famous architect and what with Alvar's unpredictable skill in the art of living, we had not taken the suggestion very seriously. Anyway, here they were; they arrived by plane from Bagdad on the morning of Christmas Eve and caught us in bed. They too got a room at the Winter Palace with a view over the river and through this double association the hotel became a home from home for *Daphne*'s crew as well. Mona had a holiday from cooking, I sat in the bar with Alvar, and Edries, dressed in his blue seascout uniform with shorts, made the acquaintance of the luxury-hotel world of décolleté women, wine-drinking dinner parties, dancing and nightly roulette-playing – need it be said that such sins aroused his severe disapproval?

The hotel guests, who for the first days bore the stamp of modern democratization, underwent a noticeable change just before Christmas: ambassadors and bankers from Cairo, one or two stray cousins of European ex-royalties, two high-ranking English officials from the Sudan, in short the relics of a bygone age's fashionable world seemed to have arranged to meet at the Winter Palace to spend Christmas in Luxor. The hotel management also took great pains to provide a worthy setting for the festival: we northerners watched in astonishment as dining-rooms and lounges had their walls 'papered' with white cotton-wool, red Father Christmas figures, silver stars and pictures of snowed-in cottages. A real Christmas-tree had been imported by air from Cyprus and in addition tinsel was hung in cypresses, which gave a surprisingly good illusion. This homage to the atmosphere of a northern Christmas certainly seemed a little paradoxical in a country whose natural features so closely resemble the real Christmas landscape round Jesus' crib. But tradition is evidently stronger than all historic considerations: Europeans no doubt celebrate a Santa Claus Christmas even in Bethlehem.

As the members of our party preferred to spend an Egyptian Christmas which differed from what we were used to, we decided to have Christmas dinner on board *Daphne*. The saloon was decorated with laurel leaves, picked by our police guard in the town park, and in my capacity of host I put on a magnificent Arabian sheik costume which I had bought during our visit to Palmyra. For Mona's culinary art and *Daphne*'s tiny cabin the evening was an acid test: there were seven of us and the dining-table was no bigger than a newspaper, but all went well and the spirits under our skylight, open to a biblical sky of stars, were undoubtedly higher than those round the elegant banqueting-tables in the hotel. Alvar improvized a ballad three pages long in *Daphne*'s guestbook, ending up with the profound lines:

> One should go against the current
> from Tell el Amarna
> to Karna
> (*k* left out by poetic licence).

Not surprisingly, the ruins of Thebes gave us full employment during our ten days in Luxor: despite the enormous damage, the town still possesses the largest and most remarkable collection of ancient ruins that any place can show. One needs months and years rather than days and weeks to see even summarily everything that has been preserved of antiquity's wealthiest city, but not even he who contents himself with seeing the most important can make do with one or two hasty visits: these temples and tombs speak at once so directly and so abstrusely to us that we feel the need of returning, of again and again trying to wrest from them the elusive meaning which at the next second we think we can seize with our hands.

Most majestic of Thebes' ruins is the Karnak temple. It lies a mile or two north of Luxor and was easy to reach either by one of the nice old horse-cabs which waited outside the hotel or by our Lambretta. We had the privilege of being shown round the huge temple precincts both by the chief inspector of archaeology at Luxor, Dr Labib Habachi, and by the French archaeological fantast, Robichon, who has lived for ten years in a hut within the temple area. I discussed the temple's architectonic language of form with Alvar, watched the sunset by the sacred lake with Astri and Juan, and sauntered about alone both by daylight and by moonlight along the sphinx avenues, through the broken seals of the pylons, among the Osiris figures in the temple courtyards and in the forest of columns in the vast hypostyle hall. Yet I seem to have got hardly a superficial general view of this temple, which was the state sanctuary of ancient Egypt and the centre of the mighty Amon cult.

French archaeologists have worked almost unceasingly for more than sixty years in the Karnak temple, but are now being ousted by the Egyptians. At present it is chiefly the great pylon gates which are the object of the archaeologists' care, for when they went to repair one of these massive structures which was beginning to fall to pieces they discovered that the inside of them consisted of nothing but blocks from older temples, almost all with fragments of pictorial reliefs and hieroglyphics. Now the pylons are being systematically taken apart to get at the stones inside them, after which the shells will be built up again round a cement core. The ancient Egyptians' custom of always rebuilding their temples has meant that not a single monument has been preserved from the Middle Kingdom, but the French archaeologist Chevrier has already pieced together, from the puzzle of stones from the pylons' interior, two smaller procession kiosks of very high quality from the XII Dynasty and this is only a beginning. Far greater temples will rise up by degrees beside the Amon temple, restored to the world by the patient work of the archaeologists.

This will be, however, but poor compensation for all that the archaeologists have destroyed. For it is one of the tragic sides of our modern reawakening of the past that historic interest wears away its object, devours it, instead of – as it means to – lifting it out of the mill of time. The sand, the Nile slime and oblivion were the real friends of the ancient Egyptian monuments and if they had been allowed to go on holding tombs, mummies and temples in trust, these would have lasted till Doomsday. But ever since the interest in antiques arose in Egypt – beginning with Napoleon's campaigns – the ancient era has been mined from old Thebes like coal from a richly veined mine. Mummies, paintings, reliefs and statues have been cut up and offered for sale in easily transported bits, to be scattered over the globe, the more important pieces to museums and collections, the simpler ones to the souvenir shelves of private homes. The fate awaiting all these fragments in a troubled world is of little concern: they already lost their chief value when they were torn out of their setting. But even the remaining excavated monuments are threatened by comparatively swift destruction. The paintings of the opened tombs absorb the dampness in the air and are starting to flake. Countless tombs, which on being discovered fifty or a hundred years ago were resplendent with the brightest and clearest colours, are nowadays bare caves; one of the most beautiful and interesting tombs in Thebes, that of Queen Nefertari, has recently been shut to the public in order to delay at least the deterioration that has set in. As for the temples, they have suffered more severe damage during the last fifty years than during the previous five hundred. As long as they lay sunken beneath the slowly rising level of the ground, nothing happened; but as the river-bed, in common with the whole of modern Egypt, lies about thirteen feet higher than it did during antiquity, the water seeps down into the excavated temples' foundations. This water is full of earth-salts and corrodes the bases of the columns, the walls and the granite statues as though they were made of sugar. How many more centuries will the temples at Karnak and Luxor be still standing before they collapse on top of their crumbling bases? The answer depends very largely on the willingness and ability of the Egyptian State to carry out enormous drainage work and to keep the pumps going for centuries.

The Luxor temple is apt to be overshadowed by the mighty buildings at Karnak. It was not really until our down journey, when we stopped at Luxor for the second time, that we could form an idea of this building's special character, through Dr Robichon's imaginative explanation. I shall have more to say of this in a later chapter. But in the log-book I find a note about this temple which concerns something other than ancient Egypt: 'Found Islam, vultures, *el hilm.*' It was an experience which is typical of what we mean by *understanding* – feelings filtered through thoughts – so perhaps I may try to give a brief account of it.

Seventy-five years ago Luxor was a small village which, like a stifling jungle plant, had taken possession of most of the temple ruins. The village also had a mosque, which stood in one of the temple courtyards. By degrees the archaeologists managed to free the temple from the greater part of the parasitic buildings, but the mosque was stubbornly defended by religious fanaticism and is still there. For no apparent reason it stands on a narrow left-over platform of the higher ground-level and can be reached only via an earthen embankment from out of the village. It was late on a Friday afternoon when I visited the temple, all the tourists had gone back to the hotel for dinner and I was alone among the columns, relief walls and Osiris statues. Suddenly two prayer-criers, each in his minaret above my head, began an antiphony as the population, with quiet dignity, came to the hour of prayer in the mosque. I sat down on a block of stone and watched the vultures wheeling above the temple ruins and minarets on huge, tireless wings, like symbols of the powers of destruction and indifference. Yet a calm confidence lay over this holy-day in the ancient land of suffering, a peace that passeth all understanding. All at once I seemed to understand Islam, the special oriental peace which enfolds centuries, desert, river, villages and petty human destinies in its arms. This peace comes from an almighty Allah, who has all will, insight, responsibility in his hand and thereby frees mankind from all unrest. Through daily prayer the Moslem experiences this higher being, sees the insignificance of his own striving, humbles himself, is purified, attains *el hilm*, the soul's calm, which in these countries is so strong that from the subjective experience of the individual it expands into an objective value. Everything here breathes this peace: villages, towns, the whole countryside is permeated with acceptance, with a yielding to nature's laws or Allah's will, however one likes to put it. The result is a kind of friendship with life, a concord, which is foreign to us reformers who want to set the world to rights. A religion created for a world without hope, a faith which helps one both to live and to die under wretched conditions.

But at the same time as, on this afternoon at the Luxor temple, I tasted Islam rather as one samples a drug, I felt with every fibre of my being that I was an utter stranger to this kind of happiness. I was grateful for the heritage of hope and disquiet that Greek culture and Christianity had given me, for the torment without which I could never live. Icarus' defiance and Jesus' doubt and agony on the cross are both equally alien to Islam, but in them lies a force which will transform the world.

It has rightly been pointed out that archaeological finds give us a distorted perspective of the ancient Egyptian community. Since tombs, mummies and temples have been preserved, while dwelling-houses of sun-dried bricks and everything else that could testify to the everyday life of the common people have vanished, we get a hopelessly one-sided view of an existence which may not have been anything like so strongly overshadowed by stone gods and the thought of death as we imagine. This unjust displacement of interest is especially noticeable in Thebes, where two temples are all that is left of the great city on the east bank of the Nile, while the city of death on the west side offers an almost inexhaustible wealth of monuments.

From a tourists' point of view, everything is very well arranged for those who want to visit western Thebes: they have only to cross the river and draw up a suitable programme in proportion to their interest and the time available. We often had ourselves

rowed across by the Nubian boatmen together with our
Lambretta and then drove about between the different temples
and groups of tombs which lie scattered over an area of about
three miles wide and two and a half miles deep, measured from
the river. When our friends were with us we did as all other
tourists: hired one of the many motor-cars which, for a flat rate
of £2, drives a party about wherever it wishes all day long,
miracle cars which might well have been grave-finds themselves,
excavated examples from the car-fleet of the Pharaohs.

If one wishes to visit the chief sight, the famous Valley of the
Kings, more or less in peace, one must be early off the mark –
after eight o'clock, when the electricity-works which illuminates
the most important of the royal tombs is set going, and before
ten, when the main stream of tourists begins to flow. Otherwise
western Thebes is so big that one can for the most part go about
undisturbed and even in the Valley of the Kings it is only three
or four tombs to which the guides conduct their hustled flocks,
the chief of them of course being Tutankhamon's unassuming
but romatically well-known crypt. Other tombs, such as
Horemheb's classically beautiful or Seknaht's endless and
mysterious one, are visited only by a handful of experts; and an
expedition to Thutmose III's out-of-the-way tomb, impressive
in its strict style, still arouses, with its strenuous descent and
brooding mustiness, much of the excitement one likes to associate
with the royal tombs of Thebes. Here one understands the
fascination always exerted by these rock caves hidden away in
lonely clefts, full of gold and the mystery of death. Plundered of
their main treasures even during antiquity and so deeply im-
printed in popular imagination that they recur in countless
variations in the Thousand and One Nights, they have in our
day again become a living myth through gripping detective
stories and illustrated weekly magazines. It is almost impossible
to ward off the question irresistibly conjured up by the sensational
finds of Tutankhamon's unopened tomb and the secreted
mummies of the Pharaohs in the deep crypt of Amenhotep II:
what unrevealed secrets and buried treasure are still hidden
among these rocks?

From the Valley of the Kings it is not far to Deir el Bahari,
where Queen Hatshepsut had her rock temple hewn into the

sheer cliff and laid out broad terraces like steps down to the valley. With this world-embracing architecture, open to the sun, the plain, and the sails gliding on the distant Nile, an architecture so unlike the usual shut-in burial temples, Deir el Bahari shows that lightness, originality and freedom to create new forms were not taboo in the Egyptian art of building. But then this temple is, in common with the Step Pyramid at Sakkara but unlike all other Egyptian buildings, linked with the name of an architect. The creator of Hatshepsut's rock temple was called Senmut and he also played a political rôle as the queen's favourite.

This naturally awakened professional fellow-feeling in Alvar, and when he saw in the guide-book that Senmut's own tomb beside the temple can be visited, he was seized by an overwhelming desire to descend into it in order to pay tribute to his deceased architectural colleague. Unfortunately, we had no torches or even candles with us, only a box of matches. Mona and Elissa refused to budge another inch after the first bend in the stairs, when the distant gleam of light from the doorway disappeared, but Alvar, Edries and I pushed resolutely on. The staircase was very long and an eternity passed before it widened out: to the left lay a small, empty room glistening with incrustations of salt and on the right was a peculiar, caricaturish portrait of Senmut carved into the wall. But the stair-corridor went on obliquely downwards and three men, all of whom want to show how game they are, do not give in straight off. We had the impression of having descended at least as deep as twenty storeys in a block of flats and of having come at least a hundred yards inwards on the horizontal plane when we reached a new chamber; it had a roof with reproduction of stars and celestial bodies. But a new staircase opened up in the other wall – it was as if we were dreaming and ahead of us was a staircase without end.

'Senmut was evidently a sly dog,' Alvar said. 'In life he was used to stealing in to the queen and he wanted to lie near her in death as well: I bet you anything that this corridor leads towards the innermost burial chamber of the rock temple.'

Spurred on by this secret triumph of architecture, Alvar was all for continuing, and as our box of matches was still far from empty we had no objection. After a laborious descent by the light of another dozen matches we reached a third, unfinished chamber.

Had Edries not found a candle-end on the ground we might almost have believed that we were the first human beings since antiquity to have penetrated down here. Edries lighted the candle, and while Alvar and I examined the chamber he went on down a new staircase. It was now that the dramatic climax occurred, understandable only if one considers that our nerves were slightly on edge and the lighting was very dim. After a few minutes Edries came stumbling up the steps with his eyes starting out of his head.

'There are two dead people down there!' he stammered.

What the strong and manly Alvar thought I cannot say. For my own part, I felt the wingtip of Terror brush past me, but plucked up courage to follow Alvar, who grabbed the candle-end from Edries and strode resolutely down the staircase. It was not long and the fourth chamber – at last the actual tomb – soon opened up ahead of us. There we came upon two very embarrassed people, a young couple. We even recognized the young man: it was a French architect who was staying at the Winter Palace . . .

Who says that architects have no feeling for setting and tradition!

After our experiences in the Valley of the Kings and Deir el Bahari we felt the urgent need of a lunch siesta. In this respect, too, western Thebes is well organized: there are two or three so-called 'rest houses', of which Cook's is at Deir el Bahari and another, the Anglo-American Rest House, near the Ramesseum. At both one can eat the hamper brought from the hotel while studying the tourist behaviour of the various western nations. Man is a kind of snail, who normally lives in a protective and supporting shell, the everyday environment we have formed and that forms us. When we no longer have this shell around us we become absurd in the same way as naked people. In western Thebes' setting of rocky desert, large solemn temples, tombs and eternity, the tourist, with his clothes full of buttons, his home jargon and his clumsy attempts to hold his own through intelligent or witty comments, becomes an utterly ridiculous figure. These ageing Frenchwomen with pretentions to Parisian elegance, these severe Englishmen who kept silent so that nobody would assume familiarity with them, these fish-out-of-water Americans with film cameras and bored wives, what did they think of us as we sat there like loud-voiced Nordic barbarians, filled with our democratic self-esteem and roaring with laughter at Alvar's juicy comments on the incident in Senmut's tomb?

Outside the rest houses the tourists are stormed by children and adults who offer false antiques for sale. Nowadays the vendors are compelled to have a sign with the word IMITATIONS among their treasures spread out on the ground, but by a strange coincidence a child usually happens to be sitting in front of the sign when the most opulent-looking customers approach. Actually, after one has haggled for a while, the prices are low enough to warrant the purchase of a sample of this traditional local homecraft – bits of reliefs, scarabs, pieces of mummy sheaths or the god Bes with giant phallus. The imitations are often so skilfully done that the tourist with any imagination can delude both his better judgment and his friends at home. There is no doubt that the descendants of the grave-robbers are still capable of tracking down genuine antiques, but those are more likely to be sold through the antique dealers in Luxor and the really valuable things are smuggled to Cairo.

But I must return to the sights of western Thebes, which of course I have no intention of enumerating in detail, but whose main groups I cannot help commenting upon. In some ways, the greatest experience here is the private tombs, or the tombs of the nobility, as they are called, as distinct from the resting-places of the Pharaohs. To date, about 20,000 such tombs are supposed to be known, but if one considers the thousand years or more during which the wealthy inhabitants of this great city interred their dead here, one can be quite sure that there are many tombs as yet undiscovered. Most of the known burial-chambers were plundered and destroyed a very long time ago and are today mere empty holes in the rock, but in perhaps a thousand of them larger or smaller remains of the adornment are still there – mostly paintings, as the stone at Thebes is not the kind suitable for the coloured bas-reliefs found at Sakkara. Of the painted tombs, nowadays barred up and shown by custodians, there are really no more than about fifty which the ordinary, non-expert tourist has any occasion to visit. A comparison may perhaps be drawn with the descent into Italy's Etruscan tombs, except that the latter – which are about a thousand years more recent – are, with their archaic angularity and far from refined sexuality, incomparably more primitive. The Thebes tombs sometimes give an almost neat and pretty impression, with their bright colours, their graceful figures of girls and their vivid narrative style. Here the weightless, intellectual side of Egyptian pictorial art scores a triumph: the effect at times is akin to modern painting's play with form and colour, especially when one sees isolated fragments of the paintings, such as are found in books on art with coloured reproductions. This free interpretation of the tomb-paintings as works of art is inevitable for us, but we should bear in mind that it corresponds to the fellahs' method of making excellent sandals out of old car tyres. The tomb-paintings of Thebes were created with the same magic intent as the reliefs of Sakkara; through them certain imagined happenings took place automatically, so to say, inside the closed tombs. It was the religious pictures, those which reproduced the mysteries of the Osiris cult, which were the most important, but with their stereotyped repetitions they interest us less than the pictures of the deceased man's imagined life in the underworld, these vivid depictions of the idealized continuation of existence complete with flowering gardens, festive boards, industrious servants, musicians and pretty dancing-girls.

A special group is formed by the tomb-workers' tombs at Deir el Medineh, where the craftsmen who decorated the burial-chambers of the Pharaohs carved out and painted tombs for themselves in their spare time. It is pathetic to find again in these small, humble tombs the refined court style and the great Pharaoh motifs in miniature. The tomb-workmen's little town close by has also been excavated and is one of the very few places where one can study ancient Egyptian domestic architecture for the common people. The resemblance to a modern fellah village is striking, the houses enclose in the same way a cramped inner courtyard, from which a staircase leads to the upper storey.

Finally, there are the Pharaoh's burial-temples, which stand in a mighty line on the edge of the cultivated plain far from the secret tombs in the Valley of the Kings. Ramses III's huge temple at Medinet Habu, Ramses II's Ramesseum and Seti I's temple at Gourna are all well preserved: of others there are only fragments left. The famous Memnon statues belonged to Amenhotep III's burial-temple, where, in the usual way, they flanked a pylon, but even at the time of the Roman emperors the temple had disappeared and the statues stood, alone and paradoxical, on the plain, regarded with amazement by the tourists of that age, who scrawled their names on their socles in the same way as the new tourists two thousand years later. Details like this help us to understand the immense age of the Egyptian monuments: in their presence both the Emperor Hadrian and ourselves become modern fellow-believers.

There are also features in the temples' reliefs which remind us of something we are apt to forget when confronted with the extreme refinement of Egyptian culture: that we are dealing after all with an almost primeval age, beyond the grasp of our mentality. One of the reliefs at Medinet Habu shows prisoners-of-war being led forward to the triumphant Ramses and two mounds piling up, one consisting of chopped-off hands, the other of severed penises, whose numbers are carefully noted down by the scribes present.

The Ramasseum is the Theban temple that appeals most directly to a westerner's aesthetic sense and we could not resist rounding off every expedition to the west bank with a sunset visit among these colonnades in order to take part in the transfiguration and apotheosis that for a few short moments each day turn Egypt into the Garden of Eden. Yet we knew that the beauty of the Ramesseum is due to the whim of time and decay, which have made of this enclosed and immeasurable Egyptian temple a kind of Parthenon in a more robust style, by lifting away the outer walls, allowing the columns to open up to the landscape and limiting the building to a nucleus. Here the sunlight finds its way in everywhere and one can sit as in a theatre, where a broken recumbent granite colossus and a god's head without a nose illustrate the drama of the death of civilizations with consummate effect, while the sprouting green of the tilled plain shows the renewal of life.

Several times during our excursions in western Thebes we had passed a village of very unusual appearance: it was obviously inhabited by ordinary fellahs, but with its brand-new, whitewashed and arched houses resembled a Cycladian rather than an Egyptian village. One day, unable to control our curiosity, we swung in with our Lambretta to an architectonic space which one never sees in Egyptian villages, but which was undoubtedly a public square. The village was only partly inhabited and a young man who came up when we stopped explained that its name was New Gourna. He spoke scarcely a word of English but led us eagerly to a house near the market-place. In this way we made the acquaintance of Hassan Fathy, an architect, a teacher at the academy of art in Cairo and the creator of New Gourna.

The use of tombs as dwellings in Egypt must go far back in time, and the cave community which has established itself in western Thebes under the name of Gourna is probably composed of direct descendants of those who once hewed and decorated the old tombs. Their feelings of ownership in the matter of antiques are at any rate ineradicable and, faced with the impossibility of keeping an eye on their manipulations with the tombs as long as they went on living among them, the authorities in charge of ancient monuments decided during the 1930s to move the entire population to a new and modern village outside the burial area. Apart from wanting to put an end to the treasure-hunting and the sale of paintings piecemeal to tourists, the government wished to do away with a social eyesore which gave foreigners a poor opinion of conditions in Egypt. A large credit was granted and Fathy was commissioned as architect to build the new Gourna.

He set to work very ambitiously. A community with public square, mosque, two primary schools, vocational school for adults, sports ground, open-air theatre, market-place, in short a model village of a type never before seen in fellah-Egypt, took shape on his drawing-board. Thanks to unremitting energy and burning enthusiasm he did succeed, despite war, changes of government and revolutions, in carrying the scheme through: after untold difficulties the main part of New Gourna is now completed and the houses are ready to receive their new inmates. An unexpected complication has arisen, however: on one pretext or another the people have refused to move in. Now they make out that there is no room for the water-buffaloes and donkeys, now that they cannot leave their neighbours. The truth is that all illegal chances of gain are threatened and the fellahs are afraid of the moral turning over of a new leaf which the rôle of inhabitants in a model village implies. When we visited the village only about a hundred families, mostly those who had taken part in the building work, had moved in – the others had promised to come when the whole thing was quite ready.

'It's a question of patience,' Fathy said, full of confidence. 'We have to convince them that they will be better off here.'

He himself had settled down in one of the fellah houses, built of sun-dried bricks like the others, and lived here as a prophet of his idea. There was no doubt that he had succeeded, on a small scale at least, in realizing his dream of the fellah-village's social rebirth on a traditional basis. His devoted work, personal contact with each family, modesty and authority had prevailed on the 500 or so people who already lived in the village to comply with his ideals: they were spirited, honest, polite, clean, progressive, social, successful, quick to learn, content, democratic and obstinate in the right way.

'They're fine lads these, a bit cheeky and hot-tempered, but otherwise all right,' Fathy said of two broadly-grinning youths who were hard at it bricklaying in what was to be the vocational school. 'Last week they gave a good thrashing to some hooligans from the old village who came to molest us. The elder one in his spare time has built himself a really good house down by the market-place, he's thinking of getting married . . . '

We heard an echo of welfare preachers all over the world, descendants of the priests of former times who praised the Christian sense of their parishioners just as unctuously as the missionaries of socialism now preach their gospel. But Fathy's architectonic ideas certainly sounded attractive. He considered that the clearance of the fellah-villages should be based on the fellah's own work and not on industrial building materials. The raw material for the traditional sun-dried mud bricks is to be found everywhere and houses built of them need not be inferior if they are rightly planned. By means of simple trade schools he wanted to teach the peasants the ancient art of vaulting, which can be studied even in the Ramesseum's storerooms, and by example he tried to stimulate the peasants themselves to plan their new houses better. Baking-ovens and fireplaces Fathy had made the same in New Gourna as they had always been, but flagrant inconveniences were done away with: humans and animals no longer lived together, but there were special stalls joined to the houses; dung-heaps, which are hotbeds of flies, were covered over and the fuel, which in normal villages is kept on the roof at great risk of fire, was stored in covered lofts above the manure-heaps. I am giving all these details because no problem is more acute in present-day Egypt than the question of the clearance of the fellah-villages. Fathy's solution pays the greatest possible regard to traditions, to everything of value in the old community cells. New Gourna is the prototype of a modernization which wants to avoid the humdrum sameness of industrialism and which tries to maintain contact with handicrafts, the fellowship of the village and the true life-values. Fathy told us with sorrow that his efforts to interest the men of the new régime in these ideas had failed: in high quarters in Cairo they would not hear of sun-dried bricks and spontaneously self-built villages; they preferred to go in for terrace-housing, mass-produced materials, centralized planning.

Unfortunately, I think the officials in Cairo are right. In the great Egyptian need, New Gourna is a romantic whim, an undertaking which has succeeded because the government has staked a great deal of money and Fathy his conviction on it. Otherwise, the road to a higher standard of living for the masses leads inescapably through industrialization, rationalization and mass production, however catastrophic this may be for the aesthetic and individual factors. The task of modern architecture, therefore, is not to cling to the pre-industrial conditions but, on this side of the great change in production, to try to lessen its drawbacks, to conceal the stereotyped and breathe new life into the soulless. Fathy's illusion is that his work can be victorious through its own power, that New Gourna can become a seed which in due course will be the means of other equally splendid villages spreading all over a splendid Egypt of the future. In fact, New Gourna rests entirely on his personality, his presence; the minute he moves away the village will, within a few years, be absorbed and merge beyond recognition into the old fellah-Egypt – until the time is ripe for the industrialized Egypt which will inevitably come.

This view did not prevent us from taking great pleasure in our acquaintanceship with Fathy and in his gentle manner, so full of implicit faith, of showing us his creation. We chanced to mention

Ramses III's archers, Medinet
Habu, Thebes

The Pharaoh Sesostris I worshipping the god Amon
Re. Relief in the processional kiosk, Karnak

The falcon god
Horus gives the
Pharaoh Seti I the
symbol of life.
Sketch for unfin-
ished relief in the
king's tomb, Thebes

Luxor's famous snake-charmer

The turning-point of our voyage, the Great Cataract at Wadi Halfa

Alvar Aalto's name and noticed with some astonishment that Fathy had not the vaguest idea who he was. As I suspected that my dear compatriot was unlikely to appreciate such innocence in a fellow-architect, should they happen to meet, I laid it on rather thickly:

'What! You don't know the world's greatest architect after Imhotep and Senmut, who is at present in Luxor?'

Fathy must have rooted in a reference book, for the very same evening he paid a call on Alvar at the hotel and invited us all to lunch the following day at New Gourna.

After lunch we inspected the bright, pleasant primary school, saw free vaulting with mud bricks according to a 4,000-year-old technique and in addition had the luck to see a dress rehearsal for a festival which the people of Gourna were to present on the following day before the Luxor tourists in order to collect money for the new school. The first part of the programme consisted of stick-fencing between the young men of the village, a peculiar sport which looks like a ritual dance but in its import resembles European fencing with foils. The handling of this traditional weapon, the wooden stick with a core of iron, has given rise to feints, parries and named movements which make competition possible in front of expert judges. The second part of the entertainment was something far more foreign to the performers than to the audience: it was a play about love and jealousy, interspersed with folk dances and songs. Women had neither wished nor been allowed to take part and so the heroine had to be played by a young boy, who was teased so unmercifully by his pals that it needed every ounce of Fathy's authority to make him appear. The performance was given in Gourna's open-air theatre with its horse-shoe rows of seats for the audience, an architectural creation of a value as yet beyond the grasp of western Thebes' descendants of the grave-robbers. If the world-wide tendency for all to think alike continues, however, it is probable that even the next generation of Gourna inhabitants will perform *Hamlet* at their theatre and their children may actually understand the remarkable problems of constricted sexual complexes and life's mental anguish.

'Aren't there any blackguards left?' Alvar asked after the show, and our hosts raised their eyebrows. 'I mean some fellow who goes and digs up his mother-in-law and sells her piecemeal as a mummy to the Americans?'

'Oh yes, there are of course troublesome elements among those who are still living in the primitive cave dwellings. It will take years before we manage to re-educate them,' was the answer.

'We had better go off and see them before it's too late,' Alvar said genially, whereupon we thanked our hosts for their hospitality and went off to the burial-city.

Before I finish this chapter about our visit to ancient Thebes, I must tell of our descent into Petamonab's temple-tomb and the key to the mentality of the ancient Egyptians that I believe I found. The reason why this tomb made a deeper impression on us than both the royal tombs and Cairo's Pyramids was probably that we came face to face here with a really untouched and primitive ancient Egyptian setting of quite a different kind from that offered by the places exploited by tourism. For it cannot be denied that the sale of admission tickets to the Cheops Pyramid, the electric light which transforms Tutankhamon's sarcophagus into a shop-window and the eloquent dragomans with their hordes of tourists have a lamentable way of robbing the monuments of the magic that even the nineteenth-century travellers could still sense so strongly.

I had been given a special letter of introduction by the superintendent of antiquities in Cairo to the supervisor of the monuments in western Thebes, Inspector Ibrahim, and on this account he had arranged to meet us one morning in his office. For some reason he was not there and after having waited in vain for an hour we set off to wander about on our own. This misunderstanding was our good luck, as the worthy inspector was so remorseful over his forgetfulness that on the following day, when Mona and I met him by chance, he offered to show us any monuments we liked, 'even those that are closed to the public'. This gave me an idea: in the Guide Bleu I had read some surprising lines in small print after the description of the usual, well-known monuments: *The finest and most important tomb in the whole of the Theban necropolis, including even the royal tombs, is the temple-tomb of Petamonab, which unfortunately, owing to work in this part of the area, is quite inaccessible.* I now told Inspector Ibrahim that we would like very much to visit Petamonab's tomb. His reluctance was plain: visits to the tomb were really forbidden and moreover they were both difficult and dangerous; he himself had not been there for several years. All this of course merely whetted our curiosity and we did not budge until we were assigned two proven guides, who, armed with paraffin lamps and rope-ladders, conducted us to a lattice-door deep down in a shaft.

The door opened into a large rock hall, where fallen stones, pieces of sarcophagus, mummy bindings and clay cones with hieroglyphics lay scattered over the floor. The guides took off their ankle-length galabias and we started off down a sloping passage at least ten feet wide, the walls of which were covered with inscriptions. We realized now why the men had undressed: the deeper we went the hotter it became. Even though we knew that it was Egypt's scorching summer heat that was spending the winter down here, we could easily imagine that we were descending into a burning Inferno. The passage divided, twisted sharply, became an endless flight of steps – it was a labyrinth without a plan and without an end. Soon we came upon the first mummies of the thousands which have been buried down here. Thieves hunting for amulets had stripped off their bindings, many bodies lay in pieces, but some were fantastically well preserved, with fine, manicured nails and ascetic, spiritualized faces, whose inscrutable, lofty expressions inspired a deep respect.

Twice we came to deep, vertical shafts, which we descended with the aid of our rope-ladders. The passages and stairs continued. The air, which from the outset had been charged with the peculiar reek of ammonia from the urine of the countless bats – a smell which permeates all Egyptian tombs and temple chambers – gradually grew so heavy and pungent that we could hardly breathe and our eyes started to run. The mummies obviously contributed to the smell with the natron and the aromatic substances which the ancient embalmers stuffed into stomachs, chests and heads. At last we reached the deepest, innermost chamber, a high, vaulted room. We were rather crestfallen to find that it was empty and less interesting than all that we had seen in the passages. On the way up we again passed hundreds of yards of inscriptions, vast reliefs and, here and there, sculptures of gods hewn out of the actual rock. When, after clambering for an hour and a half over fallen blocks of stone and stumbling along passages and up and down staircases, we found ourselves once more in the entrance hall, our guides urged us to sit down and breathe quietly for fifteen minutes before leaving the tomb – their experience had taught them that otherwise one is apt to faint from reaction when breathing the fresh air. But the psychological readjustment to the world of the living took a much longer time than the physical, and if, after an hour or two, we managed to rid ourselves of the purely bodily nightmare of suffocating confinement, the memory of this expedition remained as a pointer to an inner dimension which one finds recurring in all Egyptian creations.

Oswald Spengler's work *Der Untergang des Abendlandes* has many pages which are debatable, but it also contains profitable thoughts, of which the discovery that human beings during different cultural epochs have experienced space in different ways is one of the most fascinating. The feeling of Gothic and baroque architecture for infinite space, made rhythmical by movement, perspective and screening-off, is just as apparent as the way the Greeks imagined the world as a collection of plastic bodies at different distances from each other and Arabic-Byzantine architecture is allied to the space-conception of the cave. According to Spengler, the Egyptian feeling for space is characterized by *the way*: just as the Nile was the straight, obvious way through Egypt, the temples and the creations of pictorial art were axially conceived in relation to straight procession routes. Such an interpretation may seem correct if one studies the archaeological literature about Egypt and it was on this that Spengler based his ideas. The descent into Petamonab's tomb awakened in me a question which had lain dormant ever since I visited the Pyramids and the Cairo Museum: is it not *the nucleus* rather than the way which marks the Egyptian formation of space?

Visits to the interiors of the Pyramids and tombs convince us that the Egyptians were obsessed by a love of confinement which is the direct opposite of the claustrophobia, the feeling of suffocation, that torments us in these cramped passages and chambers. We should remember that both pyramids, rock tombs and even temples during antiquity were shut off by barriers and doors, they were not accessible by ways along which one could walk, but were shells in which one *imagined* the dead Pharaoh resting as a kernel in the centre of the Pyramid, just as one knew that the god, embodied in the cult image, dwelt inside the temple walls in a sealed chest in the innermost chamber. The common people presumably could never see their gods, but the knowledge that they were there in the temples was enough. This imagined nucleus recurs in everything the Egyptians created, even in the sculptures, which give one the feeling that the entire outer form encloses a conceived centre, the statue's soul. The magic effect the Egyptian statues exercise even on us is due to this very nucleus, intensely present the whole time to the sculptor and round which he creates his forms. This also gives the Egyptian buildings and sculptures their extraordinary weight: they can, like the Sphinx and the Pyramids, lose their shell yet still preserve their entire authority. While a Greek sculpture or building lives in its skin-like surface, the Memnon statues speak with a voice which comes from within.

The visit to Petamonab's tomb rounded off our first visit to Thebes very effectively. When, after ten days of varied study of the monuments and the pleasant company of our friends, we decided to continue our Nile journey, it was not because we thought we had seen enough of the ancient capital, but because so much else awaited us along the winding and adventurous course of the great river.

CHAPTER IX

To the First Cataract

The morning of December 30th was filled with preparations for departure. Surrounded by cardboard boxes full of provisions, luggage and a case of Carlsberg pilsner, which we had not yet had time to stow away, we waved good-bye to Astri and Juan, who were going back to Stockholm. The luggage and the pilsner belonged to our new passengers, Elissa and Alvar, who, braving our alarming accounts of navigation on the Nile, wanted to come with us for three or four days. Luckily, the wind at first was as lazy as it is in the North early on a summer's morning; only a few light puffs filled our sails now and again and we could devote ourselves to putting the stores away and installing the professor and his wife in the after-cabin, which Edries had temporarily vacated. We also had time for several discreet groundings, suitable as a mild warning to our unsuspecting guests of the kind of adventure that was inevitable. Alvar at once began to keep an illustrated log-book, chock-full of nautical terms. Over his shoulder I could read: '§1. No glass yet at the first grounding, sheered port and starboard. Depth 4' 4".' The gentle hint resulted in the Master's being served instantly a foaming glass of his life's elixir.

Not far from Luxor is the beginning of a district which is dominated by sugar production. There are three large sugar factories in Upper Egypt, all owned by the industrial pascha Ahmed Abud: Nag Hammadi, Armant, which we were now approaching, and Kom Ombo, whose acquaintance we were to make later – involuntarily but all the more thoroughly. These factories are only in operation during the short period of harvest, as the sugar-cane must be treated within thirty hours after being cut. For six weeks, therefore, work goes on feverishly all round the clock, both out in the fields, on the river and in the factories, where the machines run non-stop. The whole of this vast apparatus, which employs tens of thousands of people, had just been started at Armant. We saw battalions of white-clad men hard at work on the man-high canes along the river bank, while others were loading specially built barges, each with ten small railway trucks lined up edgeways. Tugs were bustling about on the river, towing the filled barges to Armant and leaving empty ones at the fields.

The wind increased, but we did not run aground so often, thanks to the guidance we had from the many craft on the river. After only two hours we reached Armant, the Hermontis of antiquity, whose monuments were swallowed up in the 1860s by the sugar-mill, which lies not far from the river. A huge crane was lifting the laden railway trucks, which rolled up to the mill in a constant stream. We sailed along a surprisingly neat strand promenade, lined with well-built houses, reached the pascha's magnificent villa in Swiss chalet style and were again out among the sugar-fields. The absence of the villages and fellahs of the usual Nile landscape, the fields of sugar-cane stretching for mile after mile and resembling bamboo forests, and small inlets where a solitary rowing-boat lay moored beneath slender palms, while blue mountain peaks could be glimpsed in the background – all this formed a totally new environment which almost made us feel we were sailing along the shore of a South Sea island. The ideal sailing wind tempted us to set the big balloon; *Daphne* made top speed and we got past all the shoals – no wonder spirits ran high on board.

We had told the police in Luxor that Matana was our next port of call and shortly after sunset we reached this small industrial centre, where we tied up alongside a big barge. But its skipper must have had a special reason for not wanting police-guard on board during the night, or perhaps he was just a dangerous kind of practical joker. He asked us at once why we stopped at Matana when the town of Esna was so near.

'You see those lights over there – that's the Esna dam, only four miles from here. The river's straight and deep; you can be there in an hour.'

It was tempting to get to Esna and perhaps pass the lock the same evening. We should be able then to devote the whole morning to the temple . . . But was it certain that the channel was easy and free from risk for such a deep boat as ours? Mona was against going on, our passengers had no views on the matter, but when the bargee again assured us that it was all right, Edries and I decided to take the chance.

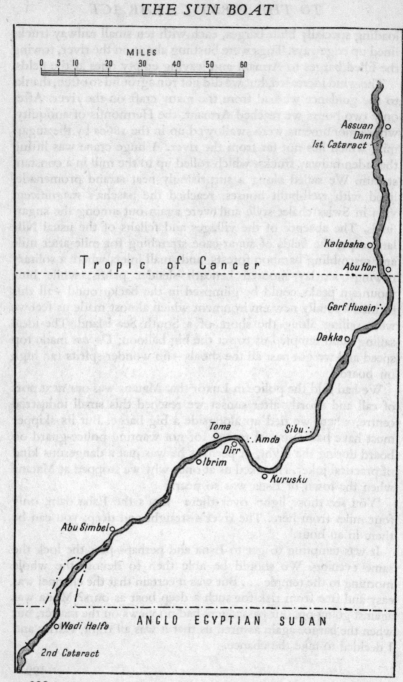

MILES

0 5 10   20   30   40   50   60

Assuan
Dam
Ist. Cataract

Kalabsha

Tropic of Cancer

Abu Hor

Garf Husein

Dakka

Toma
Sibu
Amda
Dirr
Ibrim
Kurusku

Abu Simbel

ANGLO EGYPTIAN SUDAN

Wadi Halfa

2nd Cataract

A delicate new moon lay like a boat in the heavens – or like
the horned crescent moon on the head of the goddess Hathor.
The shoreline was but dimly visible and the sparse lights of the
villages paled under the bright starry sky, but straight ahead of
us, beyond a slight bend in the river, shone the necklace of electric
lights on the Esna dam – quite near, we thought. Edries took
soundings, I stood by the mizen-mast steering with my foot,
Mona was disapprovingly quiet and Alvar tried to find the
Andromeda nebula with the prism binoculars. All went well for
half an hour, until Edries reported one and a half fathoms. We tried
to go over towards the starboard bank but in that direction it only
got shallower. Things went better on the other side and we nosed
our way cautiously to port, ran aground, backed off, ran aground
again. We got floated again, but before we could get steerage-way
the strong current had swept us on to a large sandbank. There we
stuck fast, in much the same way as at Daphne Island.

Mona could now control herself no longer: why couldn't we
have had our dinner at Matana in peace, why did I insist on taking
such risks, why did I have something in my nature which *always*
enticed me to leave the substance for the shadow . . . Remarks
like this are also a kind of encouragement – or at any rate a goad.
The engine, Edries and I mustered our last ounce of strength,
we backed and pushed and wrenched – all without result. Happily,
our guests saw the funny side of our predicament and Alvar
studied with interest the different methods we tried out in order to
get floated. When neither engine nor current helped, we launched
the dinghy and rowed like galley-slaves against the strong current
to get the anchor out. Straining every nerve and muscle, we then
wound in the anchor-chain inch by inch, certain that the boat was
moving. But it was only the anchor which slowly ate its way
through the sand. We put out again in the dinghy through the
swirling current to sound the extent of the shoal. Just as we had
managed to fight our way back to *Daphne*, one of the rowlocks
snapped off. If Edries in a flash had not flung the painter to Alvar
we would have been carried away into the darkness at a speed of
five knots, unable to get back. Over three hours had passed since
we ran aground and now we gave in reluctantly. Mona served an
excellent ravioli dinner with Chianti and the gloom lifted. Better
luck tomorrow. We turned in, exhausted, Edries slept on the

floor under the table in his sleeping-bag; it had been arranged that he was to find lodgings ashore during the time that the Aaltos were with us, but on this night it was easier said than done.

Edries and I got up in the chilly dawn and could hardly believe our eyes when we looked about us: the whole of this reach of the river below the dam was filled with sandbanks and it was amazing that we got as far as we did in the darkness. We wondered whether the malevolent bargee was taking a morning stroll along the shore to gloat over his work, but there was not a soul to be seen, only the houses of Esna far away near the dam. To make a long story short, we managed after four hours' toil – spurred on by Mona's taunts, such as: 'Perhaps this will teach you not to be so rash!' and 'If women had their way, the world would be a much more sensible place!' – to turn the boat ninety degrees and get afloat with the help of the current. Worn out, but quite pleased with ourselves, we steered cautiously towards Esna and about ten o'clock met an aiasa manned with seamen, soldiers and Esna's chief of police who had come to help us. It was one of *Daphne's* prouder moments when the rescue party in its turn ran aground and we could pull it off and tow it to the lock.

Having passed the dam, we tied up alongside a house-boat in the town. The courteous chief of police led us to a grey-painted, covered van which was furnished with a grating over the tiny windows – plainly the local Black Maria. He spoke no English and for a moment we wondered if perhaps we had misunderstood the situation and really were guests, but we climbed in all the same. When the door was again opened we were relieved to see not a prison yard but the upper portions of Esna's temple, which lies in a deep pit in the middle of the town. The ground here has risen more than thirty feet through the 'cultural stratification' of the centuries and so far only the large colonnade had been laid bare; considerable remains of the rest of the temple are presumably still under the cluster of houses which hover on the brink of the yawning shaft. The building is from a very late period, begun by the Emperor Tiberius and completed under Trajanus, but it is utterly Egyptian in its architecture – an eloquent witness to the cultural authority of the Nile land. For of all the Roman Empire's vassal states there was only one which withstood the victorious inroads of Hellenism and made the emperors forget the splendour of the Corinthian columns, just as there was only one culture which made even the Greeks feel a trifle like barbarians: ancient Egypt. Alvar was fascinated by this colonnade right in the middle of the modern town, I could see his architect's fingers itching to design a town-plan for Esna with a terraced public square, in which the temple hall would stand as a gateway to a modern Community Centre. Altogether, Esna seemed a pleasant spot in all its primitiveness; it was an active, surprising and charming town. We made our way back to the river on foot and Alvar, on passing a shop, found something that is very unusual in Mohammedan towns: a bottle of Italian vermouth. Edries found something still more unexpected: a dark-skinned cousin who was a schoolteacher in the town.

Despite these distractions we got away from Esna by one o'clock. The wind was fainter than on the previous day, the sun blazed down and all the afternoon we led a Riviera life in swim-suits, while villages and palm-groves glided past. For us, who were already rather bored with fellah villages, there was nothing unusual about the scenery, but our guests were all agog and photographed so fast that they barely had time to reload their cameras.

'We have not seen bad architecture now for several hours,' Alvar commented towards evening.

In particular, it was the villages' good lines he appreciated, the horizontal walls and the roofs, the dovecotes' tower clusters, the pylon shapes of the mud-brick buildings, sloping naturally inwards, and the colour of the houses – always due to the clay, but therefore also varying, as the tones of the clay are different in each village. For once, the misused word *organic* fits this architecture: as the needs of the family grow, a room-cube is simply added, and when they lessen, it is left to wither and crumble away. One sees as many decayed parts of a house in a fellah village as dead branches in a forest.

On our map we had found a small square with the words *El Kula Pyramid* near the village of Bisalya, which we approached just before sunset. Sure enough: an unmistakable triangular silhouette appeared behind the palm-trunks on the shore. While we were looking through the glasses at this phenomenon, unique in Upper Egypt, we heard whistling and shouting: on a low, bare sandbank by the sloping shore stood some police-soldiers, waving. They were evidently our night watchmen, who had been sent out from Esna. We made fast and gratefully left *Daphne* in their care so that before nightfall we could have a look at the mysterious El Kula pyramid. We clambered up the bank of the Nile and made our way along narrow paths between green fields o the outskirts of a straggling village: there lay the pyramid, which seemed to shrink at every step we took. When we got up o it we found a monument no higher than a four-storeyed house. It was rather carelessly built of small blocks of stone but had all the signs of a step pyramid. Edries asked some men who had ollowed us out of curiosity what they knew about the monument and was told that a European expedition had been there seven years before and in its futile search for an entrance had destroyed one entire side of the pyramid. If the Egyptian authorities had not said stop, the whole thing would have been pulled to pieces, the men made out.

There was indeed an enormous breach in one side. The thought that this pyramid was still guarding its secret stimulated Alvar intensely. After we had climbed it – easily done, as it was like a staircase with steps two feet high – he began to hunt about for the entrance.

'What we must find is a row of stone blocks supported in such a way that those underneath can be removed without causing the others to collapse . . .'

As the whole pyramid seemed to me far too badly built to be real, I said that it was probably a solid pile of stone, perhaps a late-antique monument erected by some Roman governor with a passion for antiquity.

'Pity,' Alvar said. 'Just when I was sure I had found the entrance.'

I have not yet dared to tell him that two months later, when I again met the Egyptian archaeologist Zakaria Goneim, the discoverer of the new step pyramid at Sakkara, I asked him what he thought about the El Kula pyramid and was told that it is one of the oldest in Egypt and undoubtedly has a secret entrance.

While we were busy with our pyramid research one or two men came up and said that the richest man in Bisalya, Sheik Tourist, had invited us to his house. The name piqued our curiosity.

TO THE FIRST CATARACT

Arrived at his house in the quickly falling dusk, we were met by his eldest son, who conducted us in through the column-flanked gateway to an ordinary mud-brick house. Two 500-candlepower gas lamps changed the reception-room into a film studio; the sheik, a dignified old man who had been a deputy in Farouk's parliament, asked us to sit down on one of the benches covered with oriental rugs, a shrill, scratchy gramophone was set going and glasses of tea were brought in by a coal-black servant. After the first exchange of conventional phrases Alvar asked, through Edries, how it was that our host had a western name?

'Why should only Europeans be tourists?' the sheik said, and then asked what Alvar's own name was.

'Sheik Alvar,' came the answer, and the two men exchanged an amused smile of understanding.

Edries stayed on at the sheik's house for the night in order to solve the problem of a place to sleep, while we returned to *Daphne*. It was New Year's Eve and Mona waved her magic wand and produced a delicious New Year's dinner on our little paraffin stove. The evening finished on a gay note, to the accompaniment of that volatile, jocular and pithy philosophizing in which Alvar is a master. Here I must touch on something which the reader may already have surmised: there is no doubt at all in my mind that Alvar Aalto is one of the few really great artists of our time. The innermost emotion I have felt at the sight of the Town Hall in the small Finnish industrial town of Säynätsalo and of one or two wall surfaces at the Jyväskylä University is something which otherwise I have experienced only in the presence of the greatest works in architecture of past centuries. Association with Alvar has for me, therefore, a value which far exceeds the pleasure taken in intelligent and stimulating company: it gives me an insight into both his own creations and into the problems of art in general. During this New Year's symposium at El Kula it struck me that if it was already a privilege to be sailing on the Nile and seeing the monuments of ancient Egypt, it was still a greater one to be doing so together with the man who creates what are perhaps the finest temples and pyramids of our own age. We spoke quite a lot on this evening of Egypt's monuments and I was impressed, as so often before, by Alvar's unique relationship to history and the past. We know that the pioneers of modern architecture are not anti-traditional: Le Corbusier's love of the Greek temples is no less than that of the neo-classic architects, it is merely freed from imitation of the external forms and concentrated on the actual principles of building. Alvar, too, has a marked feeling for traditions, but it is plain that he is less interested in the old buildings than in those who created them, that he is more concerned with Senmut, Pheidias and Michelangelo such as he imagines them than with the constructive or formal features of their creations. For him the living human being is in the centre, neither the heroic superman in pursuit of the absolute nor the neutralized Welfare State man, but an independent, dauntless type of human being, curiously composed of great qualities and small obsessions, which I rather suspect Alvar got to know among the rowdy urchins in the Jyväskylä of his childhood, though he has subsequently completed the right spirit of brotherhood with both Anatole France, Brunelleschi and Catullus.

In any case, it is this special type of personality which determines Alvar's entire attitude to life and art, he bears it within him as a yardstick with which everything is measured: will this train of thought, this anecdote, town-plan, book, piece of furniture, building or fellow human being hold good in the eyes of the idealized street-fight companions of his youth?

In other words, one can say that Alvar's life and work have an entirely ethical tendency: in him the aesthetic side, like all astute theories and analyses with scientific pretentions to truth, which attempt to influence life and architecture, is subservient to an incorruptible and definite human ideal.

If one knows this 'secret' of Alvar's, one is not surprised that he is the most untheoretical and concrete person imaginable. He does interest himself in abstract ideas, but only so far as he can assimilate them, use them for his aims. Everything he has read and heard—classical quotations, technical building inventions, analyses of political economy, jokes in *The New Yorker* – pop up when he needs them, but only as obedient servants. He does formulate ideas himself: most of his creations are actually based on an original architectonic idea, a brainwave he has had, but it never becomes an idea illustrated by a building; on the contrary, it is a building which acquires life and meaning through the idea. In this capacity to hold his own against an intellectualized culture and never to lose contact with the human and concrete aspect, lies much of Alvar's greatness as human being and artist.

Edries found us fast asleep when he came back from the village at dawn on New Year's Day. We got ourselves up by degrees and started off in the clear, calm morning, accompanied for part of the way by our pyramid, which moved along with us beyond the palm-trees on the shore. Alvar sat drawing in our guest-book, Mona and Elissa were busy in the pantry and Edries was beaming from ear to ear after all the hospitality he had received from Sheik Tourist. The only one who felt a gnawing anxiety was the skipper: why was *Daphne*'s kelson covered with water high above the ballast-pigs? The boat had always been as tight as a bottle and something must have happened during the grounding of the day before. True, we had a good pump and the trouble of pumping once a day was not a disaster, but I had an uncomfortable feeling that south of Cairo there was probably not a single boat-yard where a keel-boat like *Daphne* could be drawn up on dry ground for repairs.

After a good three hours the town, or rather the large village, of Edfu appeared beyond a bend in the river, overshadowed by the huge temple. Like so many other villages, Edfu keeps at a respectful distance from the Nile, to which it merely sends out a long street lined with hovels. We made fast to a rusty iron motorboat which plied between the village and the railway station on the east bank, and having got hold of two soldiers to guard the boat we set off gaily in a rattling, bobbing landau up to the temple. Edfu's temple is better preserved than any other temple in Egypt: it looks almost newly-built. One need not study the Guide Bleu to know that the temple dates from the Ptolemaic age: the coarse design of the reliefs and the far too uniform, monumental planning show that it was built during an era when the old method of building had already become a style. But the huge granite images of the temple's lord, the sun-god Horus in the form of a falcon, must be much older and probably stood in the old temple long before the time when the Greeks, in the age of religious syncretism, put Horus on a par with Apollo and called the town Apollinopolis, 'Apollo's town'.

When we returned to our floating home after three hours of intensive temple study we were all rather tired and hungry. A good lunch and an hour's rest under the awning before Alvar and Elissa had to leave us and begin their journey home – this was what we were looking forward to. Everything seemed quite normal as we stepped aboard, but when we slid open the companion hatch we were met by an incredible sight: beer-bottles, shoes and a suitcase were floating about on a level with the table, the cabin was half full of water . . . I hopped down into the equally flooded engine-room and began to pump frantically while Mona, Alvar and Edries, armed with pails, formed a chain from the cabin. All discussions were put off until the water began to sink and we saw that we were masters of the situation. After an hour and a half the boat was dry and I could see that the water was coming from the stern, somewhere near the casing of the propeller-shaft. If we pumped every half-hour we could keep the water below the flooring. So as not to darken the few hours that remained of our time with the Aaltos, we pretended that everything was all right; Mona served the longed-for lunch and we drank the health of *Daphne*, whom Alvar, in the spirit of religious syncretism, renamed the Sun Boat. But the thorn of anxiety and desperation kept pricking us: what were we to do? Edries went across the river with Alvar and Elissa to see them off at the railway station, we waved goodbye with one hand and pumped with the other, glumly aware that we were sentenced to slave-labour night and day if we did not want to see our craft swallowed up by the Nile. How light-heartedly we had taken for granted the joy, now so unattainable, of lying in our watertight boat, how uncomplainingly we would resign ourselves to every other small vexation, if only we could regain this elementary security! One of the first steps we took was to send a soldier to Edfu for the chief of police. After at least an hour he arrived, listened to our tale of woe, scratched his head and said:

'Two weeks ago a ferry capsized here at Edfu and ten persons were drowned. I can't take the responsibility of your lives, what would the governor say if you were to be drowned here in my district? I insist that you abandon your sinking boat at once and move to the hotel. By the way, have you got any postage stamps from your country? I'm a collector and I'd like to have some European ones . . .'

Such a monumental tendency to see things purely from his own point of view might have amused us at any other time, but I must admit that we had not enough sense of humour to look out the desired stamps. With Edries' help we began instead to negotiate with the skipper of an aiasa moored alongside. The man, a stocky athletic type, offered to dive down under *Daphne* and plug up the hole with putty. He did not want any money if he failed, but asked for a pound if he made the boat tight. We would gladly have promised him ten, but had very thin hopes of his succeeding. The man dived and snorted, dived again, but the water continued to gush in. Until suddenly it stopped! We pumped the boat dry and waited suspiciously for half an hour, but *Daphne* floated as calm and tight as in days gone by. In our gratitude we doubled the promised reward and our rescuer, grateful in his turn, dived once more to make sure that his work 'would hold for seven years'.

We were so anxious to get away that we started the engine at once and cast off. Luckily, I kept a watchful eye on the kelson and saw that the water began to pour in the minute the propellor was turning. The fellow had merely smeared mud round the shaft-casing, which might perhaps have held for seven years if we had never started the engine. We made fast again and he had to re-do the temporary caulking so that we could sleep through the night: to leave Edfu was out of the question. But an idea had been taking shape in my brain: had we not a letter of introduction from the big sugar company's head office in Cairo to the managers of the sugar-factories? And had we not at Armant seen a large crane unloading the railway trucks from the sugar-cane barges? The sugar refinery at Kom Ombo was only some forty miles south of Edfu and was sure to have a similar crane ... After endless trouble I put a call through from Edfu's police station to the works manager at Kom Ombo, Husein Kamel, who not only confirmed that their crane could lift a boat five times as heavy as *Daphne* ashore but also promised that we could be towed to the works by a barge-train if we were all ready to leave the following day at one o'clock.

So a long day at Edfu ended after all on a bright note and we tumbled into bed, exhausted; we slept like logs until awakened in the morning by the squeaking, whining sound of the *shadoofs* as the watering-men began their Danaid work – a kind of oriental chamber music which is never far away in the Nile land.

The *shadoof*, which consists of a pole on a swivel with a bucket on one end and a lump of mud as a counterpoise on the other, is no doubt as old as Egypt; we already see it on the reliefs and paintings of the tombs, but much more easily in reality, as it is still the commonest means of raising water to a height of about five feet. The shadoofs often work – as here at Edfu – in two storeys and can then overcome a difference in level of over ten feet. But there are also two 'modern' water-raising devices in Egypt. When, according to tradition, the great Greek mathematician Archimedes visited the Nile land in the third century B.C. he was seized with pity for the fellahs, who toiled with the ancient shadoof, and constructed two machines: the so-called 'Archimedes' screw', a long barrel containing a spiral which 'winds' the water up, and the so-called *sakia*, a water-wheel of clay buckets which is driven via a primitive cog-wheel system by an ox or donkey. Archimedes' screw is commonly used when the difference in level is less than three feet and the sakia when the height is considerable. The sakia is the most efficient but also the most costly of the water-raising machines, well-known also in other countries round the Mediterranean. But the shadoof, which is the cheapest and the simplest device, will probably outlive the others and compete for a long time with the engines which are cautiously beginning to show themselves by the Nile.

The sugar company's barge-train arrived punctually at one o'clock, a small tug and three sugar-cane barges, all manned by men who were sitting cross-legged and chewing tirelessly at sugar-cane as though for payment – or perhaps it is more correct to say instead of payment, as the possibility of living on the sugar-cane's nourishing juice is a compensation for the low wages in Egypt. We were forced to steer out to the train by our own engine and our wound opened up again, but now that help was near, it did not feel so hopeless to pump the boat dry every half-hour. The skipper of the tug told us to make fast fore-and-aft and then he ordered full speed ahead. He was extremely polite and seemed full of concern for our welfare; no wonder, as Edries told us later that 'for safety's sake' he had begun by telling the captain that I was the ambassador of my country and a close friend of the owner of the sugar refineries, the industrial magnate Abud

Pascha. We had a quick and comfortable passage. The shores we passed were mostly pure desert in character or consisted of steep cliffs. At Gebel Abu Chega we had to force a very shallow and difficult channel which I doubt very much if *Daphne* could have got through alone. Several times our keel scraped hard against the bottom and we were anxious as to whether ropes, bollards and keel would hold when the tug dragged us across the shoal with irresistible force.

Unfortunately, it was getting dark when we reached Gebel Silsala, the ancient Egyptian quarry from which a large part of Thebes' temples was taken. We caught a glimpse only of Horemheb's famous rock temple and the fantastic chaos of hewn-out cliffs. The tug's skipper evidently knew every twist of the river, as he guided us safely through the dark until, at about ten o'clock, we saw the floodlit unloading dock of the sugar mill. Fully-laden barges were crowded under the huge crane's arm and a Décauville haulage track took the sugar-cane to the factory two and a half miles from the river. Men rushed up and moored *Daphne* to a small boatshed where the Pascha's shining mahogany motorboat lay under a linen cover, and we turned in, having divided the night into watches because of the pumping.

Next morning we went up to the factory to pay our respects to the chief himself, Husein Kamel, and ask his advice about repairs. As elsewhere in Egypt where modern industry makes it necessary for western-trained officials to live among the peasant population, a special bungalow village enclosed by high walls had been built next to the factory at Kom Ombo. It implied a removal from one world to another when, after a long palaver at the closely-guarded gate, we stepped from the filthy, poor workers' village into the managerial park with its raked paths and white bungalows glimpsed between shady trees and surrounded by newly-mown lawns. Husein Kamel, who received us in the office wing, turned out to be a suave man of the world of the type that is becoming common in the former colonial districts: well-dressed and supercilious, he also shared the oriental ideas that during the last century and a half had amounted to complexes about Europeans. His treatment of us was very subtle. On the one hand, he kept us waiting for a long time before admitting us and showed a studied lack of interest in us and our journey, but on the other

he languidly rang up the factory's engineer and told him to put
the entire workshop and the best mechanics at our disposal –
free of charge, naturally, 'as the factory is not a repair-shop for
tourist boats.' We could hardly have been made to feel smaller,
but we had no choice. We thanked him, bowed and took our
leave.

Mr Osman, the engineer responsible for the repairs, was a
small man with a melancholy smile and weighed down with the
cares of work. He came down to the riverbank with a dozen
workmen and first considered lifting *Daphne* with the large crane
and doing the repairs in half an hour – the maximum length of
time for which the unloading of the sugar-cane could be stopped
without inconvenience. But there was also an older crane which
was still usable. Perhaps after all it was safer to try to get that
going in case the repairs took longer . . . A steam-engine was
set going, the crane screeched and two nooses of rope as thick
as one's arm were lowered under *Daphne's* keel. Knowing *Daphne's*
shape and distribution of weight I insisted – in vain – that one
of the ropes be placed farther forward, but Osman was obstinate.
The result was that the boat lifted at an angle of forty-five degrees
with the bowsprit in the water and the propeller in the air. There
we hung precariously, on tenterhooks lest the boat at any second
should slide out of the loops. It appeared that the constant
reversing of the engine every time we went aground had been
too great a strain for both the propeller and the rear end of the
shaft. The whole thing had to be dismounted and taken to the
workshop, which meant that the engine too had to be moved
from its position.

I will spare the reader unnecessary technical details and merely
say that for five days we remained hanging in mid air, with the
stern gaping open once the propeller and the shaft had been
removed, forced to sleep half standing up in our sharply-tilted
bunks, wakened in the night by creakings as *Daphne*, rocked by
the wash of passing boats, slid down an inch or so out of the
loops; in the daytime we were driven to despair by the sweltering
heat and the gnawing anxiety as we watched the primitive
mechanics and the unhappy Osman, whose smile grew more
melancholy with each day that passed, taking more and more of
our engine to pieces. We doubted – with good reason – if they

could put it together again in working order. We began to see
that no one would be surprised – would hardly react at all, in
fact – if *Daphne* met her fate in Kom Ombo. An engine, a boat,
an individual is of very little importance in a world where everything is in vain, where all human and material values are consumed
and man must learn above all to accept life's vicissitudes. 'Abandon
your boat and move to the hotel' – the words of the chief of police
at Edfu rang in our ears, but we clenched our teeth in protest.
We lashed *Daphne* to the sliding loops with every rope we could
muster, we went up to the workshop and stood watching as
new castings were put on to the worn-out shaft and to keep our
spirits up we decided to make an excursion to Kom Ombo's
stately double temple.

Of all Egypt's temples, Kom Ombo's is the most beautifully
situated, raised like a Parthenon on a high Acropolis above the
Nile, as full of atmosphere when you see it from the river below,
lifting its columns above the airy tops of the tamarisks, as when
you look down on the glittering stream through the wide temple
gateway of the crocodile god. The temple was only ten minutes
from where we lay, or rather hung, and in addition had a pleasant
surprise in store for us. As we entered the temple precincts we
saw a string of diapers hanging up to dry near a wooden hut, and
inside the temple's hypostyle hall we found a young man sitting
perched up on a high wooden scaffolding copying the hieroglyphics. He was Adolphe Gutbub, an Alsatian from the French
Institute, who was collecting material during the winter months
for his doctor's thesis and was living at the temple with his young
wife and new-born daughter. When it grew too dark for the
sedulous scholar to go on reading his big stone book, we all sat
round the table drinking Nile-water tea and talking of the sugar
refinery, the art of embalming crocodiles and of spelling mistakes
in the hieroglyphics. I have the excellent Adolphe Gutbub to
thank for three profitable suggestions which I was very glad of
during the rest of the journey: he aroused my interest in the
archaeological fantast Robichon at Luxor, he told me about the
Pharaoh mummies in Cairo, which may still be seen by visiting
statesmen and professors of archaeology, and finally he dropped
me a hint about the most fantastic of all books on Egypt, Vivant
Denon's notes from the Napoleonic campaign.

At long last came the hour of liberation, when propeller and shaft were again in place and *Daphne* could resume her natural floating position. We made a trial run below the temple with Osman and two mechanics on board. Everything seemed to function normally, but a lurking suspicion made us accept a bargee's kind offer to tow us up to Assuan the following day without using our own engine. The distance was only thirty miles and we could do with a few hours free from the cares of navigation in which to clean up the boat after all the bare, muddy feet which had been tramping about for the last few days. We had a quick, restful passage upstream past shores that were for the most part uninhabited. Up in these parts the fertile Nile valley has shrunk so much that there is hardly a green patch or a tree to be seen, only rocks and desert sand.

The arrival at Assuan makes all the greater impression. It begins with a curtain of slender palms on both sides of the river, an oasis silhouette with desert in the background. Then high mountains shut in the river valley to the south and the Nile is turned into a lake, in the middle of which a fertile island spreads out its shady gardens: Elefantine, the Syene of antiquity, at the foot of the First Cataract. Here, on the borderline between two worlds, the fertile agricultural Egypt and Africa's endless wilds, there has always been a trading centre, where the merchandise of the black world, gold, ivory and slaves, has been bartered for the industrial products of the civilized countries. Nowadays most of the population have moved over to the east bank, where the modern Assuan lies with the governor's residence, hospital, schools and bazaar streets. We cast off from the motor-barge and steered by our own engine in between Elefantine and Assuan to the tree-planted embankment lined with aiasas, barges, houseboats and derelict paddle-boats. Where should we tie up? In a travel brochure I had seen pictures of the Cataract Hotel's idyllic setting by the river and decided to make for it. Some boys in a primitive rowing-boat pointed out the way and we went on cautiously through the sound between the ancient temple ruins on the southern point of Elefantine and a high, sheer granite cliff with Pharaonic reliefs hewn into it. For us who had travelled a thousand miles on the calm, broad, rock-free Nile past water-worn limestone and sandstone cliffs in yellow-grey tones, it was a strange and rather frightening experience to see ourselves surrounded by smooth red and black slabs of granite, between which the water cascaded towards us with a hundred outstretched arms. The cataract has admittedly been tamed since the building of the big dam at the turn of the century, and an engine-driven craft can make its own way up to the 130-foot-high Jacob's ladder of the lock, four miles above the town, but between the calm basins, where the water is deep, the current still forms small rapids. Above the first of these basins is the Cataract Hotel with its innumerable balconies and large veranda, a cross between a rambling seaside bungalow and a Tibetan monastery. We put in beside a red granite slab which might have been in a northern archipelago, automatically carried the anchor ashore to a cleft in the rock and felt in an extraordinarily good mood. It was by far the best, most peaceful and cleanest mooring-place we had known since entering the Nile. The hotel, where we could eat, bathe and sit on the veranda with the fine view across the Cataract, further increased our content. We forgot all our past trials and revelled in a few care-free days of rest before continuing up to the dam.

When one reads in 19th-century travel diaries of all the well-preserved archaeological sights at Assuan – including newly-discovered noblemen's tombs above the town and the Elysian temple island of Philae above the Cataract – it is depressing to think of the enormous destruction which the last fifty years have brought with them. We made outings in various directions from our mooring-place. Our Lambretta took us to the old quarries from which the granite for Egypt's countless obelisks, sarcophagi, columns and statues was taken. Everywhere in Assuan there are traces of the ancient method of 'blasting': rows of holes into which wooden plugs were driven and then watered, so that when they swelled they split the rock with irresistible force into the desired blocks. In our dinghy we rowed over to Elefantine, where only the foundations of the god of creation Chnum's temple are left but where we, like thousands of tourists before us, made some excellent finds among the stones and gravel: a painted votive figure and an oil-lamp of terracotta, which we could have bought for a few piasters in the bazaars but valued twice as highly for having found them ourselves.

We were, however, charmed more by Assuan's scenery than by the monuments. We went for long rowing-trips every day among the rocky islands of the Cataract; some of them are inhabited, while the smaller ones consist only of bizarre, hollowed-out and rounded blocks which reminded us of sculptures by Arp and Henry Moore. Once we carried our featherweight glass-fibre dinghy right across the narrow but long Elefantine Island to avoid rowing back against the current; the villagers could hardly believe their eyes when they saw us coming with the large boat tucked nonchalantly under our arms.

Another of these expeditions took us to a little private paradise which must surely be unique: an island in the Cataract belonging to the Adda family. A flock of gazelles first drew our attention as they gazed out inquisitively from between some boulders, to vanish into thin air when we approached. Then we found the villa, half hidden beneath roses in bloom, and the garden with its flaunting mass of flowers. Apart from the granite base, the island is man's work throughout: incredible quantities of rich soil have been dragged here and are kept in place by high stone walls.

'*Mario, vai prendere gli ospiti!*'

To our surprise we heard an Italian voice from one of the balconies on the roof and saw an elderly white-haired woman leaning over the balustrade. A man in light overalls came down from the garden and got ready to row across to the hotel. This was enough for two 'semi-Italians' like Mona and myself. A few phrases exchanged with the white-haired lady resulted in an invitation to come ashore and look at the garden. Soon the rowing-boat returned with a group of guests, among whom I discovered an Italian diplomat who had been in Finland before the war, and the upshot was that we stayed with the friendly Addas the whole afternoon. The family really lives in Alexandria, where they have industries, but since they bought the island in the Cataract from an Englishman twelve years ago they spend a few months every winter down here.

Like all qualities, beauty is something relative which is built on comparison with that which is less beautiful: a fine day necessarily entails many wet ones. If contrast has any strength, then the Addas' island is by far the most beautiful thing one can imagine. Blossom, greenery and shade beneath the pitiless sun, a quiet idyll surrounded by the wild chaos of the Cataract, a paradise with heavily laden fruit-trees, flowering roses and ripening strawberry-beds in the middle of January, a reserve of luxury and the enjoyment of life right beside the misery of the overpopulated villages – each comparison adds a new side to the island's advantages. Peace, the rustle of leaves, the glitter of water between the tree-trunks and the wafted scent of unknown flowers: during a stroll along the winding paths of the island I thought of all the need and privation which makes people out of opposition build such pictures of happiness. I thought, too, of the pessimism hidden in all beauty, the deep pessimism of the Greeks which accepts life's hopelessness and therefore creates a reserve of joy.

A pedagogic fate would have it that on the very next day we were to see the opposite environment: a world which dares to be ugly because it is not pessimistic. It all began by our needing a little distilled water for *Daphne's* batteries. Edries and I went first to Assuan's charging-station for car batteries and then to the chemists'; at both places they were equally astonished at our errand. Ordinary tap water was all that was ever used either for batteries or medicines, but perhaps the general hospital could help us? It was not hard to find the hospital, the whole street outside was filled with submissively waiting patients. The sitting human beings of the Orient – the mere sight of them says more about their attitude to life than all historical and psychological analyses. Stuck fast to the ground, like stones over which sand-storms can blow – or the wind of time itself, while they sit stubbornly on. Huddled, resigned, yet importunate figures, which no soldiers can drive away, as they wait outside hospitals, law-courts, railway stations or granaries. With some hesitation we pushed our way through this crowd to the interior of the building, where a janitor with a bloodstained apron instantly led us into a room in which four doctors calmly sat smoking, playing cards and drinking coffee. When the general disappointment that I was not a wealthy foreign patient had subsided, the head physician was quite willing to sell me distilled water. How much did I want? A quart! Impossible, a gill at the outside. There *was* a whole bottle, but you never knew what emergency might arise during the next few weeks . . .

Rather depressed by what we had seen of the big State hospital, we walked slowly away. More out of curiosity and obstinacy than because the distilled water was so vital to us, I decided to make a last attempt at the little Swiss missionary hospital I had noticed on the way to the Cataract Hotel. In this way I was allowed a glimpse of the world that does not need beauty because it is optimistic. Three Christian doctors – two Europeans and a young Egyptian – worked here under conditions which made me think of Albert Schweitzer's famous hospital at Lambaréné. With extremely limited material resources they daily treated hundreds of sick people who otherwise would have been left to their fate. The head physician, a woman, got the mistaken idea through my doctor's title that I was a medical doctor and took me the rounds of the hospital, during which time I saw more misery than in the whole of my previous life. Coverings were lifted off the sick to show me tumours, twisted limbs, suppurating sores, and in the post-mortem room I saw a young woman whose liver had been eaten up by bilharzia worms. Yet this visit was a great and positive experience. Although I have never dared to call myself a Christian I was filled with joy at having been born within a tradition which can see all this without despairing, which can live with such ugliness because it can be overcome, alleviated or at any rate given a meaning by an all-embracing love. Great though the Greek gods were, living in their abodes of bliss, and tempting as it may be to imitate them by living in a place such as the Addas' island, was not Osiris, who was tortured, died and rose again, greater? Is not the form of godlike imitation to which the three doctors at the missionary hospital at Assuan devote themselves a more satisfying way of life? I think it says a lot for our age that the exclusive worship of beauty which was still so predominant a generation ago is beginning to disappear: we are less afraid of what is ugly than our grandparents were.

The next act in our journey's drama was as follows:

We started early in the morning from our mooring-place below the hotel. One of the police-boats went ahead to show us the way through the Cataract's labyrinth of islands, rocks and eddies, for in the strong current it would have been perilous to run aground. I thought of the dramatic descriptions of the Cataract in the 19th-century travel books: boats have always been able to force a passage, but before the dam was built it took hundreds of men in harness two days of strained effort to pull craft up through the rapids – or to hold them back on the way down. After an exciting trip of three miles and a half we began to hear the roar of water and glimpse the dam as one vast wall, below which the foam drifted in sun-glistening clouds and the water gushed in a thousand jets. For the last half-mile before the lock the channel is led through a sheltered side canal.

We passed the first lock-chamber, but when we entered the second and put the engine in reverse in order to make fast, it happened! A sound from the engine-room as though from a giant coffee-mill, a bumping and slashing at the stern and then just the normal hum of the engine. It took a while for us to realize what had happened. The mechanics at Kom Ombo had fastened the bolts between the cardan joints and the shaft so carelessly that they had come undone; the propeller-shaft had snapped off in five or six places, the leakage in the stern had opened up again and the propeller fallen out and locked the rudder. Our situation had never appeared more hopeless, with *Daphne* sinking and out of control hundreds of miles from the nearest shipyard in Cairo. As we pondered this dismal fact, deep down in the Assuan lock, a cheery Swedish voice was suddenly heard from up on the quay:

'Hallo, *Daphne*! Want any help?'

By a freak of chance, *Daphne* had never, during the six years that had passed since she left northern waters, been in a more convenient place for an engine breakdown. Not a hundred yards from the scene of our disaster there lay, marvellous to relate, a large Swedish engineering workshop with several Swedish engineers and mechanics. Some of them had been curious when they saw our masts glide into the lock and, having read about *Daphne*, recognized both her and her owner. We, on the other hand, were embarrassingly ignorant of the fact that the Swedish firm of contractors *Sentab* in Stockholm had undertaken to blast four tunnels through the granite at the Assuan Dam for the big power station that was under construction. The repair-shop at the lock had been put up to look after the excavators, lorries and drills which were used in the tunnelling work. The man in charge of the work was a young engineer, Björn Monsén, who now, from up on the quay, spoke reassuring words to us: we were to continue the lockage up to the dam, where a crane on caterpillars would come and lift Daphne's stern out of the water so that a new shaft could be fitted in. Kind, comforting, ever-confident Björn; you became our friend during the days that followed, and I want once again and before my readers to thank you for what you and your firm did for us at Assuan – without your helping hand we should have been lost.

We lay for three days at the great dam with our stern suspended in a crane, while Sjö-Olle Olson and two of his workmates turned a new shaft, caulked the leakage with pitch and re-did everything that the Kom Ombo workshop had botched and which was wrong in every detail. During this time we got to know not only the hospitable and friendly Swedes – about twenty families – who were living down here but also some of the vast irrigation problems connected with Assuan.

The electric power station was estimated to be ready within the next few years and was being built in order to utilize some of the millions of kilowatts which had hitherto poured to waste out of the Assuan Dam. It is in itself a big building enterprise, but it is overshadowed by the project which – to use journalese – is 'to build the biggest dam in the world's biggest river and form its biggest artificial lake'. Let me hasten to assure the general-knowledge reader that I have just looked up an encyclopaedia and found that the Mississippi with its 4,219 miles is somewhat longer than the Nile and that equally huge dams have been planned both in the old and the new world. The fact remains that the dam project above Assuan is one of the boldest plans that civil engineers and politicians together have devised, a matter of life and death in a double sense for Egypt.

The facts behind the scheme are as follows: the Nile is Egypt's only real natural asset, its water feeds, directly or indirectly, almost the entire population. I mentioned in a previous chapter how the old system of agriculture by flooding had been replaced by irrigation all the year round from dams and canals. This rationalized agriculture has allowed the population figure to rise to 22 millions. But the improved public health and standard of living of the present day mean that nativity is increasing still more and according to advance calculation within only thirty years the population of Egypt will have been doubled to 44 millions. The only possibility of feeding all these people is to go on rationalizing the exploitation of the Nile, both for irrigation purposes and for industry. An enormous volume of water still runs to waste out into the sea: not until the middle of October does one dare to start filling the Assuan Dam and not until February are the Nile's two outlets into the Mediterranean corked up. In order that all the water can be used and a reserve created from rainy to dry years, English experts planned a series of works at the upper course of the Nile. The levels of Lakes Albert, Victoria and Tana were to be raised, a canal dug past the swamp area, The Sudd, and a large number of dams built. The project had two big faults in the eyes of the present Egyptian government: it would take a long time to realize and it involved close co-operation with the Sudan, Ethiopia and British Central Africa.

In this situation the plan for a high-level dam at Assuan came as a brainwave. On Egyptian territory, six miles above the present dam, there is a pass which, if it is blocked, can dam up 5,295 milliard cubic feet of water in a lake 310 miles long. By means of this dam it is possible once and for all to abolish the Nile floods and turn the whole of the Egyptian Nile into a vast irrigation canal with a constant level and without an outlet into the sea. Huge electric power stations can be built and with some of the current water can be pumped up to new arable districts in the desert. The advantages are palpably enormous and must be especially tempting for a dictator who wants to do great and remarkable things for his people. The project has in fact been pertinently called 'Nasser's pyramid': no Pharaoh has created a more impressive monument than this dam will be if it materializes.

But the difficulties cannot be overlooked. They are partly financial and entail the necessity of getting a gigantic loan from abroad. When we were in Egypt it was still thought that the U.S.A. and the Soviet would vie with each other to advance the money – an illusion which, when it broke, caused Nasser to seek prestige and economic compensation by nationalizing the Suez Canal. Another difficulty is to reach an agreement with the Sudan, whose territory would be partly flooded by the lake; and anyway the Sudan might take it into its head one fine day to build a high-level dam of its own to irrigate its desert areas and then it will be hard to fill the Assuan Dam. A European expert, employed by the Egyptian government and a specialist on dams, pointed out during a talk we had with him at Assuan, that the technical difficulties too are great: at the pass, where the dam is to be built, the bed of the Nile is very loose, and it is therefore not possible to build a stone or concrete dam of the usual type. Instead, a method – considered possible but not yet tested – has been devised of blocking up the river with sand and earth in an embankment about half a mile wide. Finally, the whole of Egypt and its population – which, thanks to the dam, may well be multiplied many times over – will live in a situation comparable to that of inhabitants on the rim of a volcano. If the dam bursts, not only all human beings and houses but probably a good part of the soil of the Nile Valley will be swept out into the Mediterranean by the huge mass of water. An earthquake, an atom bomb or an insidious infiltration of water can cause the catastrophe. On the other hand one can say that even the present Assuan Dam on a smaller scale implies a similar danger, but that neither German bomber-pilots nor Israeli saboteurs have brought themselves to attack Egypt in this Achilles' heel.

One circumstance at any rate which speaks strongly for the building of the high-level dam: it is wholly in line with the country's traditions. Egypt is a gigantic work of man's hands, a swamp that has become a garden. From earliest times, seemingly impossible and stupendous schemes have been carried out, from the building of the man-made mountains we call the Pyramids and the transformation during the Middle Kingdom of Lake Moeris into a water reservoir for the Nile to the great works of more modern times such as the Suez Canal and the laying-out of Port Said on completely artificial ground. If any country deserves to contain the world's biggest dam, it is Egypt.

We lacked neither social life nor occupation during the three days *Daphne* lay at the Assuan Dam. The Swedish engineering families took it in turns to ask us to dinner, we were shown round the building-site of the power station and had everything explained to us; we followed the progress of the tunnel blasting and went for short outings in the vicinity. The most memorable of these was our row in the dinghy to the sacred island of Philae a mile or so from *Daphne*. The old travel books describe it as perhaps the greatest experience of the whole Nile trip. Surrounded by whispering palms, lined with well-built quays, dominated by the goddess Isis' great temple and adorned with colonnades and pavilions, it was the place one cherished most in memory after getting home to Europe. When the Assuan Dam was completed at the turn of the century Philae's temple, in common with several other Nubian temples, was drowned deep under the water. Its inhabitants are gone, palms and flowers are dead, but each summer, when the reservoir is drained almost dry, the temple island rises again as a guest into visible reality. As this was January we knew that Philae was flooded, but we wanted to visit it in any case. One afternoon we rowed straight across the dam, and with the help of our excellent General Staff map it was not hard to find our way. First we passed a labyrinth of narrow sounds, small islands and granite aits, where women were washing clothes on the rocks and boys with fishing-rods drifted about in rowing-boats – a strange blend of Negro-Africa and Finnish archipelago. These rocky peaks form the upper parts of what was formerly one large island. Philae lies in the sound between this island and the steep bank of the Nile. To our surprise we saw two square, quay-like stone platforms sticking up: they were the tops of the Isis temple's large gate pylons with hieroglyphic texts, licked by opaque, green waves.

We made the dinghy fast to one of the pylons and stepped aboard as though on to a barge of stone. There was little to see apart from the water-mirror's straight border across the threshold of the dam towards the flaming sunset sky, but the knowledge that we had the sunken temple underneath us was a great romantic experience. Its inaccessibility was right in some way, for one can never set foot inside an Egyptian temple without feeling it as profanation. Soft, protective water, darkness and silence – that was the right setting for these buildings, which had already half merged into invisibility. Out of reach, yet near, they now rested as though in a world of their own, fish glided cautiously up to the innermost rooms of mystery and the statues could sink down deep into themselves.

Philae is a place where we have special reason to listen to the voice of the past: it was here that ancient Egypt died, for this island was the last reserve where, by a whim of history, priests skilled in the secrets of the old religion and the hieroglyphics lived on into the Christian era. Philae's Isis temple had become the national sanctuary for the warlike Blemmyes, who ruled Nubia and were of political importance to Byzantium. When the temples of Egypt were closed by order of Theodosius and the images of the gods were shattered, Philae was excluded from the edict and the goddess's mysteries were celebrated here far into the 6th century.

There is also another reason for us to show Isis special respect. As the great goddess of mother love, worshipped in all the provinces of the Roman Empire, she could not be banished by Christianity but was transformed into Jesus' mother. The Madonna worship is the direct continuation of the Isis cult. So the same is true of the gods as of human beings: they do not die but go on living in their descendants. Appearance, characteristics and inner self are repeated in those who continue their work. Jesus Christ would not have been the one He is had not the redeeming death god of Egypt gone before Him, and the Virgin Mary would have had no meaning without Isis.

Night had come while we sat on the stone platform surrounded by the sky's and the river's stars. The place was so undefined, the time so limitless that for a moment I tried to imagine I was sitting on the roof of one of Notre Dame's clock-towers, while far below me a city which long ago had the name of Paris lay covered by the waters of the great Seine dam. Notre Dame, who was she?

One of the forgotten Mothers who always reappear in a new guise.

CHAPTER X

Nubia

The Swedish mechanics were so kind that they worked until three o'clock in the morning on our last night at Assuan and on 14th January *Daphne* was again seaworthy with a new shaft and new cardan joints. We could start on the stage of our journey that in memory's perspective I do not hesitate to call the zenith. Nubia came to mean something more to us than a new part of Egypt or a mere continuation of our Nile navigation. We encountered a new land with a new population and we began a new journey under utterly changed conditions.

The very scenery changed character as though by magic. To be lifted up 130 feet through the Jacob's Ladder of the Assuan Dam and suddenly, after hours of toil with ropes and fenders in the dripping lock-chambers, to steer out on to the great, calm reservoir, was to be lifted unexpectedly on to Egypt's roof, where everything was brighter, cleaner, more spacious than in the working and living quarters on the floors below. Only now did we realize that the Nile flows along the whole time in a valley, the river's canyon that has been hollowed out for millions of years. Mostly the rocky walls keep a mile or so away from the present river-bed, but sometimes they rise sheer out of the water. At Assuan one climbs up out of the green valley and from then on steers across an endless, grandly beautiful desert plateau.

The navigation alters just as radically. While we had enjoyed the hazards of sailing on the Nile, when they had not been too irksome, here in Nubia we knew that the past months had after all been a constant mental strain. The feeling of liberation was indescribable when we discovered that we were no longer sailing on a river but on the world's least known and most paradisian Alpine lake: the volume of water held back by the Assuan Dam forms not only a basin immediately above the cataract but also a flooded area about 180 miles long, which in places is so wide that we were not always sure which point we were to make for. The joy of no longer having to struggle against the current, of having a safe depth under our keel – and, almost best of all, of floating

on clear, blue water which invited us to dive into it, after the
sewage of the lower Nile – these were joys which we knew that
Daphne felt as much as we. Our hard-used little ship took a deep
breath and stretched herself, proudly aware of being the only real
sailing-boat with a deep keel and rigging for a hard tack on this
entire lake.

What further emphasized our having entered a new land with
other living conditions was the fact that the railway and the road,
which up to now had kept us company, came to an end; from
Assuan the ordinary travellers' only chance of getting any farther
is by river steamer, which goes up to the Sudanese railway's
starting-point at Wadi Halfa. In other words, Nubia is a buffer
zone, joined almost as loosely to Egypt as to the Sudan, an in-
voluntary natural and social reserve, forgotten by the authorities
and inaccessible to tourists. The surprising thing is that this
isolation has been more of an advantage than otherwise to the
Nubians; they have escaped the colonial conditions of the Sudan
but also the Egyptian social diseases of over-population, overcrowding and proletarianism as a result of Pascha rule and
agriculture on enormous private estates. One is reminded of the
poor but free Swiss peasants in the feudal Europe of the Middle
Ages; like these, the Nubians have been prone to earn their living
in foreign lands, partly as soldiers, partly as trusted servants with
well-born families, but as soon as they have made enough money
they return to their villages, where they govern themselves
without any help from foreign governors, proud of being cleaner,
more honest and more law-abiding than their equals in the outside
world. One could also liken them to the inhabitants of the Greek
islands, who are themselves widely travelled but are seldom
visited in their out-of-the-way villages by strangers. None of the
Swedes at Assuan had been to Nubia, though they had been living
on its border for over a year, and we ourselves could only have
visited the places the river steamer touches at if we had not had
Daphne. We were now compensated for all the vexations we had
undergone by the ideal way of getting to know Nubia which our
floating home and our Nubian travel companion Edries gave us.
Edries' joy at seeing his homeland again infected us, we saw
Nubia very largely through his eyes, which perhaps partly
explains our partiality.

A fine northerly breeze was blowing as we stowed away the last lot of stores and gratefully waved goodbye to our Swedish friends at Assuan. At last a sail across open water! Light as a soap-bubble, *Daphne* floated out from the stone quay of the dam over the glittering water. The bow-wave hissed, the dinghy bobbed along behind and the balloon-sail was stretched like a bow against the cloudless sky. The shores of Assuan, ravaged by industry and blasting, disappeared, we sailed along a barren, rocky coast without an atom of life and after barely an hour reached a sound between sheer rock walls. Several broad, white lines had been painted from the water up over the rock on both sides of the river – the survey marks for the high-level dam. A house-boat lay by the shore, evidently the living-quarters of the German experts who were working on the project.

Soon we sighted the villages, of a completely new type. While the Egyptian fellahs crowd together in cramped communities, where the chief concern is to take up as little of the tillable ground as possible, the Nubian villages spread out in long, horizontal strips on the sterile hillsides. Living quarters, shady loggias, poultry-house, cow-house, stables and privy, all separate from each other, are grouped round a large built-in yard, a complete and varied dwelling, whereas the fellah has to make do with one or two rooms, in which humans and animals live together. But the building style, too, is different. Here in Nubia the contrast makes one realize for the first time what an extremely agricultural race the Egyptians are, fettered even mentally to the dark soil and a vegetative rhythm of life. The peasant, whose existence is regulated by the laws of sowing, harvest, irrigation and by the farmer's almanac, lives in one sense in the abstract, according to customs learnt by rote. In all countries and in all ages he is a person who lacks spontaneity, his duties and cares deprive him of a carefree spirit and thus of the gaiety and light-hearted acceptance of the present moment which we usually associate with a childlike or artistic nature. This peasant attitude to life gives both the Egyptian and the Chinese cultures their basic characteristics, both are meditative old-man's civilizations without any bubbling intoxication of life. In Nubia it is apparent that one is approaching the domains of the wild hunting peoples, the childish races for whom ornaments, brightly-coloured clothes, feasts, singing and

dancing are essentials. Even the architecture witnesses to this
attitude. The monumental gateways of the houses are painted in
gay harlequin triangles and furnished with imaginative crenellations, on the façades bits of mirrors and dinner-plates have been
pressed into the wet mortar and no family lacks a shady loggia
where they can sit and talk away the hours under a roof of
vividly painted palm-trunks.

The Guide Bleu describes Nubia in some detail, but unfortunately misleadingly, as the information given refers to conditions
before the raising of the Assuan Dam in 1934. Over half of the
temples mentioned are now under water and invisible, many
villages have disappeared and the others have been moved to
higher positions. As we were anxious to reach without delay the
places that were really worth seeing, we did not bother to stop
anywhere on this first day of sailing, but our binoculars helped
us nevertheless to study the landscape fairly well.

A question one inevitably asks oneself at the sight of this
sterile countryside and these treeless villages which from a
distance melt right into their stony environment, is how the
population can support itself in such surroundings. The question
is almost as naïve as when the stranger from afar asks how people
in Northern Europe can live in the snow. The water which was
now covering Nubia's fields subsides in the spring and the
villagers have all the summer to sow and harvest the crops that
man and beast can live on during the winter. But this explanation
is not the whole truth. The Nubians have never been merely
farmers and their scant inclination for hard manual work is
noticeable all the year round. They have always lived mostly on
income from without, in the old days soldier's pay or trading
between Egypt and the negro countries. Slave traffic was their
speciality and even if the shipping of black ivory to Cairo ceased
at the beginning of this century, there are still elderly servants in
the Nubian houses who are called, and in practice probably are,
slaves. Those who may wonder why the Nubians, who themselves are almost negroes, were the most zealous of the slave
hunters, have further cause to ponder the inner identity of hunter
and hunted in the fact that it is these very Nubians who have
gradually replaced the slaves as servants in the upper-class
families of Cairo and Alexandria. They are highly valued for

228

trustworthiness and cleanliness but not for diligence and endurance. Their wives who live at home in the villages do not overstrain themselves either. Instead of toil-worn fellah women, aged before their time, one sees in the Nubian villages nothing but gay, pretty girls with gold rings in their noses or fat matrons who sit on raffia mats in the shady loggias, chattering like magpies.

Anything more desolate than the Nubian winter landscape can hardly be imagined: not a green speck, not a tree, only an endless, dead, rocky desert against which the blue, living surface of the water is in abrupt contrast. At times the sand desert becomes more dominating and vast, bright-yellow dunes mould themselves over the rocks like snow over the fellsides. We saw villages menaced by enormous waves of sand – like Alpine villages under huge crests of snow. For a long while we sailed close against a towering sand-dune which rose straight out of the water; on its clean, smooth surface we could study an intricate pattern of different tracks. It was like a page out of Nature's own guest-book, with signatures which would be obliterated by the next south wind. Nearest the water two purposeful ribbons twisted, one of pointed, cloven donkey-hoofs, the other of bare human feet; round them, in playful garlands, ran a dog's tracks, which showed a marked interest in the light traces left by a thirsty gazelle on its way down to the water. The birds' promenades began and ended abruptly, with one or two delicate marks at the side from the wing-tips, while snakes and lizards had left endless coils where we almost thought we saw the impression of scales – as though the track itself had been a long, serpentine body. After half a mile or so we saw the originators of these tracks: the donkey with two sacks on its back, the circling dog, sniffing in curiosity, and a women with an enormous bundle on her head. In her heavy, black clothes with a veil over her head she looked from a distance like an old crone, but when we had caught up with her we caught sight of a pair of slender, swiftly moving girlish legs under the multitude of tucked-up skirts. As we passed we glimpsed a pair of bright, young eyes and a flashing, white smile under the veil.

The breeze blew all day long and after a six-hours' cruise we reached Bab el Kalabsha, i.e. Kalabsha's gate, at sunset. The river here breaks through between high cliffs and forms a wild, romantic stretch which is unusual for the Nile. As we glided soundlessly along under our sails through this chaos of rocks, a little village appeared for a moment between one or two steep, dark islands like stage scenery between huge curtains. Perhaps it was this theatrical presentation and the unreal, reddy-brown sunset light which, just as plainly for us all, lifted this sight out of reality – as though we had seen a vision and without warning been snatched away into other time and space. Mute, almost terrified, we sat staring at the apparition, until the village vanished into the jaws of the rocks.

Then darkness fell quickly, while we went on beyond the gateway. We could only faintly make out the silhouettes of houses on either side of the river and an occasional lantern; Edries told us that the people here have their supper at sunset and then go straight to bed. We too decided to seek shelter for the night. We struck the sails and went cautiously by engine in towards the steep bank, where a quay-like ledge, overgrown with lush, well-watered clover was caught in the beam of our torch. As we were making fast, one or two friendly old men with lanterns in their hands appeared. They bade us welcome and told us that the great temple at Kalabsha was under water now in the winter but that a smaller temple, higher up, lay only a few steps from our mooring-place. From force of habit we asked if there was a police soldier who could guard *Daphne* during the night, but the old men replied with a laugh that Nubia has no police – everyone here lives in peace and goodwill. This turned out to be quite true. During the whole of our stay in Nubia we saw not a single police nor armed officer of the law, we could step ashore in the villages without an escort instantly tacking on to us and we lay as safe and unguarded o' nights as when we used to drop anchor in the sheltered bays of the northern archipelagos. This, in conjunction with the Nubian Nile's lake-like character, freed us from the necessity of mooring the boat to the bank. At Kalabsha we revelled in being able to ride at anchor offshore in the faint night breeze and hear the water lapping against the boat. Our awakening, too, was different from what it had been previously on the Nile and more like a morning in a Finnish archipelago: while still half-asleep you have felt gentle tugs at the anchor-chain and the swing of the boat as the morning breeze keeps veering; then you begin to hear the ripple of the waves against the bows and at last you open your eyes and see a dancing glitter of sun-cats on the cabin roof. While we drank our morning coffee on deck we could leisurely study the diverse morning activities of the village – the scorching summers have engendered the habit of concentrating life's outwardly visible business into the first cool hours of the day. Small garden-plots were watered with shadoofs, donkeys and goats were led down to drink and a bunch of schoolboys assembled with lunch-packets in their hands to wait for a ferry which took them across to the other side. Quite a large sailing-boat, laden with bulging sacks of grain and two live cows, made a tack up to us and the helmsman, a dignified Nubian with white moustache and turban, introduced himself in good English as the village chieftain of Kalabsha and asked if he could do anything for us. This knowledge of languages, which we encountered everywhere in the villages and which soon ceased to surprise us, is due to the fact that nearly all Nubian men, as I have mentioned, have been in service in Cairo and Alexandria, many of them in European families. One cannot go far in the villages without coming across grey-haired men who in dress and behaviour resemble the Magi but speak fluent French, English or Italian.

Our very first glance out of the cabin when we woke up had shown us a white-clad man who was sitting on the shore and seemed to be waiting for us. When at last we rowed ashore in the dinghy he stood up and pointed to a brass disk he wore on his arm. SERVICE DES ANTIQUITES we read below a few Arabic twirls, and he told us proudly in reasonably good English that he was the official temple guard. This dignity, however, gave him very little work. Months elapsed between tourist visits. Much worse was the fact that his real trade, that of a builder, was at a low ebb as a result of the rumours about the new dam.

'Three times I have helped to rebuild Kalabsha,' Ibrahim the builder told us. 'The first time was in 1902, when the old Assuan Dam was completed. Then we had to move higher up again in 1912 and yet again in 1934, when the dam was raised. But when the new dam is ready we shan't be able to go on living here, all our fields will be under water for good and so no one bothers even to repair the old houses . . .'

Discussing this and other gloomy topics, we strolled to the

231

little rock temple of Beit el Ouali, built by Ramses II and decorated with martial reliefs in a free style influenced by the Amarna art. Especially curious is a scene with negroes in a palm grove; a black warrior is being borne home by his comrades, wounded; his children run towards him in tears while his wife unsuspectingly prepares food under a tree.

But the village itself interested us more than the temple; we wanted to see what these houses, which we had studied from the river, looked like inside. The inmates had no objection when Ibrahim described our errand and in several houses we were sprinkled with perfume as we stepped across the threshold. Edries was so blissful that his feet hardly remained on the earth. He remembered Nubia from his childhood, of course, but it was another matter seeing it again with a grown-up's eyes, being able to compare it with the rest of Egypt and find that everything here was really much better.

Most of the houses had a large guest- and reception-room with low benches round the walls; cushions and fine fabrics were placed on them before the guests were invited to sit. The refreshments consisted of dark, stewed tea, dried dates and – surprisingly – American rice crispies in the original packet. The furnishing of the other rooms was extremely meagre and comprised only chests, low, collapsible tables, large, unfired earthenware jars and raffia work: mats, baskets and dishes. We had no idea that the houses had an inner sanctum, the women's bedroom, with furnishings all of its own, until a lucky chance allowed us a peep into one. We caught a glimpse of some girls in a doorway. Mona began to joke with them and their feminine curiosity soon overcame their shyness. There were four of them, all very pretty, dressed in light, colourful dresses and with large, golden half-moons hanging through their nostrils. None of them was yet fifteen, but it appeared that they were married and that two already had babies. Their husbands were of course in Cairo, but dutifully sent home £1 each month and visited them once a year – both the monthly allowance and the marital achievements seemed to be what was normal in Nubia. It was rather complicated talking to them, as etiquette debarred Edries from asking them anything himself, but a twelve-year-old brother of one of the beauties acted as intermediary and by means of this double chain of interpreters we made friends to such an extent that Mona was allowed to look into the room, and afterwards we men. In our amazement we thought at first that it was a general village store, for it was crammed from floor to ceiling with a medley of a thousand objects. On rods near the ceiling hung neatly folded clothes, the walls were covered with rolled-up raffia mats and plaited raffia dishes, on long, narrow shelves stood rows of coffee-cups upside down, with empty red cartridge-cases on each, sweets were threaded on to long strings, old preserve tins which had been given a handle balanced on nails and in the middle of the wall facing us an American pin-up girl, with a plunge neckline, sat enthroned in an elaborate frame cut out from fifty Navy Cut cigarette packets. By degrees we made out that the room was the bedroom of one of the young wives and that she herself had decorated walls and ceiling, inspired by the same kind of collecting mania and love of things as little girls are when they fit out a doll's house – except that everything here was a hundred times finer and more ingenious. All the young Nubian woman's meagre possessions, from the sleeping-mat and her best dress to boxes of matches, soap, biscuits and lumps of sugar, here had two distinct purposes: practical use and decorative value. It was a strange experience in this way to see our industrial mass-products exalted to individual dignity, to see them loved and treasured as precious objects. It was, if anything, a lesson, a reminder that we in our abundance possess far too many objects, that we are losing touch with most of what passes through our hands.

When we got back to *Daphne* we realized our own wealth, our immeasurable store of objects on board, and we were happy to be able to share a trifle of it with our new friends. A copy of a Swedish illustrated magazine, carefully cut into pieces, now adorns a dozen homes in the village, our old sparking-plugs have become toys for Nubian children and a tattered Finnish flag waves from the village chieftain's gaily-painted boat in sunny Kalabsha.

In one respect our stay in this village resembled our experiences in Greece: we were adopted by the first person to meet us as we stepped ashore. Ibrahim, the builder, regarded us almost as his personal property and he tended us during our walks as if we were three self-willed goats. He was by no means a bad herdsman and I was very sorry that Alvar was not with us on this stage of our journey; he would have appreciated to the full both the Nubian architecture and Ibrahim's views on the art of building houses 'which are all better than the others'. Despite their uniformity, the houses of Kalabsha varied as much as the fruit on an apple-tree. Apart from the changing position on the rock terraces above the river, the planning of the houses had always been solved a little differently and the really individual touch was lent by the painted ornamentation. Some houses had broad red and yellow bands painted as a socle, others had a flaunting pattern of large, irregular triangles laid as a net over the whole façade, while the stricter ones had cubistic white paintings sparsely applied to the clay-coloured surface of the walls. These latter paintings in a geometric style, which seemed copied from plaited or woven forms of figures (see photograph facing p. 272) especially interested us and, full of the zeal of research, we enquired for the artists. They were not far away, as it was either the housewives or their daughters in the early teens who had done the paintings. If this fact at first surprised us and seemed incompatible with the painting's high quality and adherence to tradition, we soon realized that on the contrary it explained them. Even among our own peasantry the conservative women have, through the centuries, kept alive artistic forms in the sphere that belongs solely to them – textiles.

Ibrahim's own house, which dominated the entire village, was a kind of pavilion covered with a dome, unlike any other building. It was obviously intended as an experiment and a professional advertisement similar to the houses that European architects usually build for themselves.

'I wanted to show that I can build whatever I like,' the proud master-builder declared, admitting, however, that the house was stiflingly hot in the summer and draughty in the winter – in other words, almost uninhabitable. 'But the main thing is that people admire it,' he concluded with disarming naïvety.

His most recent and beautiful building was the schoolteacher's house, which he had finished six months before. Or rather the schoolteacher's second wife's house, for our architectural studies had brought us into contact with a side of Nubian polygamy which was as surprising as it was agreeable. Nobody here keeps a harem, but those who can afford it take two or three wives and build a house for each of them. The teacher, a gentle, courteous old man in his sixties, had previously lived near the school in the centre of Kalabsha on the other side of the river, but the year before our visit he had come into a little money and taken unto himself a second wife, forty years younger than the first. Edries and Ibrahim painted the advantages of the system in glowing colours: the fortunate teacher now led two lives, one on each side of the river. In his first home he could be the learned and dignified sage whose meditations were not to be disturbed, fussed over by his wife and a shining example to his grown-up sons. In the second he crept about on the floor with a spoilt little son riding on his back and told indecent stories to his coquettish young wife. Evidently I showed too much appreciation of this way of life: Mona's face darkened and she declared that through polygamy men place themselves on a level with the animals. I could not help explaining to our Nubian friends:

'In Europe we have the same system. Those who can afford it build themselves two houses for two totally different lives, one in town and one in the country. Sometimes we also have a boat on which we live a third life. But we always take the same wife with us, for she changes just as much with the new environment as we do ourselves.'

A less controversial subject was that of building costs in Kalabsha. Ibrahim told us that whenever we liked he was willing to build us, for £50, a complete farm with monumental gateway, living quarters, open loggia with palm-trunk roof, guest-hall, storeroom and stall for the animals; the site on the edge of the rocky desert cost nothing; all we had to do was to pick out a fine spot by the river.

'Then you can come here every winter when it's cold in your homeland. Perhaps the dam will never be built and Nubia can live ...'

But Edries, who could never resist teasing Mona about women's rights, added:

'And the doctor can take a second wife in Kalabsha to run the house for him. All she would need is £1 a month like the other wives ...'

Everything I had just gained by my diplomacy went by the

board and the male sex shrank back to the level of rams and chimpanzees.

But we soon had more serious things to think of. Ibrahim took us to the village storekeeper's house, where a seaman lay ill; perhaps we could help him? In a dark hovel we found a hefty young man on a bunk; the whole of his right arm was swollen and a badly infected wound in his hand had been covered with slices of onion and bandaged round with some woollen rags. We did not need to be doctors to see that the man had severe blood-poisoning which had already spread through his body, as he had pain in the glands of his armpits and groin. We explained to his employer, the storekeeper, that the sick man must have medical care at once if his life was to be saved. We were told in reply that the next steamer to the town did not leave for three days. What we had seen of the scandalous conditions at the state hospital and of the appalling overcrowding at the missionary hospital at Assuan made us very doubtful of the seaman's chances of being treated even if he got there. On the other hand, we had penicillin on board *Daphne*, three doses all ready to inject which had been given to us by a doctor friend in Sweden. Neither of us had any experience of how to give an injection, but if ever there was a time to try, it was now. Having carefully studied the directions, and with the moral support of Mona and Edries, I told the touchingly grateful patient to raise his muscular posterior; unfortunately, the 600,000 units flowed very sluggishly and I had to stab three times before the syringe was empty. For safety's sake we also gave him some aureomycin tablets to take the next few days, and on our return two weeks later, when we spent the night in a neighbouring village to which the news had spread, we had the pleasure of hearing that the sick man had recovered.

While we were treating the seaman, other sick people collected outside the door; we handed out all we had in the way of medicine, but after only half an hour the village chieftain came to see us and asked if it was really our intention to heal only the old woman with the cataract, when the boracic acid we had given her was easily enough for ten others. Having seen so much of the idyllic side of Kalabsha, we found it salutary to see this dark side as well. It brought home to us a problem of which we had been vaguely aware during the whole of our journey.

What is it that delights and appeals to us in a place like this village? Let us say that it is the absence of everything we dislike in the modern community: an inner restlessness and spiritual emptiness, artificial needs and artificial satisfying of them, sterile egotism and standardization. Perhaps it is more correct to say that it is the opposite of these deficiencies we admire, the positive attitude which puts the development of personality in the centre of interest. On the other hand, we cannot close our eyes to the material misery, mostly in the form of disease and early death, which oppresses these people. No appreciation, however glowing, of surviving idylls should blunt our consciousness of the Nubian and Egyptian peasants' right to benefit by the helping hand of medical science and technology. But there is one condition attached to this help: it must not result in our replacing their material destitution with our spiritual poverty.

We often complain that religious and ethical values in the west have been largely uprooted by the unjustified and optimistic belief in reason and evolution produced by the technical progress of the nineteenth century. Now that rationalism has been weighed in the balance and found wanting and there is no longer any warfare of principle between science and religion, we realize what we have lost but cannot win it back overnight. If this conception of our present dilemma is correct, we should pay special heed to the 'underdeveloped races' who still retain their ethical attitude to life; we must not hand them the naïve illusions of trite materialism and dead rationalism together with the valuable medical and industrial aid they so badly need. We have a chance of gaining time for humanity if we spare these people our own mistakes and instead embody them in the modern world in a mature way. Least of all have we reason to look down our noses at the backward population of the Nile Valley: however lacking in bookish education and social progress it may be, it is much further advanced on the human plane than the barbarians of the west.

We should like to have stayed longer at Kalabsha, but Edries was impatient to get to his home village and after two days we continued our journey. It was ten o'clock before we got away but a fresh breeze allowed us after only two hours to cut across the Tropic of Cancer. Rather disappointed, we found that it had not left any visible trace on the banks of the Nile. On the other hand, the heat had been increasing day by day; this January cruise under the cloudless sky of Nubia had, for us, summer's plenitude of lavish sunshine and a pleasant heat which was never sultry. At the Tropic of Cancer we bathed for the first time in the Nile; at least Edries and I did – Mona was on the brink of tears at the thought of the perils that beset us in the form of bilharziasis and typhoid. But the sun was so scorching and the water so inviting that we could not take notice of either her or the worms, but floated along in *Daphne*'s rippling wake for several miles.

The day also offered a new kind of temple experience, which in a delightful way combined sailing and archaeology, *Daphne* and ancient monuments. About three o'clcok we sighted one or two huge Osiris statues on the shore to starboard and steered cautiously up to them. Edries could jump ashore on to the actual temple courtyard, where he made the rope fast round the nearest column. We had come to the rock-temple of Garf Husein, built by the indefatigable Ramses II on a level which at present corresponds to that of the raised Assuan Dam. Not a living soul or a house was to be seen, only the desert, the river and the Osiris figures. It was in itself a great experience to take possession of an Egyptian temple in this way, to encounter only the void left by those who had once prayed there. But how were we to get into the temple halls, which were hewn out of the rock like a deep cave and closed by a rickety door of wood and wire netting? After hesitating for a moment, we carefully loosened the screws of the hinges and, armed with our hissing gas lantern, stepped respectfully into the presence of the six giant statues of Ramses II which flanked the pillars of the colonnade. The side walls were adorned with the customary bas-reliefs and through a vestibule at the end we came into the holy of holies, where an altar and four god statues loomed up in the glow from the lantern, frightening in their superhuman severity, wildness and muscular strength. A series of small rooms beside the cult-chamber were empty and resembled burial-chambers at Thebes.

Having screwed the door back on to its hinges and returned to *Daphne*, we found that she had unexpected company: a black fish, as big as our dinghy and not in the least afraid of us, was nosing about among the rocks by the shore. On our return voyage I saw in the Cairo Agricultural Museum an embalmed specimen, three thousand years old, of the same fish and found that it was the sacred perch of the Nile, *Lates niloticus*, that we had had the honour of meeting. We continued our run before the light northerly wind and for an hour we raced a small but uncommonly swift aiasa. Not until we put up our big balloon, which before we had been too lazy to set, did we pass the aiasa, while its laughing, black-skinned crew danced and sang on their narrow deck to honour us.

As the sun dipped towards the horizon about half-past five we sighted the large village of Dakka, where a modern pumping-station works on a raft in the river and wide green cornfields extend into the desert. Two trees, the only ones in the village, stood a hundred yards apart on the bank; we made fast to one of them and went for an evening stroll up to the fields. Only a young man and two dogs came with us to show us the way; the Nubians have none of the Egyptians' often brazen curiosity. It was amazing to see what lush crops sprout from the desert once it is watered. Our guide told us, however, that not all desert earth will do: only in places where the Nile for thousands of years has mixed a certain percentage of humus soil with the sand does it pay to water. Soil of this kind, which lies too high to be watered by the old means but can be made fertile with modern motor pumps, is to be found all along the Nile Valley and that is what Nasser has in mind in connection with the big dam project.

We set off again in the early dawn and came before long to Dakka's big temple, of which only two gate pylons protruded from the water as at Philae. We had to be content with sailing over the sunken temple, peering in vain down through the water for its colonnades and statues. The slanting rays of the rising sun lent a fantastic appearance to the landscape on both sides of the broad waterway: black mountain peaks stuck up out of the sea of sand, casting mile-long shadows; it was as if the desert were filled with pyramids right to the horizon, as if we had come to an inner, unknown Egypt with dynasties and mighty Pharaohs a hundred times more numerous, a primeval Egypt which none had yet discovered.

The day was hotter than the previous one. We northerners did not complain, but Edries was almost prostrate and I puzzled over the odd fact that southerners on a temporary visit to the North are in the same way more insensitive to the cold than the country's own sons. At ten o'clock we passed the dead Byzantine town of Akmindi, which, with its city walls, streets and church ruins, would have been worth a visit. But in Egypt one becomes so surfeited with ruins and with the brutalized remains of people's lives and work which the centuries leave behind them, that one has interest only for the ancient monuments that have a living face. Perhaps, too, we were half aware of the averseness that the westerner feels when he sees how utterly the mighty cities and rich monasteries of the Christian era have been shattered, how indifferent this land has become to its short Christian interlude. The happiness we feel at the sight of the smallest ancient fragment on Greek soil or of Rome's deeply buried pre-Christian relics, is due to our having come upon the husks of seeds which have borne fruit. In Egypt most things bespeak human striving which has been in vain.

About noon the breeze died. We were left lying in the blazing sun south of the village of Nag Uman Haquabat and had another long, pleasant swim before going on by engine. The map and the Guide Bleu told of several temples along this stretch of the river, but they were submerged. About one o'clock, however, we sighted a mighty pylon façade on the starboard bank: El Sibu's temple. *Sibua* is the Arabic word for lioness, a name which the temple got from the avenue of sphinxes in front of the entrance. We found this avenue submerged and could steer cautiously up to the pylons between the sphinx heads projecting out of the water. Waiting his chance on the bank was the nicest temple-caretaker we had ever met, an old man of eighty with a handsome white moustache, a thousand wrinkles in his black face and eyes which twinkled with a gentle humour. I say waiting his chance, for it appeared that we were the first tourists for two years and that since the war the old chap had sold a total of six admission tickets out of his book; we had not the heart to produce our pass from the Chief Superintendent in Cairo entitling us to free admission to all monuments, even if the money did go to the state. He greeted us in fluent Italian and honoured me by calling me in turns *Eccellenza* and *Marchese* – it appeared that thirty years before he had been in service with the Italian consul in Alexandria.

A still older but equally hale and hearty man, the caretaker's uncle, came on the scene and also started speaking Italian – we felt quite at home.

After we had photographed the handsome old men in the partly submerged temple court and chatted about the water which rose higher every year, they took us to see the interior of the temple. The design is similar to that of the Garf Husein temple, but El Sibu is of special interest in that there still remain so many of the paintings and small extensions which were built on when the temple was changed into a monastery during late antiquity. Most of the old Egyptian buildings have in this way known a Coptic period, but almost everywhere the Arabs have destroyed the Christian ornamentation and the archaeologists have removed every vestige of it. At El Sibu hieroglyphics are mixed up with Coptic inscriptions, saints and angels with the phallus god Amon Re. Especially well preserved is a depiction of the twelve apostles in red linear style, probably from the sixth century.

It was cool in the shade of the Osiris colossuses and our two hosts were so entertaining, humorous and considerate that we should like to have stayed longer with them. A messenger from the nearby village brought a greeting from the village chieftain; he hoped we would stay the night. But the calendar and Edries' longing for Toma drove us on. We sailed on for another fifteen miles until the setting sun forced us to seek shelter for the night.

A group of submerged palms stood out in the water in front of the little village of Nag el Biteiha. We anchored between the trees and the bank, rowed ashore in the dinghy and were met by the sheik of the village, a man of perhaps fifty, dressed in a snow-white garment to his ankles and as dignified as a cardinal. He was in addition the village storekeeper and owned a house with a large open loggia on to the river. As the brown twilight thickened, we sat there talking to five or six of the village elders. The postmaster, a venerable old negro, had read about us in a newspaper, and as he also read every letter which passed through his office he knew that the chief of police in the adjacent Korosko had received orders from the governor at Assuan to look after us. We took the unintentional hint *ad notam* and decided to sail past Korosko without stopping: Nubia for us was to remain the land without police. Tea was served out of silver pots and we felt like guests of a rich merchant in the Arabian Nights, sitting there on soft carpets and talking of the caravan routes to Dongola and Kordofan while the stars grew bright above the desert. Not even the passenger paddle-steamer from Wadi Halfa, which passed by on the river with a long row of lighted cabin windows, broke the spell; the wash, which rippled for a long time among the stones by the shore, was the waves of the sea in the tales of Sinbad the Sailor.

At Korosko, which we passed early the following morning, the Nile swings to the north-west, turning south again after a bend of twelve miles. We used the engine here to avoid tacking and so reached the little temple at Amada by ten o'clock. It lies quite isolated on the sloping shore not far from the river. A tiny inlet, where mimosa bushes stood dropping their golden balls into the water, offered an ideal anchorage; through the clear water we could see the sandy bottom undulating in a delicate pattern. The Amada temple is small but unusually beautiful and pure in style. It dates from the early heyday of the New Kingdom, the reigns of Thutmose III and Amenhotep II. As there was no caretaker or human dwelling in sight, we climbed up on to the roof and from there down into the hypostyle hall, which was closed off with lattice doors. Having admired the strict reliefs, we climbed out again in the same convenient way and remained sitting for a while up on the roof. It was a clear morning with an unusually fresh, light air. From the other side of the river piping childish voices could be heard reciting in chorus; they were so far away that we could not make out exactly where they came from, but they must have been from the village school. To the west, the desert sands extended, endless and mute.

Only a few miles left now to Edries' home village of Toma. There he had lived until he was ten, when his mother died and he was sent to his father, who was in the service of a prince in Cairo. That was eleven years ago, but Edries clung to his childhood memories with a love which the years in the great city had merely increased. The nearer we came to Toma the more we heard about his mother, about cousins, games and happenings in the past. Here he had ridden through the desert for a whole day as a lad of six together with his grandfather, taking with him a kid which he killed with his own hands on a holy sheik's grave as a thank-offering for his having recovered from a severe illness. Here was the neighbouring village of Derr, which had long been the largest and wealthiest he could imagine, as it had several houses built of stone. At last Toma came into sight beyond a bend in the river, quite a large, well-built village with perhaps two hundred farms. But Edries hardly recognized it. No wonder: the pride of Toma, the rustling palm grove of his childhood, was but a withered clump of reeds far out in the water with yellow, dying leaves. The Egyptian engineers at Assuan are proud because every year they have taken bigger risks and raised the water-level still another six inches above the resistance calculations made by the English engineers; it means more water for the cotton and rice fields in Lower Egypt during the hottest weeks of summer, but death to the Nubian palms which have to stand so long in water. After some hesitation Edries pointed out his grandfather's house. Unlike all others, it was not built of mud bricks but of square, hewn stones; but then his grandfather *had* been village chieftain for fifty years until he had died recently and been succeeded by his son, Edries' uncle.

We anchored near a gigantic sycamore tree, whose gnarled roots extended down to the water. It felt almost like rowing straight into the most moving chapter of an autobiographical novel as we went ashore in the dinghy. The whole village lay deep in calm and silence, no one had come down to the shore and none of those who passed recognized the returning son. Above the steep rock lay his old home with a locked gate crowned by two cornucopias, which flanked a quotation from the Koran. We knocked, and a young servant-girl opened the door and asked us to wait. After a few moments two youngish men came out, Edries' cousins. They greeted him in a friendly but quiet way; we thought of the matter-of-fact and unsentimental behaviour of our own peasants at life's emotional moments. Down here there is an added element of restraint – the Mohammedan self-control. The whole family were all equally reserved in their greeting – as though Edries had been away for a week. The only one who could not contain her feelings was old grandmother; first she held the boy at arm's length to look at him, then buried her head against his chest.

Edries' uncle, the young village chieftain, had a complexion as

black as boot polish and was extremely careful of his dignity.
He invited us into the guest-hall, which was so fine that the
ceiling, instead of the traditional palm-trunks, consisted of
imported Scandinavian deal – knotted throw-out planks which at
home in Finland would never have been used where they were
seen. There was no excited conversation in Nubian between
Edries and his relations but polite talk in English about our
journey, about the rising water-level in Nubia and the paltry
compensation, forty piastres, which the government pays for
every submerged date-palm.

After this reception the hunt for *the key* began. It turned out
that Edries had a house in the village, his mother's house, which
had been shut up eleven years before and stood there waiting for
him all this time. But as it was so long ago, no one could remember which of the relations had the key. We went off together with
Cousin Soliman and Uncle Abdul to look for it. Despite our
efforts we never managed to sort out Edries' relations – it seemed
as if he had at least half a dozen grandmothers, about thirty
uncles and most of the village boys as cousins. Our hunt for the
key led us from house to house, at each one of which we were
invited in and given refreshment; everywhere the long-lost Edries
was received with restrained but unmistakable love. Yet it was
plain that the display of feelings was in reverse proportion to the
relationship: the most expansive were the complete outsiders.
One old woman after the other came up to Edries in the street
and began to wail; we found out that in keeping with village
custom they wanted to weep for his dead mother the first time
they saw the son after her decease – the fact that eleven years had
passed could not deter them from this duty. One old woman,
however, who saw that we were in a hurry, said considerately:

'I would like so much to cry with you, but I see you haven't
time today. Can't you come again tomorrow, so that we can have
a really good cry?'

Of the relatives we visited in vain to ask for the key, there are
two whom I specially remember. One was Edries' cousin Asisa,
who was a widow and lived together with her mother. Her
husband had died eight years before and she was now twenty-five,
which down here is as good as middle age. She was still very
pretty, perhaps partly because she had never had any children,

and, full of sympathy, we asked Edries if she could not remarry.

'No, it is not the custom, nobody will have another man's woman,' he explained.

Asisa had sprinkled us with perfume as we came in and offered us Coca Cola in her airy loggia. With the reluctant Edries as interpreter, Mona began to flatter her for her beauty, enlighten her as to woman's position in the modern society and put daring thoughts into her head regarding her own chances for the future. Poor Asisa, who had had it drummed into her for years that her life was over, was evidently deeply moved. She took Mona's hand, looked into her eyes as though to be sure Mona was not deceiving her, and was then completely spellbound by her. Mona, who was brimming over with sympathy and solidarity, wanted a memento of her new friend and asked Edries to ask Asisa if she might take her photograph. Edries refused: it was unthinkable for a respectable Nubian woman to allow anything of the kind. But Cousin Soliman had other views and translated Mona's request – perhaps to tease Edries. Asisa hesitated a second, then her eyes kindled, she vanished into her bedroom and returned after a while in her best dress and with a transparent veil over her hair. Allowing herself to be photographed by Mona in front of her male relations was obviously an act of very daring emancipation and we felt sure that the incident would not pass without comment once the guests were out of the way. Mona made Asisa promise, however, that she would come to *Daphne* the following day and return the visit.

'I bet you she doesn't come,' I remarked as we left the house. Unfortunately I was right: Edries told us next day that Asisa had suddenly been taken ill and could not leave the house.

Another memorable visit during our game of 'hunt-the-key' was to an uncle, who did not, however, seem to be a brother of the village chieftain. He too had a handsome guest-hall, where we drank tea while more and more relations from the immediate neighbourhood gathered round Edries. Among them was a centenarian, who was so decrepit that he did not recognize Edries; he merely let out an 'Allah!' from time to time, a cross between a sigh and a pious thought. Another ancient member of the family, however, was very spry and clear in the head. He was small and lean, had a fine, intelligent face, short white beard and round glasses; he was regarded by the whole village as a holy man and was called sheik. According to Edries he knew the whole of 'our book' – the Koran – by heart and could heal most diseases. He prescribed both salves, which he made himself, and prayers; Asisa, who had suffered from a racking headache, was quite well after she had plaited into her hair a tiny bag containing sacred quotations. The old chap greeted us with beautiful and friendly words in Arabic, but he kept his shawl between his hand and ours when shaking hands – evidently he did not wish to touch anything unclean.

I was beginning to be sceptical about the key when at last we came to a mean little house where a woman lived with a new-born baby – her husband, one of Edries' innumerable cousins, worked in Cairo. Here, surprisingly, was the key, a long, boomerang-like piece of wood with a series of nails at the end. I was amazed to recognize an object which I had seen depicted in archaeological literature as a key to the ancient Egyptian temples and burial-chambers. Later, we had many other proofs that Nubia is a profitable cultural region for relics; the drink *busa*, which one is sometimes offered, is nothing other than the ancient Egyptian ale and the little Nubian girls' plaited rat-tail hair is the same coiffure as the princesses and dancing-girls have on Theban tomb-paintings.

So we stood at last in front of Edries' house, which lay between other similar houses and had a view over the Nile. The lock squeaked as the wooden key was pressed in and the door opened stiffly; in the courtyard the sandstorms had piled up a drift, the lattice-work of the loggia's roof had partly fallen in and in the kitchen the birds had built nests in the pots and pans. On the whole, however, everything was in fairly good shape and it would not have taken much work to make the house habitable again. Edries fought to control himself, but we who knew him saw that the tears were not far away. For this boy, whose home of recent years had been the seascout barge in Cairo and whose only prop in life had been General Ragab's fatherly friendship, it was an overwhelming experience suddenly to have a village, a large family and a home of his own.

In the evening we were invited to dinner at Uncle Village Chieftain's. Alas, our hopes of a real Nubian meal were sadly dashed; Edries, who had spent the whole afternoon with his relatives in peace, had also had dinner with them – 'dishes which you don't like and sitting on the floor with women and children,' he told us. We were conducted to the guest-hall, where the table was laid only for two. The meal consisted of *consommé*, *riz à l'indienne*, *poulet rôti*, *pommes frites*, *compote de raisins* – this last, preserved grapes, was a new delicacy for us. But for the surroundings and the fact that instead of wine we were served tepid Nile water, we might just as well have been sitting at a restaurant in Cairo or Stockholm – particularly as Edries and his uncle out of politeness themselves waited on us and we were thus for the most part thrown on our own company. It was a little more sociable over coffee; we talked of the new dam which threatens to swallow up Nubia, and of the migration to the proletarian districts of Cairo and Alexandria which will no doubt be the only way out for the Nubian people. Surprised and amused, we noticed the change that Edries had undergone in his manner towards us in only half a day; he paid us one conventional compliment after the other, saying how honoured he was that we were graciously visiting his house and had deigned to partake of a meal at his uncle's. He had suddenly found a place and thereby a part to play in the community.

During the following days Edries slept on board at night – to his countrymen he was the Cairo student and the blasé travelling-companion of the Europeans – but in the daytime there was not a sign of him. For us it was pleasant to rest for a few days here in Toma. Mona stayed in bed to nurse a cold that had been coming on for several days and I buried myself in my books or went for solitary 'walks' in the dinghy in Toma's submerged palm and eucalyptus wood, where the birds sang in the treetops and a peaceful park atmosphere reigned on the shady waterways almost a mile from the shore. I also went for outings in the village together with Edries' twenty-year-old cousin Soliman, whom we called 'the Dandy' – for a more complete one I have never met. Dressed in a dazzlingly white galabia of a far more elegant cut than anyone else's, posing affectedly with a thin walking-stick in his hand, spoilt to death by a toil-worn mother and three sisters, who did all the heavy work on the farm, he devoted himself mostly to Arabic poetry, manicure and social intercourse. He particularly amused us because he reminded us very much of a friend of ours whom we hitherto had thought to be the product of advanced capitalistic conditions in one of the cultural metropolises of Europe. I know now that it is one's innate tendencies which are the determining factor, as one can just as well become a dandy in Toma as in London or Vienna.

We should no doubt have stayed longer at Toma if Edries had not shown a disquieting change. Our questions over morning coffee soon met with morose answers or mere silence. All comradely contact, all spontaneous liking for us seemed to have vanished as though it had never been. During our journey the lad had very seldom bothered about the ritual morning and evening prayers; now he not only became a zealously active Mohammedan but took on more and more of the sheik-uncle's attitude to us as unclean foreigners. When Soliman jokingly remarked that all the mammas had shown their thirteen-year-old marriageable daughters to Edries and that he had begun to inquire how much land he would inherit from his grandfather, I saw in a flash that we must either set sail at once or resign ourselves to losing our travelling-companion. Had I not known that both the General, the seascouts and university studies were waiting for him in Cairo, I should have hesitated longer. As it was, we simply weighed anchor very early one morning, and when Edries poked out a sleepy head we had already put several miles between us and the sycamore tree at Toma. That morning, for the first time, I saw his youthful and optimistic expression give place to that of an old, silently suffering negro.

With Edries sulking in the after-cabin and Mona still in bed with a cold, *Daphne*'s crew had been drastically reduced. I was alone on deck, but *Daphne* is a well-behaved boat who keeps her course with the helm lashed, and all sails were set. About ten o'clock I sighted a high, rocky point sticking out into the river; it was crowned by mighty walls, an ancient Egyptian temple pylon and dense rows of house ruins. It was Ibrim, an ancient fortress, which had been inhabited right up until the middle of the nineteenth century. As I began to strike the sails, Edries came out and gave a hand, without saying a word; a seascout does not forget his duty to the boat whatever happens. We started the engine and steered cautiously along the base of the cliff, where a line of tombs with hieroglyphic inscriptions over the doors and reliefs inside the chambers were half flooded and accessible only by boat. From a tomb a little higher up, white bones and a human skull or two had slid down and caught on a ledge of rock; evidently the town's inhabitants were buried here even in modern times. We anchored by the steep path leading up to the city gate. There was not a soul to be seen, not a tree or one green blade, only gravel and rock walls. Mona stayed on board, while Edries and I climbed up to Ibrim. Our gloomy spirits after the departure from Toma may have been partly to blame, but I have seldom seen anything more desolate or dismal than this dead fortress town, where the Ptolemaic temple and the Coptic basilica were just as much in ruins as the roofless houses and of equally little interest.

We were all the more greatly impressed by a discovery we made soon after weighing anchor again. We were moving carefully along by engine under the sheer cliff to port, when on a smooth rock-face which chanced to be flooded with sunlight from the side I caught sight of countless half-obliterated images. It took a while before Edries and Mona, who had got out of her bunk in curiosity, could make them out. But having once distinguished them, we saw more and more on other rock surfaces: giraffes, ostriches and antelopes, all in a style which reminded us of the pre-historic cave pictures in France. How old are these carvings? It is difficult for the non-expert to offer anything but guesses, but it seems reasonable to trace them back to the time when Nubia was not yet a desert of sand and stones, but a savanna where the animals portrayed could live – perhaps fifteen thousand years ago.

The business of lunch, which the housewife's indisposition loaded on to our unaccustomed shoulders, also made an appeal to Edries' scouting spirit. After we had joined forces in preparing the food, given Mona hers in bed, eaten and washed up, our friend began to be more himself again. Not for nothing was he a son of Africa's interior: together with his dark skin he had inherited the capacity for living in the present moment and in what immediately surrounded him. Toma already lay beyond the horizon; after two or three days it was as if we had never been there.

The strange desert landscape with black pyramid hills in the yellow sea of sand still predominated on both sides of the river, but the palm groves in the water grew more extensive – evidently the soil in these parts until quite recently could still be tilled for the greater part of the year. The villages were close together, but very few craft were to be seen, only an occasional small sailing-boat and no steamers – they seemed to move mostly at night.

The goal we were striving to reach on this evening was the famous cliff-temple of Abu Simbel, of which, in spite of all the photographs and guide-book descriptions, I had a rather hazy mental picture. Now we were to see this monument, which was said to be not only the most magnificent in Nubia but in the whole of Egypt south of Thebes. We had no difficulty in finding the place, even though dusk was falling as we drew near. The village of Abu Simbel lies on the port side inside a wreath of submerged palms, but on the other side of the wide bay we glimpsed a kind of huge niche in the cliff. The nineteenth century tourists had to walk for some distance from their Nile boats through fields and groves before reaching the cliff-temple, but *Daphne* could steer right up to it. We anchored by the smaller temple, where six god statues, as high as a three-storeyed house, stood with their feet in the water and seemed to lean out over *Daphne*. A hundred yards farther on we could see the big temple, whose four seated colossuses tower up to a height of eight storeys. No human dwelling, not a living soul was anywhere near; we were alone with the huge gods. As we sat on deck in the warm night the moon rose and the statues' facial expression emerged. They were broad, smiling faces, which imperturbably stared into a world invisible to man. Their mediating role could not have been illustrated more simply, clearly or suggestively: man sees that they see, but what they see is hidden. A horned owl had evidently built its nest somewhere in the headgear of the mighty: suddenly a protracted screech cut through the silence.

'A bad bird,' Edries said gloomily and made haste to say his evening prayers. Mona and I also felt the need of dispelling the ghostly atmosphere and soon a delicate Mozart concerto rose up through the darkness from our radio towards the looming giants, silent once more.

If Abu Simbel by night made a frightening impression, like an Easter Island, where mysterious, primeval time itself has taken on a face of stone, we awakened in the morning to a pastoral idyll which corresponded more to what the temple ruins of Greece usually offer. A large herd of black goats, accompanied by one or two cheerful goatherds, came in single file along the narrow, sandy margin between river and cliff. In the bright, clear morning sun the whole world was doubled by a reflection in the calm water: cliff, god figures, flowering mimosa trees and black goats were there in two editions, both equally newborn, above and below the dividing line of the shore. Soon the temple-caretaker came riding from the village on his donkey and we rowed ashore in our dinghy – including Mona, who still had a temperature but had temporarily left her sick-bed.

The cliff-temple's interior made just as deep an impression on us as its exterior. Armed with our gas lantern we stepped into the great temple's colonnaded hall, where towering Osiris colossuses formed a double line beneath the flight of Horus wings in the roof. The bas-reliefs of the walls with portrayals of Abu Simbel's builder's, Ramses II's, war with the Hittites are such a detailed and exhaustive book that the hard-pressed tourist has time to read only the most striking headings. The interesting thing about this cliff-temple's architecture is that the floor in all the rooms and passages slopes slightly upwards, the roof downwards and the walls perspectively inwards. Even materially, therefore, the temple prepares one in every detail for the inner, deeper and holier part which is hidden at the very end of the physical and spiritual perspective. This innermost cult-chamber, which only the high priest was allowed to visit at very rare ceremonies, was, as I mentioned in a previous chapter, the temple's intended nucleus. We children of this modern age, for whom there is no nucleus, clatter in unimpeded to the very holy of holies, where four partly mutilated gods are enthroned in high relief behind the altar.

The smaller temple is not inferior to the big one; if the measurements here are more modest, the quality of the sculptures is higher. As we were making ready to start about noon and I was left alone for a moment in front of the Hathor temple to take leave of this unique place, something happened which moved me more deeply than all the rest. At the foot of the colossus that depicts Ramses II's lovely queen, Nefreteri, in the guise of the goddess Hathor, stands a little princess, no higher than an ordinary human. I had not noticed her before, perhaps because she had been standing in the shadow behind her mother's legs, but now the sun had moved round so that her face with its little turned-up nose and her slim, shapely body were full in the light. It was as though she had been standing beside me, a provocative and attractive young woman. I looked round: there was no one near to smile. Rather awkwardly I stroked first the arm, then the rounded hip. They were as warm as a living body, it was as if hot, young blood were pulsating inside. On a sudden, irresistible impulse, I kissed the smiling mouth of stone.

CHAPTER XI

A Glimpse of The Sudan

Twelve miles south of Abu Simbel, Egypt ends and the Sudan begins. Our original intention had been to extend our Nile trip only as far as Assuan and we had therefore not got ourselves a visa for the Sudan, but the head of the Sudan Office in Assuan, a gentle little negro, had advised us not to bother about all the formalities and sail calmly on. The Egyptian passport control takes place at Shellal near the Assuan Dam, where the river steamer starts, and the Sudanese at the terminus at Wadi Halfa; for us, sailing with our own boat, it was easy to have nothing to do with the police.

We left Abu Simbel about noon; by our standards it was a blazing hot summer's day, even if the calendar did say 20th January. The wind was so faint that we had no mind to sail. Instead, we put up the sun-awning right over the boat and crossed the frontier by engine. At the last Egyptian village we glimpsed a few military tents in a palm grove and the green flag with the half moon floating from a staff. Now for it: would we be stopped or would we get over? Tensely, I watched the reaction at the frontier-post through the glasses. Nothing happened, the men were evidently having a siesta snooze. Half a mile further on the Sudanese fla   n the opposite bank
of the river.   negroes in shabby
uniforms car   o call in at the bank
for control.   , as though merely
returning a g   e foreign flag must
have put the   to them to fire a
warning shot   lered.

The landsc   lly been changing
character: the   iver narrower and
the atmosphe   gone. The effects
of the Assuan   ows in its normal
bed with a wa   in the winter than
during the flo   very opposite of
conditions on   ter all the treeless,

newly-built villages we had passed it was a treat to see, in the thick palm groves, villages with the charm that only centuries-old settlement can give. The evening sun slanted over the riverside, creaking sakias and swinging shadoofs were indolently at work watering the clover fields and in front of the huts the women were cooking the evening meal while the smoke rose in white coils through the greenery. But between the villages and the tilled fields lay long stretches of sterile ground with a wide view across the boundless desert.

As the War Ministry maps we had been lent in Cairo included only Egyptian territory, we had nothing but the general map in the guide book. This was no great worry, however, as the river must lead us to Wadi Halfa. Taking careful soundings, as on the lower Nile, and keeping an eager eye out for crocodiles that, according to the guide books, begin to be met with here, we steered off our last sheet of map. Sure enough, there they were: on a spit of sand lay two wooden logs in the hot sun. Before we had time to study them through the glasses they slid down into the water, scared by the noise of our engine. The skipper felt that one of the journey's Goals had been reached and that from now on *Daphne* could stretch herself among all the pleasure yachts of the Mediterranean and Baltic: when had they frightened crocodiles last?

Dusk was falling as we sighted Wadi Halfa's low line of houses with a cluster of paddle-steamers and barges at the wharves. Our attempt to moor at the bank was energetically quashed by the police who hurried up; British law and order reigns in Wadi Halfa and all craft must moor within the area supervised by the customs. We thus had no chance of avoiding the passport officers, but we counted optimistically on not being turned out once we had got so far. The excellent pontoon quay opposite the tidy station building of the Sudan Railways was vacant, as the steamer from Assuan only comes twice a week, and we tied up at it. To our surprise there were no complications at all about our passports, we were instantly granted a five-days' permit, but the customs formalities were all the more tedious. The customs officer in charge was a coal-black negro with a face disfigured by the tribal marks which are cut into the young men's cheeks, different for each tribe. Everything on *Daphne* must be declared, counted and weighed, and we ourselves had to undergo customs examination every time we left the harbour area. Edries, who had no passport or other document, got round the difficulty by saying he was a Sudanese, which was accepted without question by the authorities. There was, anyway, some truth in the statement: his father was born in a village somewhere down towards Kordofan.

Late though it was by the time all the formalities were done with, we could not resist going for a walk to explore the town. Wadi Halfa, which according to the Guide Bleu was founded by the English and has 3,000 inhabitants, is, according to the Sudanese, an ancient trading centre with a population of 50,000. One statement is perhaps as correct as the other, since the term town can be limited in different ways. We got the impression that the place was smaller than Assuan, but much cleaner and better built than any town in Egypt. The whole atmosphere is different; there is orderliness, tidiness and an indolent peace which are unknown in the over-populated and uneasy Egypt. The shops, which were just closing, were well-stocked with ordinary British industrial products and cheap Sudanese foodstuffs, the Greek café *Elphis* where we drank a bottle of beer would not have alarmed a germ-shy Swedish health visitor and the people we met were all just as unreserved, friendly and calm as those in the Nubian villages. The easily influenced Edries was so impressed that he himself began to believe in his statement that he was a Sudanese: when he had finished his studies he would come and live in Wadi Halfa.

Spirits ran high during the late dinner on board *Daphne*. We had reached our ultimate goal, farther than we had dared to dream when we started the Nile voyage and farther (to our knowledge) than any other boat which had sailed to Egypt on its own keel. From the lighthouse at the Rosetta sandbanks we had made our way 1,200 miles up the Nile – that it was as far again back to the sea we put out of our minds on this evening. We had no need to hesitate whether Wadi Halfa would be the turning-point of our journey: the Second Cataract – during antiquity called the Great Cataract – has never been navigable for boats. But if, instead of looking back at the river voyage we had just completed, we glanced at the map of Africa, our feat dwindled to insignificance. Farther upstream, 900 miles or more, beyond all cataracts and rapids. the Nile was again navigable and continued for another 2,000 miles through jungles and giant lakes to its distant source in Tanganyika. The Nile, which the geographers of antiquity believed to rise at Syene (Assuan), resembled an iceberg, whose greatest, sustaining parts were invisible from the horizon of Egypt. Here at Wadi Halfa this Second Nile impinged on our consciousness and with it the whole of the boundless continent from whose superfluity Egypt, with its fields and riches, had come into existence.

This feeling of something mysterious, which we had reached without being able to understand, took an unexpected form this first night at Wadi Halfa. It was as if Africa's interior wanted to give us a memory of itself to take with us on our voyage back to the Mediterranean. I was awakened at four in the morning by a vague uneasiness and crept out of the cabin to see that everything was in order. There was no moon, but the stars were so big that they formed paths of light across the surface of the river, coiling light-serpents in the warm darkness. From over the water came the sound of shouts, singing, a strange warbling and the hollow throb of drums, a kind of festival sound which now grew louder, now died away. What could it be? I stood for a long time listening in perplexity, undecided as to whether I should creep back to bed or try to investigate the noise. At last I could not stifle my curiosity and waked Edries. Not even he could say definitely what was going on a mile or two away on the riverbank north of the town, but he was as curious as I. Dressing hastily, we set off to find out; Mona, who still had a temperature, did not want to come. It was a long walk we had through the silent streets under the stars as they grew paler and paler. When we reached the outskirts of the town a faint dawn light already lay over the desert hills to the east, but the drums and the shouts continued. On we went, through garden allotments and palm groves, along winding paths, across small irrigation ditches, past solitary houses where dogs woke up as we walked by; we stopped now and then to listen whether the feast was still going on, whether we had got any nearer . . . The drums could still be heard, but they were as far away as ever. At last they were silent, the stars had gone out and in the grey morning light house doors were opened by women who swept sand out or by men who went off quietly

Daphne's *crew,*
Mona and
Edries

At *Abu Simbel's rock temple,* Nubia

Edries' house at Toma, Nubia

Mona, Asisa, Soliman, Edries and 'uncles' at Toma

to their work in the town. We stood at a loss, the spell was broken and an ordinary, prosaic day was beginning. A man came towards us with a donkey; Edries stopped him and asked what had been going on. A wedding, he explained; the desert tribes sometimes come down to the river and dance all night long on the shore.

It was broad daylight when we got back to *Daphne*.

Wadi Halfa's harbour, which usually is the busiest place in the town, lay dead and silent, as it was Friday, the Moslem holy-day. As we sat over our morning coffee under the awning, *Daphne* was honoured by an unexpected visit. Two men in well-pressed European suits appeared on the pontoon, the district commissioner and the town's chief of police. Neither was a day over thirty, the former a full-blooded negro, the latter perhaps eighty per cent negro and twenty per cent Arab. They made an agreeable and cultivated impression, and if politically they had been ardent advocates of having the English turned out of the country, they were, as persons, living examples of the good work the English had done as long as they had charge of the Sudan: both men had been educated at the Kitchener School in Khartoum. The reason for the visit was not quite clear; perhaps it was the unusual fact that some tourists had come to look at Wadi Halfa, which otherwise has to put up with being a transit halt for train and air passengers. We had at all events a profitable talk with our guests about the problems of the young republic of Sudan.

This polite and quiet conversation was ended abruptly by the appearance of a third visitor. A loud-voiced, rather portly man, bubbling with vitality, caused the pontoon to rock and *Daphne* to curtsy as though to an Atlantic wave when he stepped on board: Doctor Anis, senior physician at Wadi Halfa's hospital, quarantine doctor at the harbour and airfield, made his entry.

'Ah, so here are the gate-crashers, the boat which has no bill of health and perhaps has brought cholera and yellow fever into the country, you should have called on my excellent colleague, Doctor Deib at Shellal, never mind, the chief of police seems to be here already, we arrest you and take you along to the Nile Hotel for a whisky and soda, I'm the compulsory friend of all Europeans who can't take care of themselves, two months ago there was a French couple here who had walked all the way from the source of the Nile, they stayed with me for six weeks to rest, by the way how are you, Madame looks a little off colour . . . the pulse is not good . . . put out your tongue, please, oh dear we must see to that, you need a shot of penicillin, but we've time for a cigarette before we go off to the hospital, hallo boy, you there, what's your name, oh Edries, run and tell my chauffeur to wait for a while, no thanks, I smoke nothing but Egyptian, what a very nice boat this is . . .'

Doctor Anis, who was perhaps thirty-five and mainly Arab by extraction, was a living example of the fact that the descendants of the desert tribes are not always lean, hawk-nosed, taciturn, self-willed people; a more typical representative of the rotund type of human I have seldom met – sociable, unreserved, impulsive, undisciplined, full of kindness, humour and a weakness for material pleasures. After about ten minutes we made a move, and while the chief of police and the district commissioner drove off in their waiting jeep, we and Doctor Anis got into the hospital's combined ambulance and hearse, which took us at breakneck speed to the large hospital by the river. After what we had seen of Egyptian hospitals, our expectations of this hospital in the wilds were well below zero and our surprise was therefore all the greater when we were invited to inspect an establishment which, without being at all luxurious or particularly modern, was faultlessly run, well-equipped and moreover pleasant. It consisted of a series of pavilions among shady trees and green lawns, the black nursing attendants – male for the men's pavilions and female for the women's – were dressed in snow-white uniforms and an exemplary order seemed to prevail everywhere. The fact that the Sudan in so many respects differs favourably from Egypt – we saw this from, among other things, the hospital, the well-run railway station, the tidy post-offices and the school textbooks – may seem surprising, but it is probably because the English themselves have built up the Sudan from scratch, while in Egypt, as in India, for that matter, they have ruled through a parasitic local Pascha class, which has aped the worst sides of the westerners but has arrested development and, out of sheer egotism, let the people go on living in their former destitution. Nowadays one hears so much criticism – no doubt partly justified – of the white man's behaviour as colonial ruler, that it is cheering to see that he has, after all, done something positive. For an unbiased judge it must always be counted to the credit of the English that in half a century they have succeeded in turning the Mahdi's kingdom, one of the least civilized parts of the world, into a modern state which, rather shakily perhaps, can stand on its own legs and which, under the leadership of a newly-created educated class of natives, can go on becoming civilized.

Doctor Anis, who is the first Sudanese senior physician in Wadi Halfa, had received his medical training in London and was, professionally and privately, entirely western in outlook, while politically he was an ardent nationalist. But it is plainly asking too much that such 'first generation men' should show objectivity; we let the doctor describe all the supposed wrongs the English had committed in his country – among other things, his predecessor as senior physician had often driven off on hunting trips with the ambulance, so that the sick could not be fetched – and merely expressed our conviction that in fifty years' time the Sudanese will regard these questions differently. Doctor Anis was by no means a fanatic and had life interests other than politics, as we were soon to find out.

It began when, having given Mona a shot of penicillin, he proceeded to examine whether the chill had spread to her lungs. From the waiting-room, where I sat reading a magazine, I heard through the open door the doctor's: 'Cough! Breathe! Cough!' followed by: 'You are shaped like a goddess!' and then, after a new pause: 'Your husband is indeed fortunate!' Then came Mona's calm voice:

'Göran, I think you had better come into the room!'

The doctor now addressed his compliments unashamedly to me:

'Your wife is indeed beautiful. The African women go to seed so quickly. The home of love is the north, not the hot south, as ignorant people imagine. By the way, let me show you something that will interest you.'

And while Mona buttoned up her blouse he called over a young negress who was sitting in the shade out in the courtyard. Submissively, and with frightened eyes, the delicate girl approached. She was perhaps eleven years old.

'She's here for snake-bite, but it's something else you're going to see.'

The girl was made to stretch out on the examination-table and the doctor, unabashed, lifted up the loincloth. Before our amazed eyes lay a bared lower abdomen which was nothing but one deformed, infected scar.

'This is what ninety-five per cent of all Sudanese women look like,' the doctor told us.'When a girl is seven years old tradition decrees that she be circumcised, usually it's the village barber or some old crone who does it without any anaesthetic and without any antiseptic. The clitoris is cut away, the *labia majora* are sewn together so that only a small opening remains and not until the girl is married five or six years later is she opened up again.'

Female circumcision, which according to Doctor Anis is a misinterpretation of the Moslem doctrine, was forbidden by the English but no one took any notice, and now it is one of the Sudanese doctors' biggest problems, a veritable national disease which, apart from the extreme human suffering, causes serious infection in nearly all those who are subjected to this brutal treatment. In this respect the Sudan is the worst of the Mohammedan countries: in Turkey no such operation is performed and in Egypt they content themselves with sewing the *labia majora* together and merely splitting the clitoris in order to lessen the women's sexual desire. The explanation of this circumcision is the Arabs' traditional horror that their wives or daughters might dishonour them by being unfaithful. The doctor told us that fathers in the old days used to bury their daughters alive if they showed the slightest interest in the opposite sex: 'I am killing you before you kill me' was the formula a father uttered on such an occasion.

We were not a little upset by what we had seen and heard, but the doctor had merely begun his description of woman's suffering and love life's decline on the African continent. He told us about the typical wedding celebration when the bride is smeared with oil from top to toe so that she will be slippery in her husband's arms, how he then opens her with a knife and how the two mothers stand outside the door waiting for the bloodstained cloth which is kept as a proof of the girl's virginity – a very uncertain virginity, the doctor pointed out, as even a woman who has borne a child can be sewn together again. But it is not only the circumcised girls who lose for ever any power of erotic enjoyment. In the Southern Sudan, where the population is heathen (which in the doctor's mouth meant non-Moslem), the women are just as insensitive, due to the fact that they start having sexual intercourse at the early age of seven.

'With us, all happiness and pleasure is for the man,' the doctor sighed gloomily. 'We doctors have a gigantic task here before women's elementary rights are recognized.'

There was no mistaking the sincerity of Doctor Anis' medical ideals and in spite of his erotic monomania we could not help liking him; he was a warm-hearted and generous person. From the hospital he took us to the Nile Hotel, which he considered we must not miss seeing. The hotel is down by the river and built in the best colonial style. It was naturally more unassuming than Luxor's Winter Palace and Assuan's Cataract Hotel, but spotlessly clean and with the homely charm of a nineteenth-century country villa. Doctor Anis, who was a regular customer, showed us the house as if it had been his own and let us peep into shady guest-rooms with a view over the Nile, floral wallpaper and mosquito-nets draped above enormous beds.

'An ideal spot for a honeymoon, don't you think?' was the worthy doctor's comment.

As a crystallization of his woman-inspired thoughts we found in one of the rooms, under the transparent mosquito-net, a slim, pretty blonde who had kicked off the bedclothes and was sleeping sweetly in dainty blue pyjamas. Luckily she did not wake up and we could withdraw unobserved. We were told later by the English hotel-owner that it was the air-hostess of a Dutch plane which had had engine trouble and was being repaired at the airfield. The Nile Hotel is only in the daytime the Sleeping Beauty palace which we saw; it makes a living out of the aeroplanes which spend the night at Wadi Halfa on the way from Capetown to Europe and is invaded on most evenings by tired air travellers. At lunch down in the dining-room we met the crew of the damaged plane, including the pretty air-hostess, all rather pleased with their little extra holiday while a new engine was being installed. They had flown the route for several years but had never seen Wadi Halfa in daylight.

'How is your bronchitis?' the doctor asked the air-hostess.

'No', she answered, blushing. 'I haven't time today, we have hired a motor-boat to Abu Simbel.'

In the evening the paddle-steamer from Assuan was to arrive at the pontoon, so we moved *Daphne* to the outer side of the barge. We had special reason to look forward excitedly to the steamer's arrival, as there was just a chance that one of our friends from Finland would be on board. Two months before, we had written to her half in jest from Cairo to say that there was a spare bunk on *Daphne*. At Assuan we were reached by a telegram: ARRIVING CAIRO BY AIR THURSDAY STOP WHERE FIND YOU STOP MAIRE. We had replied: WELCOME WADI HALFA BEFORE 24th JANUARY STOP MOGO (the last word being an economic abbreviation of Mona and Göran). But we did not know if the reply had reached her or if she was willing to come straight on down to Wadi Halfa from Cairo. Doctor Anis, who in his capacity of quarantine doctor, received the passenger list by telephone from Assuan, had allowed us to see it; there, among about a hundred other names, was a 'Mr Mac Gulekian'. It must be Mrs Maire Gullichsen, we thought, and sure enough, there she stood rather anxiously in the dark on the deck of the paddle-steamer and the mutual joy was great.

But the train to Khartoum did not leave until the following morning and no passenger was allowed ashore. We chatted for a while across the railing and then agreed to fetch her in the morning when the customs formalities were over. At eight o'clock next morning we returned to the steamer and asked the steward for Mrs Gullichsen.

'She went off ten minutes ago to the hospital with Doctor Anis; I think she had a touch of bronchitis . . .'

There was no taxi within sight, so our rescue patrol was somewhat delayed, but got there in time. As we reached the doctor's consulting-room we heard: 'Cough! Breathe! You are shaped like a goddess . . .' Our burst of laughter did not put the doctor out in the least, he spoke gravely of the danger of neglected colds and was delighted to hear that Mona felt a different person after her shot of penicillin the day before. Maire also was given a shot, after which the helpful doctor rang up the chief of police and asked if the Black Maria was vacant: he would like to take us for an outing in the afternoon. The chief of police agreed at once and so it was that Maire, Mona, Edrics, I, the chief of police and Doctor Anis, plus two drivers, set off in Wadi Halfa's Black Maria and in the hospital's ambulance to the Great Cataract four miles south of the town. I sent a quiet thought to Doctor Anis's English predecessor, who had been inconsiderate enough to use the ambulance for private outings.

The Great Cataract is a series of rapids about nine miles long which flows along between shattered islands, sharp rocky points and sterile shores. The rock bed consists of black granite, which makes a much more sombre impression than the red slabs of Assuan. The total drop in level is about 130 feet, but at only a few places are real waterfalls formed. We drove along the abandoned railway embankment, which dates from the days of the Mahdi war, and stopped at the third little village opposite the famous Abusir Rock, where so many travellers have carved their names in the stone walls. Here, too, is the largest of the Cataract's islands, a fertile and green oasis which Kitchener presented to the Nubian chieftain that succeeded in piloting two of his gunboats up through the Cataract during the high-water season. The island has been inherited by the sheik's son, who, in oriental fashion, has quite taken on his father's dignity and figure – nowadays it is he who performed the famous feat.

Doctor Anis, who was obviously very popular in the villages, took us to see one of his special friends, the Great Cataract's professional and official crocodile hunter. He was a man whom the authorities had furnished with gun and ammunition so that he would keep the crocodiles away from the cattle's watering-places and the women's laundry pools. He courteously offered us tea in his house, showed us his trophies – crocodile heads of all sizes – and then took us to one of his beats so that we could see the beasts in their live state. On the rocky slabs in the rapids, however, there were no crocodiles to be seen.

'It's the mating season', the doctor explained. 'The animals keep under the water, where it's easier for them to mate.'

This amateur theory, so typical of its originator, convinced us less than the crocodile hunter's explanation:

'I shot one here this morning. They're keeping out of sight today.'

But he himself offered ample compensation for the missing

animals. As so often happens with hunters, he had, with the years, taken on his quarry's appearance, movements and habits. The small piercing eyes blinked alertly, he moved with acceleration between moments of immobility and possessed the uproarious sense of humour which, perhaps on account of its many teeth, we ascribe to the crocodile. This resemblance between types of humans and different animals – there are 'horsy people', 'squirrel people', 'cat people' etc. – permitted Plato to set forth a far more varied typology than Messrs Kretschmer and Sheldon with their investigations into the connection between bodily structure, character and habits of living. Here by the Nile, however, it is plausible to think of another side of animals' character types: the animal gods. How could the ancient Egyptians worship cats, ibises, crocodiles, chimpanzees, bulls? The totem animals of the primitive tribes have been spoken of as the origin of this religion. Another theory is the practical role, such as hunting quarry, useful domestic animal etc., the different animals in the different districts might have. These theories may be correct or incorrect, but they give us no *psychological* understanding of the animal gods, no idea of *how* they were regarded. If, on the other hand, we think of the connection between animal and human, of the man who was a crocodile, it is not a far cry to the crocodile who is a god, to the extremely personal and living being that we meet in the guise of an animal. For the ancient Egyptians, that which was symbolized was always more real than the outer shell: the god was alive in the animal, the meaning present in the hieroglyphic, the intention completed in the gesture. On this afternoon we met the cataract's ancient god in his sacrificial priest, the crocodile hunter.

We stayed at Wadi Halfa for three more days and, by special permission of the district commissioner, were allowed to move *Daphne* from the harbour to the garden in front of the Nile Hotel. From there we made a trip with *Daphne* to the Bouhen temple just below the cataract on the other side of the river. The channel was very shallow and we stuck several times before we could tie up at a little stone staircase below the temple. For us, who had seen so many temples during our journey, this rather modest ruin, only eight or ten feet high, interested us mainly because of the fine bas-reliefs – whose colours, too, were well-preserved –

from the time of Queen Hatshepsut, but Maire, who had never been in an Egyptian temple, was full of enthusiasm and amazement. Close by lies another, still more ruined temple, which had reproductions of long, writhing snakes on the door-posts. I photographed these door-posts with a sand-dune in the foreground where a snake had just left its twisting track.

If the Bouhen temple was the first for Maire, it was for us the last which our journey allowed us to discover, and we thought with a certain melancholy of the many monuments which lay beyond our reach above the cataract. There lay Ikhnaton's Nubian city of Gematon with its sun temple, there was the Amon city of Napata, whose priests in the seventh century B.C. conquered the whole of Egypt and founded the XXV Pharaoh dynasty, and still farther away, 800 miles upstream, lay the mysterious Meroe with its hundred pyramids in which the Ethiopian Pharaohs rest, the wealthy, palace-adorned city where the Egyptian culture slowly flickered out and was Africanized during the dawn of the European Middle Ages. In order to press on to these and innumerable other monuments which border the Nile's sparsely fertile shores between the cataracts, it would have been necessary to exchange *Daphne* for a camel caravan or cars on caterpillar-tracks. We had neither the time nor the means to do anything of the kind and therefore steered resignedly back to Wadi Halfa from the southernmost point *Daphne* reached on the Nile.

Another excursion, organized by our friend Anis, took us by car to a series of villages north of Wadi Halfa. Here we were greatly impressed by the modern cottage hospitals and new schools, but still more by the architecture of the farms. The design was the same as in Egyptian Nubia, but the joy of decoration still greater. The doorways were surrounded by a kind of spiky bas-relief in the clay wall. There were ostriches, crocodiles, half moons and grinning demons composed in abstract patterns, all so filled with unbridled imagination and jungle luxuriance that one almost thought one saw carved totem poles, chieftain's huts and warriors' shields. Everyone knew Doctor Anis and we were cordially received wherever we went. Especially memorable was the visit we paid to a holy sheik, who had installed himself in an old fort above one of the villages. He was known for miles round about for his skill in healing barren women and lived – rather well, we thought – on gifts which those seeking help brought with them. We found him squatting in front of his cave, not unlike an old ape. The hood, which also shaded his white-bearded face, could not conceal a pair of uncommonly bright, beady eyes and he graciously blessed both us and the beaming Anis. I was a trifle surprised by the mutual esteem which characterized the relations between the sheik and the doctor, and on the way back I asked how a modern doctor regarded a quack of this kind.

'Quack?', the doctor replied. 'No, his medicine is the most natural and the best there is. You must understand the importance to a Moslem woman of having a child and preferably a son: only then does she justify her existence and acquire a place in the family, while she can be displaced at any moment if she is barren. Heirs, sons, are also the most important thing for the husbands: they keep on until they get children. This is where the holy sheiks come in, and if you look into the matter you will find that there is not one part of Egypt or the Sudan where there is not a man of this kind to be found. For the most part the women come to the venerable hermit in good faith; they are frightened and anxious, he takes them into his dark room, intones prayers and incantations, scares them or hypnotizes them until they faint or see an angel coming down from the clouds to fertilize them. Nine months later the longed-for child is born and the husband is just as pleased as the wife.'

I now recollected a story the doctor had told us the previous day about apparently hopeless cases of childlessness – he was constantly finding new themes bearing on his one great interest in life. An Egyptian engineer and his wife had been staying at The Nile Hotel and had confided in him their great sorrow at being childless after being married for fifteen years. He had then taken them under his care, given them different kinds of stimulating injections and medical advice which had not been without result: when the couple returned to Cairo the wife was expecting a baby. Was not this a parallel case to what the doctor had told us of the holy sheiks, had there not been a certain professional fellowship in the two men's greeting? I begged the favour of thereafter addressing Doctor Anis as Holy Sheik, which he smilingly granted.

So the last day in Wadi Halfa arrived. We felt a trifle sad at parting from our sheik doctor, who, with all his manifest weaknesses, was such an obvious asset both to visiting strangers and the population of Wadi Halfa. From a purely human point of view, we had come closer to him than to any other Mohammedan during our journey. This was partly due to his frank, kind nature, but above all to the fact that one could joke with him without tripping over that barrier of personal pride, religious fanaticism and complexes about westerners which hedges in most orientals. That he too regarded us as friends appeared from his invitation to visit his home before we left.

Doctor Anis lived in a modern villa with a garden by the river. His wife, a twenty-six-year-old Egyptian woman of the wax-pale, curly-haired and rather plump type of beauty which ex-Queen Narriman has made familiar in the international magazines, received us like any European hostess. We made the acquaintance of the four attractive children, one of whom lay in a pram while the others played with their favourite toys, a stuffed crocodile and an equally genuine panther. About ninety per cent of the furniture in the house was European, but there was not a single book and the only pictures were one or two photographs of relations, grouped round a gigantic enlargement of the master of the house in Arabian sheik costume, a souvenir from a delegation trip to Saudi-Arabia. On another wall hung the neatly framed medical diplomas from the Kitchener Medical High School in Khartoum and from the London University. The place of honour in the sitting-room was occupied by an enormous refrigerator – one could not help thinking of the monumental open fireplace in northern homes, equally justified by the climate.

We were at once given a glass of chilled beer, while the head of the family, who at the hotel and on board *Daphne* consumed one whisky and soda after the other, here at home orthodoxically kept to water. Dinner was one of the most copious we had ever eaten and enabled us to taste both Sudanese national delicacies and European party dishes. We were waited on by a negro boy who, surprisingly, spoke fluent Italian; he came from the former Italian colony of Eritrea.

Utterly incapacitated by all we had eaten, we sat after dinner in easy chairs, watching Mrs Anis playing on the soft carpet with her children, a goddess of fertility surrounded by swarming issue.

Joy and unclouded satisfaction also radiated from her husband as, not unlike the god Bes, he sat enthroned with rounded paunch. He raised an indolent eye towards us and asked:

'Must you really leave tomorrow morning? Europeans are always so fidgety, you live with one eye on the clock. We take things more easily, we know that after all it's God who decides everything.'

'Yes,' I answered, 'but He's a little too fond of children here in the Sudan. The ladies no longer dare to take any risks.'

CHAPTER XII

Down The Nile

What one has attained one is usually allowed to keep – or else it slips through one's fingers of its own accord. The object pursued is, as a rule, a terminal point where something new begins. Perhaps out of sheer force of habit we had never really considered the fact that every yard we forced our way up the Nile would one day mean an equally great, if not greater, effort to get down again. With the same energy, we now had to struggle back from the final goal to the starting-point, to put another 1,200 miles behind us from Wadi Halfa to reach the open sea again.

The first stage across the Nubian lake was by far the easiest. Our new passenger Maire, with her zest and curiosity, also helped us to recapture the spell. It was like turning the pages backwards in a nice book one had recently read, seeing the pictures again with more knowledgeable eyes and refreshing one's memory with all the motley experiences. We now had the north wind against us and so went mostly by engine; for only a few hours each day did we allow ourselves the time-wasting pleasure of tacking across the bays. The Egyptian frontier was again negotiated by waving gaily back when customs and health officers signalled us over to the shore. At Abu Simbel there was not a living soul at the temple; we dug the bows into the margin of sand below the Ramses colossuses and rested for an hour in the shade at their feet. Our first port of all for the night was Garanok, the Blemmyes' old capital, which we reached in the darkness but where we did not go ashore. As we left at dawn, however, we caught a glimpse of the mighty ruined citadel, like a fantastic cathedral in the desert. Edries was palpably unwilling to visit Toma – perhaps he instinctively guarded against being ensnared once more by the world of his childhood – but through the glasses we could study Uncle Village Chieftain's camel being watered by the sycamore tree and Soliman the dandy sitting and reading poetry in his loggia. At Nag el Biteiha we passed close against the village inside the flooded palm grove where we had spent the night, but the cardinal-like village sheik who had come down to welcome us was left standing at a loss on the bank. At El Sibu we called in quickly to show Maire the temple and were greeted by the Italian-speaking temple caretaker with a cordial: *Buon ritorno, Signor Marchese*! Two new Nubian villages, Abu Hor and Nag Suluka, reminded us of our pleasant time at Kalabsha: here was the same imaginative architecture, attractive wall paintings, the 'best parlour' with a thousand knick-knacks neatly arranged and the same hospitable inhabitants with a gift for languages. In the last-named village, where we lay overnight tied to the village storekeeper's aiasa, we were serenaded in the moon-light by three twelve-year-old boys who, plucking at 4,000-year-old lutes, sang: 'My girl is as lovely as nylon, her eyes are as lustrous as nylon . . .' According to Edries, nylon is 'something which the Nubians have heard is very fine and remarkable.'

It was Thursday afternoon – the eve of the Moslem holy-day – as we again approached Assuan. One little boat after the other came sailing towards us, all filled with peasants who had been in town to market and were now returning home. How changed our perspective had become during the two weeks that had elapsed since we steered in the same direction as they! We had thought then that we were setting out from civilization into the wilds, now we were returning from the peace and simplicity of a peasant land to the depravity and vexations of a big city. Even the white lines marking the planned high-level dam we regarded with other eyes: as a hostile threat to the paradise we had learnt to love. Are Nubia's villages and temples to vanish beneath Nasser's giant lake or can Egypt's water problem be solved in another and happier way by building dams higher upstream?

There was no passing through the lock at Assuan on Friday, the holiday, so we had time to visit our friends among the Swedes at *Sentab* and also to meet General Ragab, who chanced to be in Assuan with one or two members of the government to inspect the work in progress. On Saturday we moored again by the red granite slab below the Cataract Hotel's veranda and on Monday we were ready to go on to Luxor.

I had been quite well aware from the outset that the trip down the river would offer far greater difficulties than the voyage up; not only had the water level sunk further in the meantime but it would be very much harder to get floated when we went aground, with the current driving the boat on to the sandbanks instead of helping it off. It was simply a matter of not going aground at all, if we wanted to avoid misfortunes like that at Daphne Island. Faced with this dilemma we decided to give up sailing on our own and to go hand in hand with some deeply laden motor-barge which could show us the way. Edries and I went for a walk along the riverside at Assuan to see if we could find a suitable barge and soon came to one with the name of *Luxor*. We took this as a good omen and asked the skipper when he was starting.

'Tomorrow morning at six!'

So it was that in the chill, grey dawn, with the engine doing the maximum number of r.p.m., we cast off in the wake of the unusually swift barge. If its friendly skipper had not slowed down one knot we should have lagged sadly behind; now, helped by the current, we came within three hours to Kom Ombo, where we only just had time to salute the temple and our friends the crane operator and the boatmen at the sugar-works' unloading-wharf before we were round the next bend of the river. Our anxiety for the shallow threshold at Gebel Abu Chega was very happily dispelled: Edries waved a rope at the skipper of the barge and he understood the problem at once. We were towed along and *Daphne* lifted her stern in the air as the keel began to dig in; after an unpleasant few minutes we were again in deep water and could go on by ourselves. Edfu with its high temple silhouette loomed up and disappeared. At sunset we were already at Esna after a record trip, 101 miles in twelve hours – an average speed of seven-and-a-half knots.

Luxor went alongside a stone quay, the first we had seen south of Cairo – it was 2,000 years old and had been built by the Romans. We made fast to the outer side of the barge and went for a stroll in the town. After the excitement of the day the evening calm felt doubly restful and we appreciated Esna's careless charm as much as on our first visit. Having sauntered along to the pit in the middle of the town where the temple portico lies, we found at the foot of the columns a small hut which had evidently been put up during the last few weeks. It was of the same type as the archaeologist's hut at the Kom Ombo temple and so we were not surprised to come upon a youthful trio sitting

271

round a paraffin lamp: the Egyptologist Serge Sauneroy, his pretty wife Nadia and an architect by the name of Guichard, all engaged in checking the measurements of the temple and verifying the hieroglyphics before final publication. We had a gay evening, first in the hut and then on board *Daphne*, where the young archaeologist composed a hymn to our boat in ancient Egyptian, which he printed in hieroglyphics in our guest-book.

But we did not want to lose touch with our guide, so at seven the next morning we passed with *Luxor* through the Esna dam. All went well as far as Armant, but there the barge tied up to load and as it was only twelve miles to ancient Thebes we decided to continue on our own. It was a trip which cost us more trouble than the whole of the previous journey from Assuan; all our pessimistic premonitions about the difficulties of navigating downstream were confirmed and surpassed. Three times we had to row out our big anchor with the dinghy to winch ourselves free after going aground and we vowed never again to navigate on the river by ourselves once we had reached the plainly visible, but alas so inaccessible, shore below the Winter Palace's façade. Late in the evening we did actually tie up beside the Nubian seamen's little houseboat and could give them a greeting from their villages. After the happy time we had spent in Nubia it was almost like meeting fellow countrymen and they pleased us by singing 'the nylon song'. The Winter Palace was full up, but no longer with the exclusive public of Christmas week; the guests were mostly conducted parties from France and Germany. But the staff welcomed us back and in the bar we almost seemed to see the ghost of our friend Alvar.

In Luxor I had a letter from Åke Norrby in Cairo. Not content with what he had already done for us in arranging our contact with the General and the Egyptian authorities, he now appeared as our guardian angel for the voyage home. It was quite impossible for us to wait in Egypt until the spring and then sail *Daphne* back to Italy, and on the other hand we did not want to leave her in Egypt for the year we thought of spending at home in the North before our next cruise. Up to now, *Daphne* had never ridden in a train or been sent by steamer, but in the present situation the possibility of shipping her across to Genoa and her 'home shipyard' at Lavagna was very tempting. We had written

Nubian farmhouse

(Left)
Meeting in the Suez Canal

(Below)
*Ferdinand de Lesseps invites
the ships of all nations to
pass Port Said*

to Åke Norrby in the matter and he had been making enquiries about freight and sailings. A lot of ships went to Genoa, both Italian luxury steamers from Alexandria and Japanese cargo boats from Port Said and none of the lines had the slightest objection to transporting *Daphne* to Europe. There was only one slight snag, which for us was the same as an insurmountable barrier: the extortionate cost. But Åke had also written to Gothenburg and asked if the Swedish East-Asiatic Company had a boat on its way home from the Far East via Suez which could take us to Genoa. He had now had an answer and could inform us that, on very favourable terms, we could sail with m/s *Ceylon*, which, it was estimated, would call at Port Said on 7th March – it was over a month until then. On this first evening in Luxor we decided to stay quietly for another ten days at this, the most profitable and beautiful archaeological place in Egypt. Mona and Maire, who both had work waiting for them at home in the North on 1st March, would then sign off in Cairo and take the plane home, while Edries and I would take *Daphne* to Port Said.

The time we now spent in Luxor was most fruitful from every point of view. For Maire everything was new and we others could study more thoroughly what we had previously skimmed over, see new monuments among the countless treasures of ancient Thebes and make contact with archaeologists who were working there: both the Americans at the Chicago School's excellent institute and the Egyptians. But our most stimulating archaeological contact was the Frenchman Robichon.

It sometimes happens that one seems to step straight into a detective story – or at any rate light upon material which, in the hands of a suitable person, could make a first-class thriller. That we, during our travels in Egypt, came across such an unwritten book is perhaps not so surprising; there are two settings which have become almost classical for writers of detective stories – libraries and Egyptian archaeology. Silent bookshelves or hieratic Osiris statues seem to form the ideal background for an intricate murder mystery – perhaps because they symbolize so vividly a reality beneath which unknown chasms yawn. Or is it the librarians' and archaeologists' way of life, so remote from the outer world, which demands a compensating outlet for suppressed passions? In any case, we were tuned in to the right wave-length when we leaned across the Luxor Hotel's bar one evening to ask the bartender discreetly who a youngish man in a dark suit with aquiline profile and glasses might be. He was standing not far away from us together with a well-known French industrialist, a woman painter and a Parisian journalist, to whom he was explaining, in a low, fanatical voice, something which we could not help trying to catch.

' . . . the temple in man, we all bear it within us . . . cosmic principles which the Wise understands . . .', were some of the disjointed phrases which reached us through the music and the hum of voices.

'That's Monsieur Robichon, who lives in the Karnak temple itself,' the bartender informed us. 'He usually comes here of an evening; maybe he feels lonely after his friend Monsieur Varille's death.'

During the next few days we collected the following information from different persons: Varille and Robichon were both members of the French archaeological commission in Egypt. Having excavated the temple at Medamout, near Luxor, they had been instructed to carry out measurements, photographing and small checking excavations at Karnak for the scientific publication – in preparation for decades – of the inexhaustible archaeological material of this temple area. But some years before our visit the two archaeologists, who had spent years in the temples and got to know them in minute detail better than any other living person, had shocked their superiors – mainly the chief superintendent of Egyptian antiquities, old Professor Étienne Drioton in Cairo, but also all other orthodox Egyptologists – with a theory about the Egyptian temple's meaning and structural history which, if it was correct, implied a reassessment of the entire Egyptian culture and a rejection of the excavation methods used hitherto. Varille's presumption – it was he who was spokesman – was summarily denounced and he was forbidden to develop his theory in the official publications. But he found a way out: as his colleagues refused to listen to him, he began to interest laymen – art critics, authors and the intellectuals among the Luxor tourists – in his ideas and soon an Egyptological battle was raging in the Parisian cultural magazines. The traditionalists were now forced to reply, but their arguments were unexpectedly weak. At this critical juncture Monsieur Varille died as the result of an accident and everything was as before. True, Monsieur Robichon was left, but he had no real authority, as he was really an architect and moreover had allied himself with a mysterious charlatan, a Polish emigrant by the name of Lubicz . . .

Ancient mysteries revealed, the sudden death of an awkward man, an unknown East-European in the background and the keeping of the secret in the care of an overwrought and visionary archaeological hermit – with material like this, a detective story almost writes itself. We on our part had no reason to start enquiries as to whether Monsieur Varille's death *was* an accident, but we had all the greater curiosity about his theories. I sent a note to Monsieur Robichon, who invited us to visit him early one February morning.

The air was still rather chilly and long shadows stretched from pylons, columns and obelisks as we made our way through Karnak's temple area to the wide circular wall of sun-dried brick which encloses the place like a rampart. High up was a miniature house which we should have taken for a caretaker's hut if our guide, a boy from the village, had not insisted that it was the Frenchman's dwelling. We climbed a flight of steps and knocked on a wooden door. Sure enough, aquiline profile and flashing glasses met us and we stepped into a long room, furnished with Spartan simplicity but immaculately tidy; this room comprised the whole house. It was divided into three sections, which we later found corresponded to the architectural ground-plan of the Karnak temple. At the end, like a cult image, towered a black basalt head, whose mutilated nose and split skull accentuated the bitter and painfully wise features that characterize the Pharaohs of the XII Dynasty but which was also strikingly reminiscent of Monsieur Robichon. From the windows there was a view across the entire temple area.

Monsieur Robichon's life for ten years in this strange hermit's hut had left its mark. His behaviour from the outset showed two opposing attitudes. On the one hand he evinced an almost pathetic need of communication, a desire to convince and make contact – this was a person who was obsessed by his idea, he lived for it as a monk does for his religion; on the other hand, he was extremely suspicious and touchy about objections. He began by unrolling some ground-plans of the Medamout temple, on which the various building phases from pre-historic time to late antiquity were indicated in different colours. According to Robichon, the building of the temple over a period of thousands of years followed an organic and predetermined plan: the oldest temple had the form of a womb, later it became a human organism which extended into a pattern regulated by the Golden Section and other geometrical principles.

'It's sheer rubbish to connect the Egyptian temple buildings with economic or political factors, to make out that they were destroyed by war and built up during prosperity. The Pharaohs merely made the changes decided on from the beginning at the times when the astronomers said that the constellations demanded it. Nothing in ancient Egypt happened by chance, not one stone was moved from Upper Egypt to Lower Egypt or vice versa without its having a hidden significance, without its being a sign which the Wise can understand.'

At this point I permitted myself a polite question, not even an objection, concerning the invasions and ravages of war that had nevertheless occurred in Egypt's history. The prophet almost burst into a rage; without a word he rolled up the plans and thereafter addressed himself entirely to Mona, who managed to look utterly convinced throughout. To dispel the slight cloud he pulled out a book and began to read aloud in a droning voice, which harmonized well with the bombastic text and grandiose words. In this way we could form a picture of the Master of the doctrine for which Varille and Robichon are only prophets – or the Mysterious Stranger in our detective story. Schwaller de Lubicz nowadays lives in the South of France and seems to be equally successful as amateur astronomer, amateur poet, amateur doctor, amateur Egyptologist and amateur nobleman. Together with his sibylline wife he had lived for many years in Luxor, where, in the shade of the temples, they had thought out the amalgam of astrology, oracularity, chiromancy, Bible faith, symbolic physiology and Indian mysticism that they have presented in a series of books as the revealed secret of ancient Egypt. It is from Lubicz that Varille and Robichon have got their ideas, the latter after Madame Lubicz, according to hearsay, had healed him of a severe illness with the aid of ancient Egyptian medicines.

The discovery of this compromising bond, together with Robichon's personal behaviour, gave me the impression that the whole thing was either a hoax or a series of mental cases, a coalition of persons who had reason to support each other's kindred mania. But when Robichon conducted us round the temple area I saw that the problem is not so simple. For on several points it has turned out in practice – in an almost embarrassing way – that Lubicz has been right and the orthodox archaeologists wrong. The first of these is the so-called seed stones. Lubicz had observed on certain relief walls that the god figures had some small detail – a hand, a part of the head or trunk – which obviously dated from older buildings; an economical using up of old stones according to the archaeologists, a transference of the former temple's life to the new one, according to Lubicz. Nowadays the archaeologists have been compelled to yield in this matter and what is more, have begun to look for seed-stones under the temples as well. It has turned out that most of the statues conceal broken fragments of older statues, placed as magic seeds under the foundations. Robichon showed us one of these fire-destroyed granite statues which he had found below a threshold and whose 40,000 splinters he was piecing together with the skill of a wizard. He has trained several native helpers in this tedious work and now one lost statue after the other is rising again in his workshop. But before he picks up the bits, he carefully studies the message, the rebus, that the fragments express through the position they occupy, the vessels and other objects with which they are associated – all are signs and have symbolic meaning according to him. He also maintains that the level of the Nile, which has been slowly rising through the centuries, has determined the buildings' renewal and that he has found the footprints that the priests at the foundation ceremonies pressed into the wet clay on which the walls rest.

Much of what the Lubicz school contends about the strictly mathematical aspect of the buildings' design and the astronomical reasons for the lie of the axes also seems acceptable – the connection with the position of the celestial bodies at different sacral times is plain even in the architecture of very much more primitive cultures, as shown for instance by Stonehenge.

It is a little more difficult to follow Lubicz's reasoning when he states that the plain and irregular blocks of stone that comprise the floor in the Luxor temple are a secret mosaic, whose pattern is not visible because only stones of the same colour have been used, but one cannot deny that the picture he produces of them is surprising. One also feels dubious about his interpretation of the whole of this temple as a reproduction of both man in his capacity of a microcosm and of the universe conceived as a divine man – even if the many details on which he bases this view show a singleness of meaning which scepticism finally wearies of constantly dismissing as coincidences. Our walk of inspection in Thebes' various temples under Monsieur Robichon's guidance was in fact a most curious intellectual adventure. We told ourselves the whole time that these interpretations must be sheer madness, but we listened fascinated to the well-constructed and astonishing chain of proof – it is at all events a very organized madness founded on a detailed knowledge of every block of stone, which only years of impassioned study on the spot can give. If one has previously thought that the Egyptian temples give a monotonous and, in the long run, boring impression, one now realizes that they are brimful with peculiarities, problems, allusions and associations, which Mr Lubicz may not have finally solved but which in any case must have some significance.

Robichon kept repeating a line of thought which he considered crushing to his opponents: 'If you approach the Egyptian temples with western questions, you will get western answers.' The criticism hits the mark: our mentality and our habits have led us to regard the Egyptian temples as the result of the building mania of mighty princes and a wealthy priesthood, as show buildings in a modern sense. But if the Egyptians, as I have indicated previously, had no conception of the statue as image – that is, as absent reality clad in a representative material – they did not have any conception either of the building as architecture, clad in a suitable building material. We use cheap building stone inside our churches' foundations and walls, we mask servants' quarters and lavatories in our castles and all our buildings are stage scenery which represent buildings for those who have only their eyes to see with. The Egyptian temples, on the other hand, *are* buildings, right down to their invisible foundations laid in accordance with sacred rites, they are buildings down to the smallest block of stone, relief and space, whose real form is actions in the service of religion and the shaping of ideas. If one comes to these temples with western viewpoints one certainly does not discover the meaning of either the seed-stones or the other blocks. But it does not enter Robichon's head that in the same way one gets the answers one deserves if one comes to the Egyptian temples with obscurantist and quasi-mystical questions, as is shown so frighteningly in Lubicz's books.

The odd thing is, however, that these enigmatic questions have, *de facto*, been fruitful and have opened up perspectives which the archaeologists would never have discovered on their own. The explanation probably is that the Lubicz train of thought, with all its obscurity, is akin to the ancient Egyptian mentality. The mixture of symbol and reality, the proneness to see hidden meanings and connections between things which, to a logical mind, have nothing in common, all the mentality that is taken for granted in children and savages but which we have constricted until psycho-analysis rediscovered it even in the adult westerner, probably dominated the Egyptians entire cultural life. Robichon's contention that nothing in the old monuments is accidental and that everything has a hidden meaning is therefore a very good working hypothesis, just as every attempt to read, with the help of intuition and symbols, the meaning put into the stone may be fruitful and in any case deserves a thorough test.

The conclusion of this whole matter is that while science naturally cannot accept such a fantastic and dogmatic viewpoint as that of Lubicz and Robichon, it may well be fertilized by it. It is through the heretics that the Church develops and goes ahead – even our respectable, cautious and mighty church of Natural Science.

Our ten days in ancient Thebes slipped past. We sauntered about among temples and tombs, we spent pleasant hours in learned discussion with newly-found friends. But clouds of anxiety were beginning to darken our horizon and menace our return journey, which we optimistically had imagined would be as swift and effortless as the trip from Assuan to Armant in the wake of the barge *Luxor*. We noticed peculiar fluctuations in the water-level at our mooring place: one day there was deep water, the next the Nile had fallen two feet and we lay high and dry. The phenomenon turned out to be connected with the paddle-steamer *Sudan*'s regular tourist trips between Luxor and Assuan; when *Sudan* was on the way downstream, the engineers at the Esna dam let more water through so that she would float, when she was in Assuan the level was allowed to sink. Passing bargees reported that conditions below the Nag Hammadi dam were even gloomier; there, in places, it was well below five feet. *Daphne*'s draught is five feet two inches and we began to wonder how we could get down to Cairo without wings.

Our only chance was to find some kind barge-skipper who could take us in tow – we had already seen that *Daphne* quite docilely allowed herself to be dragged across shallow thresholds; she either lay on her side and tobogganed on the slanting keel or lifted her stern if it was only a slight shoal. But where was the suitable barge? We put a call through to the big United Egyptian Nile Transport Company's agent in Assuan to ask if the company had any barges destined downstream and we contacted the sugar-works in Armant, which regularly ships molasses to refineries outside Cairo. The Transport Company did have a barge which would pass Luxor. In memory of the Greek managing director's home island among the Cyclades it bore the name of *Pholegandros*, a name difficult for Arabic tongues to pronounce; we had previously met the barges *Dionysus*, *Pan* and *Zephyr*, which belonged to the same company. The snag with *Pholegandros* was that it was going only as far as Asyut. All the sugar-works could offer was the barge *Antoinette*, which would not be starting for another week; moreover, they demanded a deposit of £25 as guarantee against the damage *Daphne* might inflict on the iron barge (!) The actual payment for towage was in both cases to be adjusted at the company's head office in Cairo after arrival.

As our travelling funds had sunk as alarmingly as the Nile, we chose *Pholegandros* in the hope of finding another connection from Asyut. On Friday, February 11th, we lay ready to start at our landing-stage, waiting for *Pholegandros*. Barge after barge went past and not until about one o'clock could we read through the glasses the intricate name on a neatly painted iron prow. The barge did an about-turn as elegantly as the paddle-steamer *Sudan* used to do in front of the Winter Palace and remained stationary with its bows against the current. A rope was thrown across and off we went. It certainly felt a trifle ignominious to have been turned into a passive hanger-on behind a chugging barge, but on the other hand it was nice to sit at ease under the awning and study the passing shores through the glasses. After the sterile Nubia Egypt seemed to us overwhelmingly rich – a fertile and shady Arcady, where the villages were reflected in the river and the afternoon light gave a transfigured fullness to life. Again it was the people in this land who filled us with wonderment and questions: how was it possible for them to look so happy and healthy? Beside the mean hovels built of maize straw, at the perpetual mills of the shadoofs and the sakias, everywhere in field and village street we saw stalwart figures and smiles and heard laughter and fun as the people went about their work. Down by the life-giving, but also death- and disease-producing, river merry children and chattering women were bathing and filling their Ballas pitchers.

Only twice during the day did we graze bottom and when dusk fell *Pholegandros* sought shelter for the night at Quena. The skipper, a sinewy, thick-set man, was puffed up with our importance: the company's big chief himself, a man so remote and great that the barge-skipper had never seen him although he had always lived in accordance with his unfathomable decrees, had telephoned to Assuan and given the order for *Daphne*'s towage. In order to show his zeal, the bargee had now decided that we would start off again at two in the morning, when the moon had risen; we would then reach Nag Hammadi in the morning and pass the railway bridge when it was opened at eight o'clock. We therefore turned in early and when the barge made a start at the appointed time, Edries and I got up to see to the manoeuvres. We had little to do, for that matter: *Daphne* was moored to *Pholegandros*' side with thick ropes both fore and aft and, thus glued to the barge, followed its every movement. The night was chill and damp but the sky was starry, the moon shed its glitter across the water slipping swiftly by and the shores could be discerned as dim contours – obviously quite well enough to guide our practised skipper. In other words, everything was most reassuring and having agreed with Edries that he would take the first watch, I crept back into the cabin and fell asleep on the bunk, dressed in sheepskin and boots.

Not until *Daphne* was lying quite on her side, the crash and the shouts had subsided and I had managed somehow to emerge into the moonlight from the chaos of mattresses, suitcases and sails in which I had awakened – only then did I realize what had happened. *Pholegandros*, with the combined top speed of engine and current, had headed straight up on to a sandbank. *Daphne*, who drew more water, had instantly burst her bounds and by a lucky chance laid herself with the masts outwards instead of inwards towards *Pholegandros* – otherwise the barge's wheelhouse and davits would infallibly have wrenched our masts off. We were now lying almost on dry land – there was only one foot of water around us – and *Pholegandros* lay stuck just as fast fifty yards ahead of us. Maire had woken to find the wall beside her bunk the roof, and Mona when Maire, the ship's library and the table fell across her, but both managed to scramble into clothes in the twinkling of an eye and our gallant passenger asked meekly as she peeped out:

'Has anything happened?'

There was no immediate danger, as *Daphne*'s hull had fortunately stood the strain, but it was slightly uncomfortable lying stranded out in midstream in pitch darkness and cold. We noticed, too, that the boat was taking in water through the sun-dried planking; as the kelson lay higher than the side of the boat we could not pump. One consolation was that the water could rise only as high inside the planking as outside – one foot. The prospects of salvage were not so bright: how were we ever to get out into deep water again? *Daphne*, fully laden, weighs a good 15,000 lb and cannot be handled like a rowing-boat. As we sat against the side of the boat, shivering in the night cold and debating this problem, we heard *Pholegandros* buzzing and flopping about in the dark like a huge bumble-bee in trouble. But the Nile barges are equipped for all eventualities and *Pholegandros*, which for want of cargo had filled its ballast tanks with water in order to get the propeller sufficiently deep down, could begin by pumping out several tons of water. Then the big kedge-anchor was rowed out and with the aid of the motor winch and much toil by the crew, the barge got floated after three hours' effort. The skipper, who was very nervous and kept shouting orders in falsetto, now wanted to fasten a wire to *Daphne*'s weak fore-bollard and tug her off with *Pholegandros* – a plan which could not have failed to shatter our little craft. He growlingly submitted to my plan first to put the thickest rope to be found on the barge three times round *Daphne* from stem to stern, then to fasten the wire in this ring and finally to pull us backwards in the direction of the keel without jerking. The morning had come and the sun had risen, but it was still very chilly and I shivered like an aspen leaf as I waded about in the water trying to get the rope in the right position. At last everything was ready and *Pholegandros* let her 400 horsepower tighten the wire. *Daphne* did not budge an inch. We now tried a new method: the barge anchored, and instead the wire was paid home with the machine winch. *Daphne* still would not budge, and the barge's two anchors merely dragged through the silt. As a last resort *Pholegandros*' crew carried ashore the big anchor on to the riverbank two hundred yards obliquely behind *Daphne*. Despite the protests of the fellahs who rushed up, they dug a deep hole in the field, buried the anchor and told the fellahs to stand on the mound, whereupon *Pholegandros*' machine winch again pulled on the wire. Now *Daphne* began to slide back obediently into her rightful element.

Our relief, after the mental and physical strain of the night, at once again feeling the gentle, rocking movement in the hull and in having our home right side up, was indescribable and we gladly sacrificed not a little broken china and water-damaged provisions to the river.

If we had been suffering from any illusions as to how easy and safe towage would be compared with river navigation on our own, they were now dispersed. *Pholegandros*' skipper excused himself by saying that it had been dark; in daylight such a calamity could never have happened. All were equally exhausted by the nocturnal interlude and on reaching Nag Hammadi after an hour's run we decided to spend the night there. President Nasser had recently visited the town to present Prince Yusuf Kamal's 70,000 acres of arable land to the fellahs and triumphal arches still adorned the main street. During an evening stroll we visited the prince's palace, which was surrounded by a garden. There we met young officials from the ministry of agriculture; they seemed just as impressed by the quasi-European luxury of the princely apartments as by the handsome plans to rebuild the entire town and turn it into a model community which an architect had just completed and which were shown to us with great pride. From the viewpoint of our northern democracy it is interesting that Nasser's revolution, unlike the communist one, does not transform the big private estates into nationalized collective farms, but tries to create a self-owning small-farmer class. Obviously, Egypt's future political development largely depends on how this succeeds.

Next morning we passed through the lock, a day late because of the grounding. Two days later Asyut's twelve minarets appeared ahead: *Pholegandros* had reached its destination and we were faced with the problem of finding a new tug. We moored in the middle of the town by the so-called Cook House, erected by the well-known tourist company at the time when Cooks' paddle-steamers and dahabias catered for the tourist traffic in Egypt. Nowadays it belongs to The Nile Transport Company's agent in Asyut, an agent who, to our surprise, turned out to be a young woman. Irma Bartolo's father, an Italian from Malta, had handled this work during a long life, but during the last years before his death had to rely increasingly on help from his eldest daughter. Irma first had to learn to go down to the barges with orders, then to write reports and telephone to the company, and on her father's death two years previously she took over officially the work she had long carried out with energy and business-like dispatch. She now met us on the bank and said that she had received orders from the company to send us on by the first connection. Unfortunately there were one or two slight difficulties, so we must be patient and be her guests in the meantime.

The difficulties consisted of the Nile's water-level immediately below the dam. It had been shallow there even when we passed on the way upstream; for the last fortnight it had been three feet above the sand bar and a vast number of barges and aiasas had either stuck fast out in midstream or waited on either side of the barrier. The very day before the authorities of the dam had relented and temporarily raised the level six inches to allow the waiting boats to get away, and Irma had still this same morning sent off a large barge train with two tugs and three barges, a connection which would have been ideal for us if we had come a little earlier. As we sat discussing this in Irma's house, the bungalow-like Cook House, her servant came into the room and said that she had just seen the skipper of the barge train in the town.

'Impossible! They left the lock this morning,' Irma exclaimed, but sent her servant off to get hold of the man if he was still about.

It turned out that the train had stopped just below the shallow part and that the crew had taken French leave – no one can check the obstacles that may arise on the way and most of the barges therefore stop for a while at the villages where the crew have their families. The captain blamed the victualling, which had not been done in time, and was amazed when, instead of censure, he was met with delight. Could he go back over the bar with one of the tugs and take *Daphne* to Cairo? The inscrutable Arab face revealed nothing of what he was thinking, but after a while he answered:

'No, impossible.'

And when Irma said that he must, he added:

'I would rather be hanged.'

It took a whole hour's persuasion, threats of reporting him to the company and the promise of liberal bakhshish to make him change his mind – but the whole thing was at our own risk.

Daphne went through the lock in the afternoon and the skipper promised to fetch us the next morning at dawn. We spent a pleasant evening with Irma and her fiancé, a wealthy Coptic civil engineer. He had bought a magnificent carriage complete with horse at the auction of King Farouk's belongings and could therefore take us for a princely drive – only the cheering crowds were missing.

We slept badly in the splashing water and eddies below the lock and lay worrying about what the morning might bring. Would the tug really manage to get up through the shallows and would *Daphne* stand the strain of being dragged for over a mile in a channel which was two feet too shallow? Not until about seven in the morning did the little steamer appear round the bend of the river and it reached us with unexpected ease. The skipper was now full of optimism. He wanted to tow us with a thick steel wire, but I insisted on using our own ropes: if we ran hard aground, it was better for the ropes to break before *Daphne*. At first all went well. The shallow-draught tug sent up a shower of mud while *Daphne* tobogganed on her keel, more or less sprawling on her side. But after only a few hundred yards the tug ran aground – hard. It let out a wail with its whistle and was answered from beyond the river-bend, where its mate lay. We understood now why tugs and motor-barges nearly always navigate in pairs: they take turns in pulling each other off the sandbanks. The other tug hurried up to help, and after several hours of every possible kind of manoeuvre we got across the bar and joined the two barge trains. They were laden with stone destined to Alexandria.

Our progress with the barge train was very slow, partly because the skippers dared only to creep through the shallows with the heavily laden barges, and partly because the stops at the villages were uncommonly many – the crews' families were obviously scattered all over Central Egypt. The first night we stopped in the village of El Quseir, as I have already told in the chapter 'The Fellah's Egypt'. The next afternoon we were approaching Minya and already discussing whether we should go on by ourselves from the centre of the town to our friends the Carvers' villa, when, near the village of Beni Ali, we saw several barges stuck fast out in mid-stream.

Our skipper tried to force the passage by going full speed ahead, but we all went aground and *Daphne* had her bowsprit damaged in a slight collision with the rear barge. At other times, when the train ran on to a sandbank, I used to start our engine and put it swiftly into reverse so as not to bump into the barge, but our batteries, which had evidently been used too much for lighting, suddenly refused to act. The hard fact that from now on we were entirely dependent on being towed was rather depressing and our heavy spirits did not lighten when the skipper, after exploring with the tug and consulting with the skippers on the motor barges that had previously run aground, declared that the Nile was completely closed. Our barges were set free by the two tugs and the train was moored by the shore not far above the sandbank at the village of Beni Ali. How long would we have to lie here? Perhaps a day, perhaps a month. The government had at its disposal a kind of sand-drill or dredge, which was sent out to the rescue in specially serious cases on application by the barge companies; we could do nothing at present but wait.

After twenty-four hours the only development was that several more barges had arrived – all those with cargoes stuck fast and only the empty ones got through. Gloom sank down over *Daphne* as it was now plain that we should not get to Cairo in time for Mona's and Maire's trip home. Their only chance was to take the train from Minya and leave Edries and me to take *Daphne* on as best we could. Especially for Mona, who had been living on board for the last eight months and who had shared all *Daphne's* previous adventures, it was hard to leave her in this predicament. The suitcases were packed, but how were we to get them to Minya? In the evening Edries and I set off to pay a call on Beni Ali's omda. There was no proper road, only narrow paths between the fields. Now and then we came to wide, water-filled ditches, which we jumped over, a large canal forced us to make a long detour and not until an hour later, when darkness had already fallen, did we reach the outskirts of the village, where savage dogs on a lead barked at us. The village was very large and the inhabitants very poor. An old man showed us the way along the winding, stinking village streets, where the only light came from doors which were open on to wretched rooms in which families sat on the earthen floor round their supper. The contrast was all the greater when we came to a high wall illuminated by electric spotlights and stepped through an imposing gateway into a large courtyard, where three tractors, a harvester and various other modern agricultural machines were parked, while a fat, imperious man, not unlike King Farouk, sat in a chair in front of the office building and held court with the farm's bailiffs: we had found the man we were looking for. Beni Ali's omda was the biggest potentate of all the omdas we met in Egypt. He owned, according to what we were told, 400 acres of land himself and leased 1,000 from the state – a nice slice of arable land which yields three rich crops per year. No wonder he could keep three wives, each of whom had her own magnificent villa in the village, added to which he owned houses in Cairo and Alexandria for the sake of the children's schooling. We were invited to a whisky and soda in the nearest residence, which turned out to house the youngest wife. This dark beauty, perhaps twenty-five years old, had already grown as fat as a prime pig and even mentally gave the impression of being on a level with dumb animals. On the wall in the clumsily elegant drawing-room hung a large photograph from the opening of parliament in Farouk's time: one saw His Majesty's monumental frame on the throne and among the members the equally monumental omda of Beni Ali – naturally unanimously elected by the village's 15,000 inhabitants.

To us the omda was graciousness and kindness itself. He sent his eldest son to lead the expedition of four cars and one jeep which was to convey Mona and Maire, with their luggage, to Minya. It was a stately procession by the light of blazing torches with many bearers which carried the suitcases from the shore up to the road. Then off at breakneck speed to Minya, where the hospitable Carvers put Mona and Maire up for the night, while Edries and I returned to *Daphne*. It felt desolate and empty now that she who had been the boat's ministering and warming spirit had gone. *Daphne* was no longer a living home.

Two days passed, each morning one of the tugs went off to take soundings, but the channel was still closed. Then came *Antoinette*, the molasses barge from the sugar-works at Armant, heading downstream at a speed of nine knots; she made a neat about-turn and stopped beside *Daphne*. Would we like to go along with them? The skipper had received orders at Armant to pick us up if he came across us. Our counter-question as to how *Antoinette* would get over the sand bar was answered with a smile. The sugar barges are the strongest and quickest barges on the Nile and their skippers are regarded as aristocrats among bargees. As they do the trip between Cairo and Kom Ombo regularly three times a month they know the river better than anyone else, and in tricky passages it often happens that a whole swarm of other barges waits for the sugar barges in order to have a safe guide. We took a hasty leave of the tugs and their crews and threw our rope across to *Antoinette*. She went on a slanting line up to the bar, where it was obviously narrowest, crouched for a spring, leapt over – and *Daphne* with her, dipping her bowsprit in the water as the stern lifted.

During the two and a half days we followed *Antoinette*, Edries and I often exchanged the following remark with feeling:

'A good thing Mrs Mona didn't have to go through this!'

With her draught of four feet one inch and her high speed, *Antoinette* threaded her way skilfully through innumerable shallows, while *Daphne*, creaking and lurching, followed as well as she could. We knew that there were no rocks or reefs in the river, but the sandbanks are often very hard and we passed several wrecks, victims of the collisions that are common on the Nile. Think how easily we might crash into one of these sunken aiasas or iron barges! It was also impossible to know how securely *Daphne*'s keel was fastened to the wooden hull and how strong the bollard in the bows was. At the more difficult passages we dragged after, but often we lay moored alongside *Antoinette* and one of the crew stood with the sounding-stick just in front of our bows.

'*Bordu aima, bordu aima*,' he sang in monotonous antiphony with another seaman who was taking soundings on the starboard side – according to Edries it meant: 'We are still floating.' When the voices changed to Arabic numerals we knew that it had become shallow: 'Seven *shipr* (about five feet eight inches), seven, seven, seven, six and a half, a half, a half . . . ' Then we waited for the first bumps. It was worst when *Antoinette* stuck beam on two or three times and we rushed at her from behind with no possibility of stopping. In a situation of that kind Mona would have thrown herself between the boats without a thought.

'Now it was a *very* good thing that Mrs Mona was not here,' we sighed, trying to soften the blows with the fenders.

Otherwise it was a pleasure keeping *Antoinette* company; her whole crew were unusually nice, first and foremost the skipper – in Arabic *raies* – who was a young man with precision and elegance in every gesture. To his attributes belonged a pointed and well-twisted moustache, white galabia and fanciful turban. Once I chanced to see him when he was washing his face and had taken off his headgear: he had suddenly been changed into a very ordinary and nondescript man. It dawned on me to what a great extent the dignity of orientals lies in their clothes, also because these garments demand measured gestures and plastic, expressive bearing. How disastrously European dress affects the dignity of orientals can be studied in Turkey – and from the appearance of an engineer on a Nile barge. As an inhabitant of a city and the representative of the machine age, he is the only one on board who does not wear galabia and turban. My special pal among the crew of *Antoinette* was a scruffy old seaman who first tried to sell me a doubtful antique and then gradually gave me to understand that what he longed for in life was a little alcohol, which he had once tasted twenty years before. I gave him a few drops of vermouth and another day a little white wine – homeopathic doses which could have intoxicated a fly at most, but which made him blissful. Edries looked very disapprovingly at this sinful commerce.

The first night we stopped at the old works of Sheik el Fadl, which belongs to the sugar company but is now closed down. I went for a walk by myself past the vacant dwelling-houses of the staff and past gardens grown wild, where melancholy birds sang of the boring existence of engineers' wives who had long since moved away. The village itself seemed unusually well-to-do with many stone houses – evidently the industrial incomes have helped to raise the standard of living. I felt like the Pied Piper of Hamelin when, on my way back from the village, I was followed by at least fifty children of every age, of whom the smallest bringing up the rear could hardly walk.

The second night we lay – after a troublesome grounding which had cost *Antoinette's* crew four hours' toil – at the village of El Ayat, whose reputation is so bad that bargees who are forced to spend the night here dare not go to sleep. Edries, who said that the village's name means 'tears', was also full of evil presentiment. I therefore went off with him to the police station and got three armed guards for the night, to the great relief also of the tired men on *Antoinette*.

El Ayat lies only eighteen miles from El Hawamdya, where the sugar company's big refinery is situated, and from there it is about twelve miles in to the Cairo Yacht Club in the centre of the city. How were we to get there without the aid of the engine, which we could not start because of the run-down batteries? A little miracle saved us: a fresh southerly wind blew for once and we could sail. Edries, who had often raced in these waters, knew the channels well and with all sails set we headed in towards the ancient city of the caliphs, filled with joy and relief; despite all difficulties we had managed to bring *Daphne* safely down again.

CHAPTER XIII

A Fresh and a Salt Canal

Our winter in Egypt's perpetual sunshine had completely upset our sense of time and not until we were moored again at the Cairo Yacht Club's barge after three months' absence did we become aware that even in Egypt there were such things as seasons. The low riverbank, where the tender grass had sprouted after the flooding, had been transformed into a high embankment covered with lush vegetation, the club barge lay many feet lower down in the dwindling river-channel and the sluggishly flowing water reflected a sun which, even now at the end of February, had become mercilessly hot. Five months of constantly increasing heat and sinking water still remained, until suddenly, in the middle of unendurable July, the river bed would once more be filled with flowing, rising, life-giving water. One understands that in Egypt the seasons are not, as with us, determined by the succession of light and dark, of summer and winter, with the transition periods of spring and autumn. The flooding, which, when the ancient Egyptian calendar was introduced, took place on the day we call July 19th, is the factor that overshadows all else and it was therefore chosen as New Year's Day. One then reckoned with three seasons, each of them four months: the flooding season until about November 20th, the season of growth until March 20th and the season of harvest during the last four months.

Because of the delays during the journey down, I dared stay no longer than five days in Cairo, but I made good use of every minute. Practical matters had to be seen to, the batteries had to be charged and the masts taken down and laid on wooden rests because of the many bridges. Then I must call at the offices of the sugar company and The Nile Transport Company to ask what I owed them for towage. The sugar company contented itself with 'a nominal sum' of £2 and the transport company's Greek manager, Mr Pendaki, would simply not hear of any payment. One evening I gave a talk to the members of the Cairo Yacht Club about our trip. I presented them with the Swedish Cruising

Club's pennant which we had flown and was ceremoniously given theirs in return as a memento of the club. It was doubly profitable after all our own experiences to discuss Egypt and its problems once again with our friends in Cairo.

But best of all was to see again, with new eyes, Giza, Sakkara and above all the Cairo Museum, which made quite a different and very much more vivid impression now that I knew the places from which the various objects came. Rahotep's and Nofret's statues, filled with magic life, are not so unreal when one has visited their place of origin, Meidum. Memories of Ikhnaton's Horizon City give personal relations to the finds from Tell el Amarna and Queen Hatshepsut's sphinxes take on a greater authority when one has seen the terrace where they once lay. The talks with Robichon were recalled by the curious slab of limestone from one of Thebes' royal tombs, which is obviously the architect's working plan of the tomb and which shows complicated mathematical auxiliary constructions. Very amusing is the museum's collection of potsherds used for messages or for other notes which the people of that time were unwilling to print on the expensive papyrus. It is an archive which puts us in immediate touch with all the little ordinary details of everyday life in Egypt two thousand years ago. There are threatening letters, bills, rough drafts of speeches and a piece of lead on which a man from Alexandria, by the name of Poseidonis, has written a magic formula begging the infernal powers to assure him of 'the girl Heronous' complete and exclusive favours'.

What moved me most this time in the Cairo Museum, artistically, was the limestone head of Pharaoh Amenemhet III, the most sublimely disillusioned face I have seen, stamped with will without faith, with petrified pain and resolution. This is the Man of Destiny: so must destiny look when it takes the shape of a human being, who, as an accessory, knows from fellow-feeling the endless sacrifices, never counted, that life demands of all living things. For a modern observer, such a psychological power of characterization, such a finely-shaded conception of the tragic conflicts of the human soul, has its nearest points of contact in a Michelangelo or a Dostoievsky and shows in an overwhelming way that in the inner dimension, which is the essential one, man has not developed one iota in the last five thousand years.

Perhaps what we call progress takes place in external things, in the transformation of the world, but not of man?

General Ragab, who was very interested in the details of our journey and who showed me the same generous helpfulness as during our first Cairo visit, unintentionally confronted me with a strange and difficult choice. He wanted my journey to be crowned with a great and memorable experience and gave me to understand that he could do me a very great favour: either I could have an audience of the head of the revolution council, Colonel Nasser, or else I could see the mummies of the Egyptian Pharaohs. Neither was easy to arrange, as the head of government was a very busy man and the mummies have been inaccessible to the public for the last twenty years and may only be shown to two categories of visitors: statesmen who are the official guests of the government, and the cream of scientifically trained Egyptologists. Weeks and months may pass without any such authorized person applying and being granted admission to the resting-place of the Pharaohs.

The reason for my choosing an audience with the Pharaohs and not with Nasser was probably that, when it came to the point, I was more interested in the old Egypt than in the new – even if it would have been extremely interesting to try to sound this young and strong-willed officer's face. There is much in his actions which must arouse our sympathy or at any rate our understanding: under his firm leadership the Egyptian community is being renewed; misrule, poverty, backwardness and national impotence are being overcome – even if the road is long and the results not yet as far-reaching as an impatient propaganda tries to make out. For the bulk of the Egyptian population, the new régime has not as yet brought any other relief to their poverty than hope of better times.

The big question is merely whether Colonel Nasser is one of the wise and realistic tyrants. The fact that he is an officer need not be a drawback – so was Kemal Ataturk – and it only means that he comes from the one stratum of society in the Middle East which is at once nationally minded, occidentally trained, energetic and economically independent of the old corrupt society. His weakness for what is adventurous and dramatically effective seems more risky – the arrest of Naguib, which took place while we were in

Egypt, his eagerness to stake all on the huge project of the dam, the *coup* against the Suez Canal Company, which has occurred as I write this last chapter. The great and serious task in Egypt would be a thorough inner reform, such as Turkey has undergone during the last few decades, but Nasser is turning his eyes outwards, playing on national passions and blaming all difficulties on the European spirit of initiative which yet, *de facto*, within a century and a half has transformed the dying Mameluke-Egypt into the important nation it is today. It is a disquieting development for Egypt's real friends.

But with all deference to Colonel Nasser: what is a meeting with him compared with standing face to face with the god-kings and rulers of the world, Thutmose III and Ramses II!

Howard Carter and C. W. Ceram have made known in the widest circles the fantastic story of the Egyptian royal mummies' rediscovery in 1882. As the result of the incautiousness of some grave-robbers and the Sherlock Holmes instincts of a young archaeologist, the almost incredible secret which a deep rock tomb near Deir el Barhai's temple bore within it was revealed. Thirteen Pharaohs, who in their previous tombs had been plundered of all their treasures, had, shortly before the downfall of the Pharaonic empire, been placed together here in extreme haste to be protected from further damage. 'Kings whose names were familiar to the whole world but whom no one, even in his wildest dreams, had ever expected to see' (Carter) were placed before the astonished gaze of posterity and sent to Cairo to be examined by experts. Together with ten other Pharaoh mummies, which in similar fashion towards the end of Egyptian independence were hidden from grave-robbers in an inner chamber in Amenophis II's tomb and were later found by archaeologists, these embalmed remains of Egypt's kings form the most imposing pantheon which any country possesses.

Oddly enough, nobody grasped at first what these mummies really are: dead kings, who are entitled to the respect that is due to every deceased person as long as he means anything to those surviving. In many museums in Europe mummies of humans and animals have already been exhibited among sculptures, jars and household utensils. This is defensible, as these dead had neither names nor personal ties to anyone. Now the Pharaohs too were exhibited in the Cairo museum, dragomans tapped with their fingers on the glass pane to draw the attention of the public to Pharaoh Sekenenre's mortal wound and tourists could send home picture postcards of Ramses II's dead bird-head. These princes, at whom a world had trembled and who, even in death, had been acclaimed as gods, had suddenly been turned into curiosities at a fair. This lack of reverence continued until Egypt acquired a national consciousness of its own and those in power in Cairo began to ask themselves: why should our former rulers be gaped at in a museum when other nations do not show their great dead for money? The Pharaohs were withdrawn from view and it was decided to build a worthy mausoleum for them.

I was forewarned of all this and therefore presented myself in a suitably solemn frame of mind on the appointed day at the office of the chief inspector of Egyptian antiquities, Professor Mustafa Amer – for safety's sake dressed in a dark suit. Where, in which secret part of the museum building could the mausoleum lie? It was more commonplace than that. An officer and a key-rattling janitor conducted me to the ordinary museum rooms. On the actual staircase one flight up is a door which the janitor unlocked: we entered a large room in which oblong show-cases with glass tops under black drapes stood in rows. The mausoleum was evidently a thing of the future . . .

I jotted down one or two hasty notes each time the janitor lifted a black cloth and copy them here without further comment:

Sekenenre – club wound above right eye plainly visible, biting off his tongue. Ahmose – curly-haired, short of stature. Amenhotep I – still in his mummy sheath, has bouquet of flowers with clear colours. Thutmose I – black skin, bald, beautiful eyebrows, well preserved. Thutmose II – open mouth, half bald, one hand open, the other clenched. Thutmose III – no nose, mouth open in a clown's grin. Amenhotep II – well preserved and touchingly lovely, head backward inclined, nose slightly pressed in, a far-away and infinite expression over the closed eyes. Thutmose IV – well preserved, a lean Dante head sunk in sublime sleep. Amenhotep III – worse for wear, almost nothing but a skull. Semenkara – skull. Seti I – bald, no illusions and concentrated inwards, resembles Louis Jouvet. Ramses II – a fantastic ghost, reddish-brown complexion, not black like the others, flaming red hair, evidently the ninety-year-old's white locks dyed with henna, a bird head with sharp nose and chin, Adam's apple, choked-up eyes, chewing earth, left arm stretched out to seize. Merneptah (who pursued the children of Israel during the flight from Egypt, but obviously, despite Bible history, escaped from the Red Sea) – thick-set, resembles General Ragab. Siptah – woolly-headed negro. Seti II – Aztec profile, face fallen in, skin like cracked dough. Ramses III – massive pear-shaped head with mouth in drawn-down bow. Ramses IV – broad, flat nose, onions in eye-sockets. Ramses V – pock-marked Chinese face. Ramses VI – gaping skull stuffed with linen cloths. Ramses IX (or XII) – black, with a hole instead of nose. Queen Nefretiri – rat-tail plaits like the girls in Nubia. Queen Sitkamose – old crone with loose hair. Queen Meritamen – still in wrappings. Queen Nedyamet – young and pretty like a village girl, small turn-up nose, enamelled eyes, enquiring expression. Queen Makere – invisible under wrappings. Queen Honttatoui – terribly distorted face, embalming fluid under skin has crystallized, swollen and burst the shell: an exploding human being.

It is important to realize one thing in the presence of these mummies: only in part are they dead human beings miraculously preserved; they are just as much sculptures of a most macabre kind. In the Cairo Museum there is a death mask from the Old Kingdom, a plaster impression taken for a magic purpose from someone who had just died. It is interesting because it so clearly shows the difference between the Egyptians' real appearance and art's supposedly realistic interpretation of it. The death mask most resembles the famous 'Unknown from the Seine': it has life's own diffuse ambiguity. The portrait sculptures, on the other hand, reflect a clearly articulated idea about the dead, they are intellectual representations of them and often are far removed from any likeness to the original – the intention was to offer the dead man's soul as favourable a dwelling as possible. But this purpose, served by the sculptures of stone and wood, was achieved to a still greater extent by the embalmed body. The embalmers therefore did not try to preserve the dead man such as he was when life fled or even to recall his previous appearance. What they strove for was to transform the bodies into worthy images. They filled out the skin, gave character to the features and what they, despite their best efforts, could not achieve in skin and flesh, was realized by the craftsmen who made the manifold masks over the face and encased the dead man in shell after shell, as we see from Tutankhamon's mummy. It was in the healthy self-assurance of the golden masks, rather than in the 'inner-most face' wasted by disease, that Tutankhamon's soul was invited to live.

We, who adopt another attitude to man and seek his 'real' appearance inside all concepts of it, lean over these dead in their glass cases in an attempt to discern what they were before the embalmers and the tomb artists performed their work. The result is a meeting with the Pharaohs in all their greatness and decrepitude, a meeting which causes conflicting reactions in the modern recipient of an audience. In the main, the reactions go in two directions: one minute one is moved by the human, the next by the superhuman aspect of these dead princes.

It is a historic triviality rather than a piece of fresh news that the Pharaohs were ordinary people, but all the same it is touching to see their bodies – so like our own – marked by age, disease and suffering. The sublime and the ancient of days take on ordinary proportions, the mighty events of history are changed almost into adventures and boyish pranks when one sees in this way the end of the game. During the Middle Ages, Alexander the Great's skeleton used to be painted in monastery refectories as a reminder of life's conditions, but here in the resting-place of the Pharaohs earthly vanity is preached still more forcibly by far more majestic rulers. The mighty Ramses Miamun, whose greatness we had also seen a reflection of in the colossuses at Abu Simbel, the ruler before whom Moses fell on his face when summoned to Pharaoh's presence, evidently became at last a feeble-minded, rather ludicrous old man. The son of God, Thutmose III, who established Egypt's world dominion and whose military genius is considered to have surpassed both Caesar's and Napoleon's, is just as conquered here as any of the countless unnamed he crushed beneath his chariot. And Ikhnaton's father, the refined ruler of immeasurable golden treasure, Amenhotep III, has been plundered to the bare bone.

But the lesson of vanity is no longer as convincing as during the Middle Ages, for that which was put forward as the reverse of earthly greatness has shown a still more bitter transience. All gods have died and only man is left, and his weakness no longer surprises us. We know the stuff of which we are made and the kind of nothingness which awaits us, but just because we do not set out with any illusions the Pharaoh mummies are encouraging: this is what man is capable of. He can not only recreate nature, from the actual landscape to all the great monuments and small accessories we call a culture; the most remarkable of all is that, out of his own flesh, he is able to create gods. Pharaoh represents the first stage when a man is made into a god: through purposeful upbringing and the suggestive power of his entire environment he learnt to think, act, live and die as an immortal. Therefore he was the first man as we mean it, while all his subjects were like the brute beasts, without soul and without immortality. What happened during Egypt's three thousand years of history was that the soul and immortality spread first to the ruler's family and immediate surroundings, then to wider and wider circles. If all people today can claim a share in the divine and if the strange gods we meet outside us have been made to yield to those we bear within us, it is thanks to the development that began with the Pharaohs. A fragment of their immortality lives on in each one of us in the inviolability we call our human worth.

Nine days remained until the Swedish ship *Ceylon* on its way home from Japan was to pick up *Daphne* and me in Port Said. From Cairo's northern outskirts an eighty-mile-long canal leads to Ismailia and from there it is fifty miles along the Suez Canal to the Mediterranean. In normal circumstances this voyage might take three or four days at the outside, but after all the happenings of the last few weeks we thought it wisest to allow twice as long. Edries and I decided to leave Cairo on February 27th to be sure of not missing *Ceylon*, which was my only chance of getting *Daphne* freighted from Egypt. If we reached Ismailia quickly and without mishap, we could use up the margin for a trip with the Lambretta to Suez and the Red Srea, which I was curious to see.

We did not get away from our moorings at the Cairo Yacht Club until ten in the morning, as there had been a dance on the night before with tempting possibilities to meet my many Cairo friends once more. It was a fine, rather hazy morning, typical of

Cairo's winter; not a breath ruffled the calmly gliding surface of the river, the dew lay heavy in the grass under the trees of the Gezira Island park and over the bridges flowed a stream of people on their way to work. We steered this time through the east arm of the river between the Hotel Semiramis and Gezira's southern point, where Colonel Nasser resides in a palace surrounded by machine-gun nests behind sandbags. The beautiful park, which extends along the shore of Gezira Island, was also closed off and turned into a camping-site for an élite detachment of the Egyptian army – the new, army-trained leaders do not permit themselves any tactical indiscretions. From the medley of tall modern buildings and indescribable slums, past riverbanks coated with refuse, through the grimy litter of factory districts and the big barge harbour with hundreds of craft loading and unloading, we came out by degrees into more rural surroundings.

At Choubrah, six and a half miles from the centre of Cairo, a narrow but towering lock lies on the east bank under some leafy trees. As soon as we approached we noticed that an astonishingly strong current was sucking the Nile water in through a side sluice-gate of the lock; the canal leading from here to Ismailia is intended chiefly as a means of supplying the three towns of Suez, Ismailia and Port Said, together with the rest of the canal zone, with the fresh water that this sterile desert area lacks, and its function as a traffic-route is only secondary. It was not easy to manoeuvre in the current with our long masts, which stuck out both fore and aft as they lay in their wooden rests on deck, but I managed to put Edries ashore so that he could show our papers to the lockmen, who would then open the gates.

The lockage itself went without a hitch, but the rest of the trip on the canal was a ticklish business from the outset. We had a following current of perhaps three knots, which in the narrowest passages under bridges or between the many stone-edged gates reach five. The banks were a jumble of factory yards, rusty barges, wooden piles and temporary loading quays. One or two bridges were open, others were only just high enough to let us pass beneath. After about three miles we came to a swing bridge which was shut and much too low; it would be opened in half an hour, the locksmen had told Edries. It could be swung round a bridge abutment in the middle of the canal, from which a kind of wooden pier extended twenty yards upstream, evidently built as a place where boats could wait. I slowed down and had just reversed the engine to draw in to the pier, when a crashing sound came from our propellor. The boat was shaken by violent jerks and suddenly the engine began to race. Luckily, Edries had time to leap on to the pier with a rope and *Daphne* could be stopped an inch or so from the bridge. A hasty inspection showed that the propeller had hit against an iron girder under the water and that the propellor shaft had been shattered. The engine itself went like clockwork but it was no longer of the slightest use to us.

It was out of the question to get the damage quickly repaired and be in Port Said by March 7th. Even to procure a tug which would tow us back to Cairo would have been a slow and costly procedure. We must try to push on by every available means. The bridge opened sure enough after a while and at the same moment a barge train appeared from the direction of Cairo. We waved appealingly with a rope, but here in the vicinity of the capital we found a hardened and unhelpful spirit. Not until we had promised £5 did the *raies* order the men on the rear barge to cast us a rope – in the strong current the train could not stop, so we had to act swiftly. We caught the rope, but it was quite rotten and snapped like twine with the jerk. The train glided on out of our reach and we were again left to our own devices. There was a good tail wind – why not rig up a small sail? I raised our strong spinnaker boom, took the boat-hook as a sprit and the upturned foresail as a sail. With the aid of wind and current we made quite good headway and after only an hour arrived at the canal's second lock.

The barge train, which had to go through the lock one barge at a time, had just got through and as we steered in towards the bank we saw the raies and the engineer coming towards us – obviously wanting to help us and take us with them, we thought naïvely. They turned out to be fuming with rage. Where was the rope they had given us? As only a rotten end a yard long remained after it broke, we had thrown it into the canal. Edries was now told that he was a filthy nigger, a dirty thief and the son of a bitch. But not for nothing did Africa's hot blood flow in Edries' veins: I couldn't believe my eyes when the perfect scout was suddenly changed into a raging tiger, who, crouched to spring, bared his teeth and roared curses at the equally rabid raies on the bank. In vain I tried to pour oil on the troubled waters. I told Edries to tell the raies that I would gladly pay for both a new rope and for towage if he waited for us until we were through the lock, but neither listened to me. Fortunately, our deep keel kept us stuck fast about four yards from the bank – otherwise I am sure there would have been a murder. But we were not as much out of reach as I had optimistically thought: soon the raies began to bombard us with stones and cakes of mud, at the same time showing every intention of wading out to us, while Edries armed himself with an iron bar. As luck would have it, the crew of the barge came up and dragged their kicking, screaming foreman away.

If I imagined that this was the end of the quarrel, I was roundly mistaken. The barge train did start off and disappear as we went through the lock, but rage was still smouldering inside Edries and, unknown to me, he went into the locksman's office and rang up the chief of police in the nearby Abu Sabel. I cannot say whether he had reason to take seriously the raies's threats to murder us when we got to Port Said, but the chief of police seemed to do so. Just as we had emerged from the lock and were about to resume our makeshift sailing, two police jeeps came driving along the tow-path. In one of them sat the raies, pale and grim, between four stalwart soldiers; the police had stopped the whole train three miles farther down the canal. For us, without our engine, it was impossible at the moment to steer back to the bank, we lay in the lee below the lock and, to make matters worse, began to spin round in an enormous eddy in the middle of the canal without getting anywhere. After a quarter of an hour's futile efforts to make steerage-way I thought I would launch the dinghy, but the impatient policeman found another solution: he ordered the raies to swim out to us for a rope, after which he was made to run along the bank and tow us for over a mile to the police station at Seriakos, where a report was written. To Edries' disgust, I managed to have the raies discharged with a caution, and he padded back to his boats.

We had no choice but to spend the night at the police station. The following morning was windless, but in my desperation to get on I decided to tow the boat myself with a rope from the bank – it needed only to get steerage-way and the current would do the rest. The spinnaker boom was rigged up as a haulage mast, then we tied the main sheet to its top. Once we had got away from the shallow bank, to which *Daphne* was stuck fast by the current, all went relatively well. Edries sat and steered, while I, half running, followed the tow-path. But soon the tow-path petered out into a reedy marsh filled with deep pools of mud. Sometimes I had to wade in the slime up to my thighs, twice I fell, once I very nearly trod on a green snake which coiled swiftly away into the reeds and when at last we got near a village I was greeted by savage dogs, was forced to plod through stinking muck-heaps and, to my amazement, had stones thrown at me by the village children – we were approaching the English military base and the grown-ups had evidently not had time to re-drill their children after the signing some months before of the evacuation pact. To add to our misery, the heat was stifling on this dead-calm, cloudless day, a foretaste of the insufferable conditions of summer. The canal lay glassy and dead, there was not a sign of a barge the entire day.

After two hours I had had enough and accepted Edries' offer to take over. When we came to an abandoned barge I could jump on board and Edries ashore. But after only a mile or two we came to a factory area where the riverbank was cut off by high walls and locked iron gates. Edries was left behind while *Daphne* and I drifted helplessly on. I hauled home the sheet and tried with the help of the dinghy's oars to hold the course in the middle of the canal. A bridge loomed up, fortunately high enough to let *Daphne* pass under it, but there were one or two tense minutes as I worked with the little oar to make *Daphne* drift between and not onto the bridge-piers. Not a sign of Edries, evidently he had to make a long detour. I passed under another bridge and soon sighted a third near a little village. That too looked high enough for the propped-up masts, but when only three or four feet away from the bridge I saw that it was an inch or so too low. The next second came the crash. The bases of the masts struck the iron girders of the bridge, the props snapped like matches and the heavy masts were wrenched backwards, sweeping with them skylight, ventilators and boom supports. Luckily, the boat got caught up under the bridge in some rake or stay – otherwise I would probably have been crushed between the masts and the cabin-companion. Edries now turned up and could help. In the meantime large numbers of the population from the nearby village had collected on the bank and there was no doubt at all that our predicament was the funniest thing they had seen for years. Having temporarily lashed the masts to the deck, we took a rope ashore from the stern and asked some men to help pull *Daphne* upstream so that the swing-bridge could be opened. A forest of eager arms seized the rope, but instead of pulling us backwards they deliberately hauled us against the bridge-pier, so that the current wedged us like a lock-gate beam on to the canal. The situation now grew critical, the boat listed heavily, the bowsprit snapped off and I fell into the water in my efforts to prevent a catastrophe. The first thing I heard as my head rose above the slimy water was jubilation, then stones and cakes of mud began to rain over me. At this critical moment there appeared, exactly as in adventure stories, two riders spurring their horses to a gallop along the road. They were soldiers sent out from the police station at Seriakos and they had only to show themselves to change the whole situation. The mob calmed down and the same willing arms which had recently hauled *Daphne* to destruction drew us away from the bridge, which was opened, and we could pass. We moored to patch up the damage and above all to get the masts up on to new rests so that we could move about on deck.

Two hours later we went on, with the mounted police as escort. About five o'clock we came to the former royal domains of Inchas and passed a bridge which was opened in the nick of time thanks to one of the policemen having ridden on ahead. We put several more miles behind us in the castle park before tying up for the night by a guard-hut after what took the prize as the most exhausting and unpleasant day during the whole Egyptian voyage. That night we were well and truly protected and guarded: a dozen soldiers sat around a blazing camp-fire near us on the bank until the morning, and on the other side of the canal flamed a similar bivouac fire under the huge branches of the trees. The whole of this interlude at Inchas seemed quite unreal; we were no longer in Egypt but in a solitary Shakespearean Forest of Arden, where I almost expected Puck and Titania to appear.

From an historical point of view it would have been more correct
to think of Joseph and the children of Israel. For in all probability
it was here that the land of Goshen lay, the place where the Jews,
according to the Bible, dwelt at the beginning of their sojourn in
Egypt. The ancient Egyptian canal between the Nile and the Red
Sea – which thus allowed boats to pass from one sea to the other
via the Nile Delta – followed partly the same course as the
Ismailia canal and no doubt in the same way served both irrigation
and transport.

In the morning as Edries and I sat over our morning coffee on
deck, pondering the day's gloomy prospects, the unexpected chug
of an engine was heard away in the canal's green tunnel: sure
enough, a barge train was approaching. Thanks to our police, the
train stopped, but the skipper, who made out that all raieses have
orders never to tow any strangers, obstinately refused at first to
take us along. At last Edries resorted to his favourite saga and
explained that I was 'an ambassador' and that ominous political
complications might ensue through the skipper's stubbornness.
That did the trick and we were allowed to make fast alongside.

Our mounted police continued to escort us and succeeded in
getting a bridge which was not due to open until ten o'clock to
give us a clear passage the second we approached: now my
dignity of ambassador was openly proved and the raies doubled
his servility. At the town of Bilbeis we were also allowed to go
through the lock before all others; two thick, forty-foot-long
drag-chains were fastened to *Daphne*'s stern so that we should not
be swept forward or twisted round by the current, and we were
towed on by the three stone-laden barges. The canal has many
narrow passages, bridges and the like, where the barge-trains
make their way through with extreme caution, braking with the
help of a kind of iron hook on a long rope, which a seaman swims
ashore with and digs into the bank, scraping a long, deep furrow
in the loose earth. We now had open desert on the starboard side
but to port villages, cultivated land and a highroad, along which
cars sped past incessantly. Now and then we passed English
military camps, some of them already evacuated and all with
barbed-wire fences, watch-towers, searchlights, machine-gun
nests. At one point there were endless stacks of cases of empty
English beer bottles. The population seemed both aggressive and

corrupt; the men shouted '*klefti*' (robbers) after us in the belief that we were English and the girls made insinuating gestures, which are otherwise never seen in Egypt.

Late in the evening, after darkness had fallen, we reached the wretched hole of Gassasin, having completed about thirty-seven miles since the morning. A few dim lights showed us a row of mean hovels, but also two buildings which we were astounded to find in this setting – a small hospital and a mosque. We were told that they had been erected by Farouk after he had survived a severe car crash at this place. In the morning the raies promised that within four hours we would be in Ismailia – 'I can do it in two when the water's high'. We set off with hopes soaring and all went well for three and a half hours. But at the village of Nafisha two miles before Ismailia we were met by a depressing sight: the entire canal was choked with boats as far as the eye could see. Now we understood why there had been so little traffic on the canal during our trip: the entire available fleet was stuck here at Nafisha, where the water-level was too low. We took our place at the end of the queue, then stepped ashore and set off with our raies to reconniotre. Many of the skippers told us that they had been stuck fast here in the bend for six days and that every day they had been promised more water. When, at that moment, a police major rode up on a motor bicycle from Ismailia to meet us and ask if we needed anything, it was not difficult to answer: we need water. He promised to go off at once to the Irrigation Office to see if it was possible for the drinking water for Suez or Port Said to be shut off for an hour or so to raise the level at Nafisha – that was the usual measure taken when the wails of complaint from the bargees grew too loud.

By four in the afternoon the water had actually begun to rise. All the boats moved off, but the crush and confusion were indescribable. Most of the boats were bound to Ismailia, but the two or three which were going westwards blocked all the others, so that the barges were wedged tight in futile attempts to get past at the expense of their neighbours. After two hours the water sank again. Port Said could not be without water any longer. We had progressed about fifty yards and the situation began to look hopeless, as it was very unlikely that the water could be raised again. Was *Daphne* to be left sitting here on the threshold of freedom while *Ceylon* steered past only a mile or two from our prison? That evening spirits sank to zero on board *Daphne*, as she lay embedded among such a multitude of ship's decks that the muddy water of the canal was quite invisible.

In the morning everything seemed just as hopeless. Although a dredger was working a mile ahead of us, one did not have to study its working capacity for long to know that it would take weeks before it reached the place where we lay. Was there no way out? Suddenly I recollected that in Ismailia there was a Swedish master-pilot, Tage Schölin, who had been employed by the Suez Canal company for the last twenty years. I managed to get hold of a telephone in a nearby grocer's shop and rang him up. Half an hour later the splendid, reassuring, helpful Tage was on the spot. He took one look at the situation and declared:

'There's only one thing to do: speak to the governor.'

We drove in to Ismailia. Tage had met the governor before and my letter from the Home Secretary did the rest. After the calm, taciturn man had listened to us for a while, he gave an order to his secretary. Ten minutes later two persons appeared, a police-major and the head of the Irrigation Office. The governor spoke to them in Arabic for a while and then said to me:

'In three hours your boat will be lying down on Lake Timsah.'

Rather sceptical, but curious to see what might happen, we politely took our leave and as Tage had to go off to Suez on a piloting job, Edries and I returned to *Daphne*. We soon noticed feverish activity up the canal. However tightly jammed the boats were lying, they managed nevertheless to draw aside and form a winding passage. Along this came a small, venomous tug with the irrigation engineer and the police-major on board. *Daphne* was taken in tow and although the keel scraped bottom the whole time, she was dragged, jogging and lurching, through the entire barge fleet, whose crews lent a willing hand to mitigate the worst collisions. Three hours was a rather optimistic estimation, but in four we reached the town, where the barges lay as densely as outside. Beyond the first lock the jam eased, and we passed the tree planted esplanade with well-tended streets and stone-paved quays which comprises the centre of Ismailia.

At the second lock, where the view opens out over the sea-blue Timsah – Crocodile – Lake, we found ourselves in a veritable park with flower-beds, lush, newly-mown lawns and venerable old trees which give shade to rows of villas in a homely colonial style. These were the living-quarters of the Suez Canal company's officials; the office buildings of the central administration lay next door. There, too, was Ferdinand de Lesseps' little hut, built one hundred years ago as the first house in Ismailia. The whole of this town, which today boasts about 30,000 inhabitants, is a plant which grew up out of the sterile desert when the fresh-water canal reached the half-finished Suez Canal in 1863. Built for Europeans and with the wealthy canal company as economic background, Ismailia, like Port Said, is utterly different from the rest of Egypt, here one is in another country with another atmosphere, far removed from overcrowding, misery, dirt and the peace of Allah.

The tug and the irrigation engineer left us in the second lock and we sank down between spashing sluice-gates, still borne by the dirty-brown Nile water on which we had been floating for nearly four months. Then the gates opened and we headed out on to the open water. We had neither masts to sail with nor an engine which could drive us, our boat was scratched, stained and badly in need of repair, but even so we thought we had got off lightly. With indescribable relief we gulped in the cool, fresh wind, we saw blue, glass-clear water around us and felt *Daphne* rocking in freedom in the wash from the convoy of big ships that was passing far away on the other side of the lake.

Schölin had arranged for a seaman from the club to come and meet us with his little motor-sailing boat, which took us in tow, and after a while we tied up at Ismailia's sailing club, which has a pleasant, modern clubhouse and a handsome harbour-basin by the lake. We had late lunch in the club restaurant – fresh shrimps and bouillabaisse. Through the huge windows we caught sight of Europeans in shorts hoisting flapping sails on light, white-painted dinghies, while some young people dived into the water from a springboard. A greater contrast to the morning's hopeless depression away at Nafisha could not be imagined, the whole of this environment with its fresh, salty tang seemed as unreal as a dream.

When Edries and I returned to *Daphne* we made a surprising discovery: through the clear sea water we could see that both our fine propeller with automatically swivelling blades and the projecting part of the shaft were missing – they had evidently been left behind in the canal. We washed the entire boat with clean water gushing from a hose, we cleaned and tidied up the cabins, which after Mona's departure had been sadly neglected, and after we had had a shower and changed into clean clothes we felt in every way like new and happier people. Schölin was still away piloting, but Edries and I went for an evening stroll in the town, whose neatness and cleanness impressed us both equally. Later in the evening we ended up at an Egyptian cinema. It was a most curious picture of Egypt that this film presented, utterly unlike everything I had seen of the country. The heroes were all Egyptian engineers who handled vast machines of different kinds and the heroines were Europeanly emancipated in the matter of dress and the possibility of meeting their boy-friends, but at the same time the helpless victims of anyone who grabbed hold of them.

'It's the Americans who drill for oil with us, we have no machines like that,' Edries admitted as we walked home. 'But we're going to get them, we're not going to be done.'

I cannot help thinking of this film and its wishful thinking about Egypt as today, during the Suez crisis, I sit writing of our visit to Ismailia. The Egyptians think that they can do exactly the same as the westerners if only they can get their machines; that which lies behind the machines, the western mentality, the centuries' struggle to master reality, they have not the vaguest idea about.

Schölin, who came down to the sailing club in the morning, brought bad news: none of the canal company's tugs was going to Port Said within the next few days. How were to we get there in our helpless state? Schölin hit on a solution: not far from the club lay the canal company's engineering workshop, where the pilots' and the control staff's small motorboats were repaired. We managed to get the permission of the managers of the canal office to take *Daphne* there and found an entire gang of idle and well-nourished mechanics – without a doubt the best paid in Egypt – in a workshop which might have been an exhibition hall at a technical fair. In the well-stocked storeroom there were ready-made shafts and propellors, one of which corresponded fairly well to what we needed. *Daphne*'s stern was raised out of the water in a crane and the fitting work was started. Tage, Edries and I stayed on the spot the entire time so that our presence would bring moral pressure to bear on the friendly but bone-lazy mechanics, who had probably never been through such an ordeal before. Within five hours the job was done and we could go out on a trial run across the Timsah Lake to the channel, where Tage gave us all necessary instuctions for meetings with convoys. Small boats on the Suez Canal are exempt both from the obligation to have a pilot and from having to pay dues, but they must in no way disturb the main traffic. Then Tage asked us home to dinner in his pleasant bungalow. There too was Åke Norrby, who was an old friend of Tage's and had come from Cairo to accompany *Daphne* to Port Said. It was a party which was at once a farewell to Egypt and a reunion with the North: apart from the somewhat astonished Edries and the Biblical, starry sky outside the windows, the setting, the company at table, the food and the geniality spoke entirely of home.

Åke lodged on board, glad to make closer acquaintance with the little craft whose voyage he had facilitated in so many ways. We awoke at seven o'clock in the fine, clear morning – Lake Timsah lay blue and wide outside the clubhouse, we almost had the impression of a fine summer's morning at home in the archipelago, the shadows cool but a delicious heat warming the sunny side of the house. A bracing swim, and we started. We passed the bathing-beach, empty now in the morning, and reached the entrance of the canal by the high bank where the viceroy's old villa and the modern hospital are. Lake Timsah lies almost in the middle of the Suez Canal. In the south it communicates with the Bitter Lakes, which are silted-up parts of the innermost bed of the Red Sea and which even during antiquity made it possible to build a canal to the sea. The stretch northwards to Port Said is about fifty miles long and cuts partly through earth ridges seventy feet high. These were difficult to force when the canal was built in the 1860s, but today seem rather insignificant; in general one must admit that nature has been astoundingly well-disposed to man by laying such a low and narrow bridge between the two continents.

The traffic is regulated in convoys of about twenty ships which twice a day start from each end, meeting either in the lakes or in a newly-dug double canal half way between Ismailia and Port Said.

The canal for the most part therefore lies empty and desolate – we had it quite to ourselves on this morning. The road runs along the African side, where one or two control stations and small green fields lie beside the fresh-water canal which conducts the Nile water to Port Said. On the Asiatic side the excavated masses of earth have been collected in pyramid-like mounds. It is completely desolate and only an occasional soldier patrols along the edge of the desert – beyond the empty wastes lies the hostile land of Israel.

About two o'clock we met a south-going convoy and according to regulations kept to port. The display of flags was almost as varied as at the inauguration of the Olympic Games, with the difference that certain nations here recurred several times. The Union Jack was predominant, but the finest boats were American tankers. At four o'clock we began to sight Port Said in the dead-straight perspective, we passed a working-site where thousands of men were running about like ants with baskets of sand on their heads – one wonders why such primitive working methods are still used – and reached the basins where long rows of ships lay moored between buoys, waiting for a passage. Past the former command-station of the British Fleet and the canal company's pagoda-like palace with cupolas of green tiles, both on the African side, we made our way to the line of clubs on the Asiatic side. This part of the town is called Port Fuad and is mainly a tree-shaded villa suburb for the officials of the canal company. Åke had lived here one summer a few years before and guided us to the Greek Rowing Club – other nations have their more or less nautical clubs close by.

We reached Port Said on the evening of March 5th and the shipping agent Hull & Blyth informed us that *Ceylon* would reach Port Said on the 7th according to schedule. One day in which to see to customs and clearance, to have a look at Port Said and take leave of Egypt; we had certainly not reached our destination too early. The customs formalities were got out of the way in a couple of hours thanks to the chief of police, who came down in person with us to the customs office. The fat inspector, accustomed to procrastinating and raising difficulties, was on the verge of tears at having to deal so frivolously and quickly with something which was so obviously a matter of red tape. He begged me at least to write a letter of recommendation to the chief inspector of customs in Alexandria and say that he had raised no objections to my departure.

Port Said, which for some reason I had imagined as a squalid hole, a hotbed of the vices of east and west, surprised me by being in all respects a tidy, almost sleeping idyll, which was given life and colour by the big ships forever gliding past. With its tall veranda façades of wrought iron from the 1880s, with the tropical equipment in the show-windows of Simon Arzt's department store and with the black police in white coats, it has an air of America during the last century, of Phileas Fogg and well-ordered colonial administration. In the evening we tried to see something of Port Said's naughtiness and looked in at one or two seamen's cabarets, but were greeted everywhere by a drowsy atmosphere and the intimation that the naughtinesses were asleep and would not appear until midnight. We were too tired to stay up so late.

On the 7th came the report from Suez that *Ceylon* had arrived and would call at Port Said in the evening. Åke, Edries and I waited in readiness on *Daphne* by the Rowing Club and about half-past nine we saw the giant hulls of the convoy, lit up by searchlights against the black night, glide past dramatically one by one. We knew that *Ceylon* was the ninth ship and set off so that we could accompany her to the buoys, to which she made fast. She was dazzlingly white and towered above us – an iceberg which at first paid not the slightest attention to little *Daphne*, circle round her as we would. *Ceylon* was to unload a small consignment of goods – from what we heard later, it was *tea dust*, the droppings that are left on the floors of the Chinese tea-packing factories and which Egypt buys for a song to satisfy the tea mania of the penniless fellahs. At last a winch arm was rigged out on the port side by the after-deck, one or two spotlights were turned on us and two wire loops came down from the sky. We had had the foresight to provide ourselves with two bits of planking to distribute the force of the squeeze and we also secured the wires with ropes, so that *Daphne* would not glide out of the snare. Even so, it was quite a dizzy experience suddenly to fly up into the air with boat, masts, Lambretta and the whole of our floating home. A swing of the winch arm and we glided in over the rail of a large, newly-painted iron deck. The ship's carpenter had got ready some

V-shaped wooden rests and after a while *Daphne* was propped, lashed and splinted on *Ceylon*'s deck like an Eskimo baby on its mother's back.

Our friend Åke, having thus seen that we were taken such good care of, said goodbye, and went ashore with the shipbroker but Edries found it hard to part from *Daphne* and when he heard that *Ceylon* would remain at her moorings until six in the morning to load, he asked if he could stay until then – besides which, it was more practical for him than finding a hotel room in the town. We both had tears in our eyes when we parted and I promised to try to arrange for Edries to come with a Swedish boat to Scandinavia in a year's time when he had passed his exam. I went to my large cabin, fitted out as a Swedish hotel room; I felt very strange being no longer in Egypt, having no goal to strive for, being a helpless passenger.

In the morning when I awakened we were already far out to sea, a stiff breeze was blowing and the sky was winter-grey. I picked my way across the heaving, rainy deck to *Daphne* in the vague hope that Edries might have stowed away. On the cabin table lay a scrap of paper with one or two lines in a large, childish writing:

> 'It is difficult to me to leave Daphne. I hope I can see Daphne again. I hope you can speak with the Captain of the ship to take me the next time. I like to see Sweden and all the Swedish people. Thank you, many thanks. I like you very much. Good luck Daphne in every sea and Niles.
>
> Edries.'

I sat on in *Daphne*'s cabin while a rain squall pattered against the roof and the angry surge of the Mediterranean blended with the throb of *Ceylon*'s engines. What had become of the sun, the river's calm water and the blue cliffs with the ancient tombs? Where were all my shipmates? Soon I myself would be walking the hard pavements of big cities and *Daphne* would be asleep in a dark hangar. The adventure was over, broken off with an almost supernatural suddenness which harmonized with the whole of this voyage, so unlike our previous ones.

No voyage had ended so strangely. We had always sailed 'home' to Lavagna on our own keel, tired but proud of the summer's motley experiences. These sea voyages had filled us with self-confidence, triumph, a feeling of freedom. The memories of our daring cruises, the ever-open possibilities, the conquest of new islands and harbours, the utter lack of dependence on land-bound people and the fact that we had always managed on our own, had given us a feeling of being the equal of the gods. As we drew up our boat in the autumn and no longer needed to fear the envy of the sea god, it was not far to the temptation of the ancient Greeks, to the arrogance which they called *hubris*. The Nile voyage was something different. It had from the first made us dependent on innumerable people, on authorities, regulations and fellow-passengers, on the dictates of the river and the twisting barrier of the riverbanks. Only thanks to interpreters, police, pilots, ministers, permits and various forms of favour had we been enabled to complete the journey, we had been forced to ask for help at every step and only by adapting ourselves to hierarchies and positions of dependence had we succeeded in following the way marked out.

What was the final impression of all this? We had carried through our voyage as before. But however much we had battled for it, the successful issue gave us no real pride and least of all any arrogance: it was no credit to us that everything had turned out so well and that *Daphne* had sailed to the Great Cataract. The last few months had rather been an initiation into life's dependencies, a gradual education which, via the external forms of constraint, such as the unpredictable dictates of the authorities and the river, had led us step by step to an awareness of the deeper and more essential dependencies, those which had given us solidarity with fellahs and Nubian peasants, opened our eyes to social problems and in another way spoken to us through the ancient Egyptian monuments. It was not freedom and individualism that Egypt had taught us, but dependence and respect for that which controls man.

I thought of my first impression of the Nile landscape: that the gods are necessary here so that everything shall not be meaningless. 'Who is the great lord who can live in the garden of paradise without being worried by the destitution?' When we came to Egypt we thought it was for the sake of our own adventure, our high enjoyment. Now that our journey was over I was not so sure. We had indeed had both adventure and joy, but in some way it felt unreasonable that all these police who had watched through long nights, all these helping hands and all the letters with orders that had paved the way, should have served something so unimportant as our pleasure. Had not we ourselves worked as if we had a great and exacting task – as if we, like all the others, had been servants and been acting on higher orders? In some way everything had pointed to our journey as having had an acceptable Aim.

Sitting there in *Daphne*'s cabin, I was of course aware that such thoughts were a game, that they only intuitively tried to sound the mental climate we had met in Egypt, but I could not help continuing to spin the thread of my thoughts and ask myself Who it was that we had so devotedly served and borne along with us. Memories from the royal tombs in Thebes rose up, the boat that floated below the celestial cow's star-strewn belly and had the sun as a passenger. Had not the sun always needed boats in Egypt for its mysterious journeys? And had it not stepped aboard *Daphne* every morning to accompany us day by day to the heart of its long, sand-embedded kingdom?

The rain came in driving gusts, *Ceylon* pitched heavily in the rough sea and I felt a great void now that the comforting and warming presence of the Inexorable, the Lifegiving and the Scorching One was suddenly no longer there. But I also felt a new affection for *Daphne*, who had not only allowed me to follow in the capricious wake of Odysseus, but this winter had overcome the trials of the endless river and been a Sun Boat.